The Skilled Compositor, 1850–1914

Modern Economic and Social History Series

General Editor: Derek H. Aldcroft

Titles in this series include:

The skilled compositor, 1850–1914

An Aristocrat among Working Men

PATRICK DUFFY

Ashgate

Aldershot • Burlington USA • Singapore • Sydney

Published by

Ashgate Publishing Ltd
Gower House, Croft Road,
Aldershot, Hampshire GU11 3HR
England

Ashgate Publishing Company
131 Main Street
Burlington, Vermont 05401–5600
USA

Ashgate website: http://www.ashgate.com

ISBN 0 7546 0255 9

British Library Catalguing-in-Publication Data
Duffy, Patrick
   The Skilled Compositor, 1850–1914: An Aristocrat among Working Men
   (Modern Economic and Social History)
   1. Typesetting—History.   2. Printers.   3. Skilled labour.   I. Title.
   331.7'686225

US Library of Congress Cataloging-in-Publication Data
The Skilled Compositor, 1850–1914: An Aristocrat among Working Men
      p.   cm.
   1. Typographers—Great Britain—History—19th century.   2. Typographers—
   Great Britain—History—20th century.   3. Type and type-founding—Great
   Britain—History—19th century.   4. Type and type-founding—Great
   Britain—History—20th century.   5. Great Britain—Social conditions—19th
   century.   6. Great Britain—Social conditions—20th century.
   Z250.A2 S58 2000
   686.2'2'0941–dc 21   00–061792

This volume is printed on acid-free paper.

Typeset by Manton Typesetters, Louth, Lincolnshire, UK.
Printed and bound in Great Britain by TJ International Ltd, Padstow, Cornwall.

Modern Economic and Social History Series
General Editor's Preface

Economic and social history has been a flourishing subject of scholarly study during recent decades. Not only has the volume of literature increased enormously but the range of interest in time, space and subject matter has broadened considerably so that today there are many sub-branches of the subject which have developed considerable status in their own right.

One of the aims of this new series is to encourage the publication of scholarly monographs on any aspect of modern economic and social history. The geographical coverage is world-wide and contributions on non-British themes will be especially welcome. While emphasis will be placed on works embodying original research, it is also intended that the series should provide the opportunity to publish studies of a more general and thematic nature which offer a reappraisal or critical analysis of major issues of debate.

Derek H. Aldcroft

Manchester Metropolitan University

Contents

List of tables

List of illustrations

Preface

This book represents a modest contribution to the growing body of literature concerned with the life experiences of ordinary workers. Rather than rehearse once again the theoretical debates of the many eminent labour historians, the purpose here is to try to identify particular and unique aspects of the skilled trade of the compositor. It is left to others to judge just how their actions and behaviour influenced labour relations in the wider context, the work serving as the starting-point for further study rather than serving to provide definitive answers. It is hoped that this text might encourage others to pursue some of the ideas and facts, taking a closer look not just at the stresses and strains of labour in the nineteenth century but also at the pride and satisfaction gained in this important trade.

For at least two reasons it is entirely appropriate in this millennium year to give some attention to the skilled compositor. In a recent poll of 100 of the world's most powerful and influential people, Johann Gutenberg, the inventor of printing from movable type, was voted the most significant figure over the last thousand years, contributing more to civilization than any other person. The second reason why this study is appropriate now is that for the first time in its long history, the supremacy of the print medium as the primary means of the communication of ideas is challenged. Instant transfer of data by satellite, the Internet, electronic books and many other yet-to-be-exploited technologies will undoubtedly have an impact on the ancient art of printing. While it would be very unwise to speculate what will happen to the printed word, what can be said with certainty is that the days of hand setting metal type are all but over: the 550-year-old trade of compositor has gone for ever. For many, what will remain is the fascination with the mystery and tradition of this trade, and perhaps the aesthetic qualities of the three-dimensional printed book may ensure its continued existence.

No work of this kind would be possible without the co-operation and help of those working in libraries and museums, and I record my sincere thanks to the staff of the John Rylands University of Manchester Library, Manchester Metropolitan University Library, the National Museum of Labour History and the St Bride Foundation Library. The Working Class Movement Library, Salford deserves special mention, as this is the repository of much archive material from the printing-trade societies.

At a personal level, I wish to thank Prof. Derek Aldcroft and Prof. Neville Kirk for their help and encouragement. Also, I record my appreciation to members of my family. Thanks to Fiona, Shelagh and Philip, who all interrupted their own work to read sections of the book, providing useful critical comment. I also appreciate Patrick's efforts in keeping the computer hardware going, particularly when the monitor self-destructed in a puff of smoke. Finally I record my gratitude to my long-suffering wife Mary, who has had to put up with my detached behaviour while writing this book.

PD

CHAPTER ONE

Introduction

More has probably been written about printing than about any other trade; however, little attention has been paid to the social and economic experiences of the craftsmen who worked in it. This book seeks to redress this imbalance by examining the experiences of one printing craftsman, the skilled compositor, in the period 1850–1914. Focusing primarily on the workplace and workplace institutions, the intention is to explore issues of control, co-operation and conflict in order to determine if the compositor was, as some labour historians claim, a 'better sort of workman'.

Not only is the study of printing important because the products of the press have acted as a vehicle for change in society; it is interesting on account of the evidence that printed matter provides of the materials, technology and artistic endeavour of the trade. It is particularly appropriate at this time to provide some insights into the craft of the compositor because, after relative stability for more than 500 years, the trade has virtually disappeared over the past 20 years.[1] Not only have the techniques involved in 'hot-metal' setting been replaced by digital systems, but many other related trades such as type-founding, stereotyping, punch-cutting, electrotyping and photoengraving have also been rendered obsolete.

This is not a treatise about the technicalities of printing but an attempt to provide a context and perspective within which to study the experience of one particular group of skilled workers. The objective is to provide sufficient detail to allow labour historians to understand the trade of the printer better and perhaps encourage historians of printing to direct their attention towards the workplace experience of the craftsmen. It is hoped that providing this groundwork will encourage others to pursue some of the issues raised.

The importance of printing

A number of historians have ranked printing, along with gunpowder and the mariner's compass, as the three inventions which have had the greatest impact on European culture: gunpowder because it enabled wars to be conducted on a mass scale; the mariner's compass because it allowed accurate navigation of the oceans; and printing since it made possible the spread of ideas. Thomas Carlyle left out the mariner's compass, however, claiming that the three great elements of modern civilization were 'Gunpowder, Printing and the Protestant Religion'.[2] Indeed, in considering any aspect of printing, the quality that sets the trade apart from any other is the importance of printed materials to society. It is worth briefly mentioning some of the consequences of the introduction of printing, as this provides some clues as to why printing craftsmen gained status in society.

No social, religious or political movement can be fully understood without considering the influence of the printed word, which for more than 500 years has been the main instrument for the transfer of ideas. Printing accelerated the diffusion of ideas while reducing the need for reliance on interpersonal contact, thus facilitating the beginnings of mass culture. Religious texts were made available in every European language. Printing allowed history to be recorded and accurate maps to be produced, and for the first time large numbers of people had access to identical information, the same music and the same pictures. For the first time texts became available to unlimited numbers rather than to the privileged handful who had access to texts in manuscript form.

Before the invention of printing most texts were in Latin, but from 1500 books were produced in the vernacular. The creation of multiple copies of texts meant that languages became more standardized, making learning to read easier and reducing the numbers of corrupt texts produced in earlier times by the copyists. Standardization allowed expansion of the vocabulary, greatly aiding learning. Individuals could now own books, removing the limitations necessitated by constant memorization of single copies of hand-written texts.

Printing made texts easier to understand. In the seventeenth century print-ers introduced punctuation and diacritical marks, paragraph breaks within long sections of text and they divided plays into scenes and acts. In turn printing allowed the revival of Greek and other ancient languages, and played some part in the development of the Irish and Welsh languages. In science, the results of experiments and new discoveries could be communicated quickly, and in religion and politics, public dialogue in print became the norm. The production of texts illustrated with woodcuts and engravings allowed the rapid expansion of non-verbal communications. For the first time art could be exposed to a wide audience and the illustration of complex ideas in anatomy, biology and medicine fostered the growth of the natural sciences. Commercial and industrial development, too, is difficult to imagine without printing; the domination of the medium remained unchallenged until the advent of radio, film and television in the twentieth century.

The mass production of literature quickly brought about notions of rights of ownership of words and ideas, eventually leading to the legal concept of copyright. Once it became possible to produce an unlimited number of copies of tracts, control by monarchy, state and religious institutions and by power-ful individuals came to be of great significance. The restrictions on who should print the Bible in England (a restriction still in place today), the granting of the Papal imprimatur and the Index of Prohibited Books (1559) are all examples of the workings of privilege and control.

It is little wonder that printing offices became the meeting places for scholars. Erasmus, for example, regarded at the time as the most learned man in Europe, spent much of his time copy-reading, writing and translating in printing offices in Basle.

The compositor in the hierarchy of labour

Many labour historians have cited the skilled printer, along with the carpenter and engineer, as archetypal examples of an elite group of workers whose wages, conditions at work and sound trade-society organization set them apart, socially and economically, from the majority of nineteenth-century industrial workers. The case will be made that this assumption is not always justified because it fails to acknowledge the diversity of experience of compositors in the workplace and the uneven patterns of change within the trade.

Leaving aside the controversy surrounding the wider debate as to whether such elite groups existed, at least five specific weaknesses can be identified in the case of printing that call into question some of the arguments used by those who cite the printer as a labour aristocrat. The first, and most common, error is to use the term 'printer' in a generic sense to include all those who worked in the trade, a mistake that suggests failure to acknowledge its complexity. From the outset it is necessary to make clear that in using the term 'printer', two separate meanings are possible – the general sense referred to above and the specific function of the pressman or printer. It is an easy error to make but it should be noted that, on occasion, perhaps eight or ten different trades might be employed in one printing office, all with diverse levels of skill and all paid according to separate scales.[3] Printing-machine operatives, for example, were paid on a different scale to the compositors, they were not members of the Typographical Association (until late in the nineteenth century), and, unlike compositors, they accepted women and semi-skilled labour in the pressroom. An even greater spectrum of experience is seen if comparisons are made between lithographers, engravers and stereotypers, diversity that is further compounded when consideration is given to the class of work produced. Working in a large specialized firm producing high-quality colour printing would have represented quite a different experience from working in a 'one-man' office producing basic commercial work. Not surprisingly, this degree of sectionalism gave rise to occupational hierarchies of status and skill within the trade, making it unwise to draw conclusions based on the collective experiences of these workers.

Even within the particular trade of compositor, the main focus of this study, it is important to differentiate between hand compositors and those engaged in mechanical composition and the subgroups of those employed in the various sectors of the trade (book, periodical, newspaper, jobbing). The experience of each of these was so varied that generalizations are fairly meaningless. Differences in pay and conditions existed in each town and within offices in the same town, with book, newspaper and jobbing compositors all working to separate scales.[4] It is suggested, then, that unless the 'labour aristocrats' of the printing trade are positively identified, the whole concept of such a group becomes ambiguous and of questionable value.

A second obstacle arises in making comparisons between 'printers' and other skilled trades. Printers have frequently been grouped together with skilled engineers, builders and carpenters, suggesting common experiences based on skill and high wages, an analysis that will be shown to be defective. It will be argued that the printing trade was marked more by diversity than by common experience, and if this proves to be the case, the wisdom of making comparisons must be re-examined. It is of course likely that in other trades, too, diversity was a common feature, further complicating attempts at making generalizations.

The third problem encountered by labour historians in the past concerns the inability to identify those aspects of the trade that were characterized by continuity and those marked by change. Industrialization in printing did not follow a path of uniform change: the transition from manual craft to mechanized industry took a long and uneven course. Remarkably, many customs and practices remained untouched throughout the period, and the prevalence of small printing offices ensured the continuance of techniques unaffected by mechanization well into the twentieth century. As recently as 1962 the technical journal *Print in Britain* suggested that 'one of the most endearing facets of the printing industry is the mixed-up marriage of the archaic with the ultra-modern', with a phenomenal amount of handwork still carried out in printing.[5] However, Hobsbawm's claim that printers were substantially unaffected by the Industrial Revolution is clearly erroneous because it fails to acknowledge the introduction of unskilled and female labour, the emergence of new trades and the consequences of capitalist modes of production.[6]

In dealing with such a long-established trade, vigilance is needed to detect sudden, and perhaps temporary, change, and to see this in the context of its 500-year history. A thorough and detailed knowledge of the trade clearly helps in avoiding misunderstandings about working conditions and the polices of the trade societies.[7] The Webbs, for example, made a serious misjudgement of the unions' policy relating to the restriction of numbers entering the trade, arguing that from 1870 this was falling into disuse, a completely incorrect assumption.[8] Additionally, the Webbs claimed that, by 1890, 'a very considerable proportion of compositors had undergone no training at all, but had picked up the trade while working at the full market rate'. Compositors' work could hardly be 'picked up', and it is unlikely that any employer would pay the market rate for learners, considering the surplus of skilled labour.[9]

The fourth problem arises because some labour historians look at developments in the printing trade in a British context, overlooking influences from America and Europe. Treating the trade in isolation in this way risks missing some important connections. For example, as early as the mid-sixteenth century it is recorded that printers in England and France conferred over trade matters, chapel rules often being identical in both countries.[10] In the period under consideration, competition for trade between countries increased and working practices were influenced at least in part by standards of industrial relations, particularly in respect of France and Germany. Many of the developments in typesetting and machinery originated in America, and, to an extent, American attitudes to management and training, especially the policies of the International Typographical Union (ITU), served to influence developments in Britain.

Finally, because the printing trade unions gained a reputation for moderation, they are afforded only a cursory mention in many texts in order to support or oppose a particular viewpoint. Caution is needed because moderation should not be taken to mean capitulation to employers. Often the unions successfully worked to their own agenda and, in any case, printing employers themselves seldom presented a united front. In these circumstances errors of judgement are frequently compounded by historians who, lacking any detailed knowledge of the trade, cite work by others without critically examining the reality of the situation. Both Hobsbawm and the Webbs are widely quoted by labour historians, and yet they make fundamental errors in their analysis of labour relations in printing.

One of the aims of this study, then, is to rectify the five weaknesses mentioned through a detailed study of the trade, focusing on the experience of the skilled compositor, particularly in the workplace.

The period under consideration

This book is intended to focus on the period 1850–1914, although from the start it must be admitted that marking boundaries proved especially difficult. This is partly because with a trade as old as printing there is constant reference to past traditions. This was not a trade marked by rapid change: by 1850, printing had already been practised in Europe for almost 400 years, representing a unique degree of continuity, both in trade customs and techniques. For this reason some flexibility in interpreting the period is justified where this proves necessary to elucidate particular issues.

It must be stressed, however, that errors of judgement can arise through insufficient regard to chronology. In relation to printing, to discuss the

'Industrial Revolution' or the 'machine age' allows assumptions that can prove misleading because much of the economic and technical progress was of a stop–start kind rather than following a smooth path of transition. In part this was due to the relatively large number of small firms which benefited little from the introduction of powered presses and the mechanical composition of type.

Although the starting-point of 1850 is not seen as a watershed, there are a number of social, political and economic reasons why mid-century can be seen as appropriate. Following the turbulent decades of Chartism, the 1850s marked the start of a trade boom, with Britain enjoying unchallenged economic ascendancy in overseas trade, a fact celebrated by the Great Exhibition of 1851, which provided a showcase for newly industrialized Britain.[11] The move from country to town was well under way, the 1851 census confirming that for the first time more people lived in an urban, rather than a rural, environment, a fact of particular significance in the study of the Manchester region.[12] By 1851 the population of Manchester, the first industrial city, had grown to 338,000, with large population increases in the surrounding cotton towns.

The year 1850 also marks the mid-point in major electoral reform, which began with the 1832 Reform Act and ended with the Act of 1867, extending the franchise to two million people. Extension of the franchise and economic growth are two of the reasons given for the reduction of working-class agitation that had characterized the pre-1850 years of Chartism. Tentative, but uneven, acceptance of capitalism, according to Neville Kirk, served to fragment, rather than unite, the working classes.[13]

The period 1840–80 witnessed a whole series of important inventions which were to affect the trade for the next half-century, although the application of new technologies in printing often took longer than expected to make an impact. Increased demand for printing was partially met by mechanization in the pressroom, first by sheet-fed rotary presses, and, from 1865, by web-fed rotary machines. Attempts to mechanize typesetting in order to meet the demands created by power presses were under way by 1850 but were largely unsuccessful until the last decade of the century.

This was a time of great expansion in the printing trade, with the numbers employed in letterpress printing alone increasing from 23,000 in 1851 to 138,000 in 1911.[14] According to Mitchell's *Newspaper Press Directory*, when the final tax on newspapers was removed in 1855, there were 551 newspapers produced in the UK and by 1913 this number had increased to 2456, with similar expansion in periodical production. Representing what has been described as integrated systems of production and distribution, there are many examples of printing becoming a commodity to be sold in the marketplace.

After the company legislation of 1855–62 the popularity of joint stock companies marked a move from family-owned and -run businesses to limited

liability companies controlled by directors and run by managers. One consequence of this changing relationship between employee and employer was
the divergence of interests and the social separation between the two groups.
In printing, established firms increased in size by opening offices in other
towns. McCorquodale's, for example, in addition to their London offices,
opened works in Liverpool, Newton-le-Willows and Crewe, and in Manchester, Blacklock's, who specialized in railway timetable work, expanded rapidly,
employing over one hundred workers.

The year 1914, the terminal date of this study, is chosen because, for the
printing industry, it marks the establishment of mature industrial relations
and at the same time takes in the period of general industrial unrest between
1910 and that date, together with unprecedented growth in trade union membership.[15] It was becoming apparent that, for stronger representation, a national
alliance of trade unions was required in order to move towards national
negotiations. To this end the national Printing and Kindred Trades Federation
(P&KTF) was formed in 1903. One of its first tasks was the protracted but
successful negotiation with the Federation of Master Printers (FMP) of a
standard working week for the trade of 51 hours, followed by co-operation
between the P&KTF and FMP which resulted in the campaign 'Betterment of
the Printing Trade'. Within two years of the publication of the Whitley
Report, which recommended the setting up of joint groups representing workers
and employers, a formal alliance between trade unions and employers came
into being in 1919 with the formation of the Joint Industrial Council (JIC).[16]

Unfortunately, the period chosen for this study is not a particularly fruitful
one in terms of providing definitive answers. It is marked more by questions
than by solutions. How long could the ancient traditions of the trade be
maintained in an industrialized society? What impact would the newly discovered process of photography have on printing? How well would lithography
compare with letterpress printing? When would the composition of text be
mechanized? How quickly could the problems of automatically feeding fast-
running presses be solved? It is hoped that this work will throw some light on
these issues, even if answers prove elusive.

The Manchester region

Without ignoring national and international developments, this study demonstrates a specific concern with developments in the Manchester region. A
rather fluid definition of the Manchester region is used so that, where appropriate, reference can be made to Chester in the west, Burnley in the north,
Congleton in the south and the Yorkshire border towns in the east. It is
acknowledged that such a broad sweep does take in a number of distinctive
cultural and economic areas. Regional differences are visible within this

work. Manchester as the commercial centre for the cotton industry contrasts with mercantile Liverpool, and many of the surrounding towns display their own unique characteristics and independence.

Much historical attention has been paid to the roles of cotton and engineering within the Manchester region, with resultant neglect of trades like printing, and this work serves in a small way to redress this imbalance. Because of the size and structure of the printing industry, it is not easy to incorporate a study of printing into a local studies context. The printing trade never dominated a whole community in the way that cotton, mining or engineering did; consequently the trade leaders made less impression on community life. Large employers in textiles and engineering, such as Greg, Mason, Holdsworth and Whitworth, made a huge impact on towns by taking high-profile roles in local and regional political, civic and religious affairs in a way that was not open to printing employers.

A recurring problem in studying the printing trade is the differing scales and customs applying in each town. Each local trade-society branch had a fair degree of independence but was subject to a measure of national regulation from the Typographical Association. Manchester, the first industrial city, although not a centre of printing on the scale of London or Edinburgh, was nevertheless important. The city was a centre of regional and national newspaper production and many of the major service industries for the trade were situated in the region (paper, machinery and ink manufacturers). The Manchester Typographical Society, together with the Liverpool Society, were the largest and most influential branches of the Typographical Association. The Typographical Association's head offices were located in Manchester, as were the head offices of the trade societies of the lithographers and bookbinders.

The political and economic importance of nineteenth-century Manchester and its association with printing trade unionism provide an appropriate context in which to examine the relationships between trade union officials and employers, particularly in respect of the part they played in local and national politics. This is achieved through brief consideration of the origins of the Trades Union Congress, the Trades Council, the Co-operative Printing Society and the Ship Canal Movement. In each case Manchester played an important role, making it possible to examine the extra-union activities of officials of the Typographical Association and to draw comparisons with the political interests of branch officers in other parts of the country.

Structure and organization of chapters

Chapter Two

The aim of the second chapter is to survey the nature, growth and development of relevant aspects of printing. It is based on the premise that some understanding of the trade is necessary before proceeding to draw conclusions about the experience of its workers. Harrison, in the foreword to his co-edited book, *Divisions of Labour*, argues that the history of the worker has to be written in relation to the history of his work, a claim that provides some justification for devoting a chapter of this book to examining the development of the printing trade.[17] In a similar vein, Musson, in his *Trade Union and Social History* (1974), also argued for the necessity of having a thorough knowledge of a particular trade, because the policies and development of a union depend on the working conditions of its members.[18] It is hoped then to furnish sufficient detail about the trade to be of use to labour historians who may wish further to explore social and economic aspects of printing.

Particularly in the case of a trade such as printing, which altered little in the period between 1456 and 1800, changing business structures, regional differences, technological developments and trade customs all need detailed examination. The first section of the chapter demonstrates the importance of avoiding generalizations by describing in some detail the specific nature of the compositor's work. The development of the trade in the period after 1850, especially the growth of the Typographical Association, is considered in order to stress the growing sectionalism and the formation of a hierarchy of workers within the trade.

Following this broad introduction, three different aspects of the trade are examined: the ancient workplace institution of the chapel, apprenticeship and the introduction of mechanical composition. All three studies show, in different ways, the central importance of tradition, custom and practice in the compositor's determination to maintain some degree of control in the workplace. It will be demonstrated that the chapel played a crucial role in unifying men working in the same firm, perhaps more so than any trade society. The insistence on a seven-year apprenticeship not only served as a means of controlling the numbers entering the trade, but also ensured that apprentices were well schooled in craft tradition and practice, thus reinforcing notions of the exclusiveness of the trade of compositor. It will be shown that by the end of the nineteenth century, when the threat of mechanization became a reality, the Typographical Association was in a strong position to adopt successful strategies to resist any dilution of labour in the operation of composing machines.

Chapter Three

Building on the detail provided in the previous chapter, Chapter Three examines the occupational and social aspects of the compositor's experience. Brief consideration is given to the origins of the idea of a labour aristocracy and the relevance of the debate to the historiography of labour.

From the 1970s a number of historians have questioned the idea of a distinct labour aristocracy, and while scepticism is the general stance taken in this work, the debate is not dismissed because of the valuable insights it provides. The six conditions employed by Hobsbawm to identify this elite group of workers are used in this chapter to examine the position of the compositor in the hierarchy of labour. Level of wages and security of employment, Hobsbawm's first criteria, are dealt with separately and in detail. Differences between rates in different towns and between offices in the same town are considered in order to stress the point that generalizations, even about men in the same trade, are inadvisable.

The prospects for some degree of social security through the provision of unemployment and strike pay are examined next, revealing the importance of tramp relief as a way of distributing labour and allowing some self-esteem for unemployed men. Unemployment, through fluctuations in the trade cycle and seasonal recessions, is shown to have been a major factor in moderating the behaviour of compositors and in turn regulating the actions of the printing unions.[19]

The third element, conditions at work, illustrates how the slow change in the work of the compositor fostered increasing levels of craft consciousness. Relationships with the social strata above and below that of the compositor are then considered through a detailed study of selected marriage registers in order to judge the extent of social and occupational mobility achieved by compositors. General conditions of living are examined next, before an assessment of the compositor's prospects for advancement and the prospects for his children.

Chapter Four

This chapter explores the experience of women in the printing trade, especially those who sought employment as compositors. The printing trade has always been seen as a masculine one, although from the sixteenth century women played some part in the trade, usually as the wives or daughters of master printers or as booksellers.[20] However, gender did not become a major issue in relation to the composing sector of the trade until the nineteenth century.

From the early nineteenth century female labour was fully accepted in the pressroom and in bookbinding, but from the third quarter of the century onwards, when serious attempts were made to employ women compositors, there was almost universal opposition to any efforts to bring women into the composing room. With very few exceptions the Typographical Association successfully blocked these attempts, maintaining this part of the trade for its male members.

Because so few women were employed in this sector, the subject has received little attention from historians of printing. Yet in the wider context of the labour aristocracy debate it provides a valuable early example of women attempting to enter a skilled trade and, importantly, exposes how the trade was perceived as a masculine occupation.

The chapter is structured around the alleged advantages and disadvantages of employing women as compositors. The views of the middle-class philanthropists who pressed for the employment of women are examined, as are the opinions of the employers and trade unionists. The conclusions reached by Ramsay MacDonald in his report, *Women in the Printing Trades*, are given special consideration, as they provide a useful structure within which to examine the issues.[21]

Chapter Five

The final chapter reviews the formation, functions and development of the relevant trade unions and employers' associations in order to aid understanding of how the compositor fared in the period of maturing industrial relations. Where possible, particular emphasis is placed on Manchester, partly to stress its significance as a centre for newspaper production and partly because it was in this city that three of the major trade unions had their head offices.

First, consideration is given to the formation and slow development of the master printers' organizations. It is clear that in Manchester, the employers were by no means united in their approach to industrial relations, a factor that may have been partly responsible for the apparent strength of the trade union.

Second, the development of the Typographical Association is reviewed and the structure of the union examined, especially to contrast its regional organization with the independence of small branches and chapels.

The third part of the chapter deals with the wider issues of industrial relations and the final section of the chapter explores the relationship between the leadership of the Typographical Association and the wider business and political community in the city. The Ship Canal Movement, the founding of the Trades Union Congress, the Co-operative Printing Society and the provision of technical education for printers all, in different ways, illustrate how the rank-and-file membership and their union leaders accommodated change. Their moderate behaviour played a large part in maintaining a reputation as responsible and respectable tradesmen.

Historiography

At least three distinct, and often unrelated, approaches to the subject of this study can be identified, each with some strengths and shortcomings. The deep theoretical perspectives taken by some social and economic historians provide insights that can be easily misinterpreted by those who lack sufficient knowledge of the trade to draw objective conclusions. On the other hand, historians of printing tend to view the subject in isolation, taking insufficient account of economic and political dimensions. As David Knott has pointed out, the study of English provincial printing has lacked any coherent philosophy or approach.[22]

Justifiably, given the importance of the printed word, a great deal of research has been carried out into the design and production aspects of books, usually by analytical bibliographers who are concerned with books as physical objects or by those interested in *l'histoire du livre*, the study of the book's role and impact on society. The connection between the social and economic history of printing and bibliographical studies is of course important because the physical appearance of any printed document largely depends on the methods used in its production and these in turn are related to economic factors. Other writers have painstakingly documented the many highly technical processes and techniques involved in printing, particularly those concerning the origins and development of illustrations and letterforms.

Some aspects of the trade have been neglected. What has been overlooked or summarily dismissed is the social and economic conditions of compositors, especially those relating to conditions at work.[23] A survey of doctoral research related to printing in the USA reveals that, between 1970 and 1984, 120 research projects were carried out, and of these only three dealt with the experience of workers in the trade.[24] Little work has been done to examine the social standing of printers in the community or the part played by printers in working-class politics. The role played by women, for example as employers and trade union activists, has also been largely neglected, at least until recently.

A possible reason for these omissions is that during the nineteenth century printing was a relatively small industry employing less than one-tenth of the numbers employed in mining or building. In consequence, the trade never commanded public awareness in the way that, say, textiles did in many northern towns, or as mining did in South Wales.[25] Unlike printing, both mining and textiles had good political representation, both within Parliament and outside, which often meant that public attention was brought to contentious issues of, for example, child labour or industrial accidents through the Royal Commissions and Select Committee Reports.[26]

A small number of studies have been undertaken to redress this imbalance. Cannon's work 'Social situation of skilled workers: London compositors' (unpublished Ph.D. thesis, 1961) represents an early attempt to examine the experience of compositors. Likewise, Jonathan Zeitlin has undertaken a detailed investigation of the trade by comparing the experience of compositors and engineers, a study which emphasized wide regional disparities.[27] In 1983 David Preece examined the social-aspects effects of the adoption of the composing machine with specific reference to Bradford. Donald Bateman's recent study of the printers' chapel at the *Bristol Gazette* provides an interesting and informative account of the working lives of men in the nineteenth century.[28] In addition to these three important pieces of work, there are a number of locally based studies, for example Nuttall's *History of Printing in Chester*, and while these are helpful in providing background information, they are of less relevance to the social and economic study of the trade.

Two more general works provide invaluable information about the trade: Ellic Howe's *The London Compositor* (1947) and A. E. Musson's *The Typographical Association* (1954).[29] *The London Compositor* is essentially a collection of reprinted documents relating to the wages, working conditions and customs of the London printing trade between 1785 and 1900. The title is somewhat misleading in that the book contains a great deal of information relating to the provincial typographical societies, including the Manchester Society, and provides invaluable primary source material relating to apprenticeship ratios, wage rates and conditions of employment. Commissioned to mark the centenary of the Typographical Association in 1949, Musson's book, *The Typographical Association*, provides a great deal of information relating to trade unionism in the provinces. In Musson's own words it represents 'a plain unvarnished tale of the development of trade unionism in the provincial letterpress industry'.[30] The book contains valuable detail, although the author is inclined not to acknowledge the extent of non-unionists in the trade and perhaps to overstate the strength of the Typographical Association.

A third text, *Union Democracy*, by Lipset, Trow and Coleman, is a detailed study of the internal politics of the American International Typographical Union (AITU). Although it uses the methodology of social science, the work provides valuable insights into the organization and functions of 'communities of printers', secret trade societies and the internal political struggles of the union. While attempts to quantify social behaviour in a precise mathematical way are not usually part of the methodology of the labour historian, this work contributes a great deal to the social dimension of the 'aristocracy of labour' debate, albeit within a non-British context.[31]

The status and historiography of the labour aristocracy debate is discussed at the beginning of Chapter Three, so it is only necessary at this point to mention briefly some of the major texts. It is acknowledged that the earlier work of labour historians, for example Cole (1919), the Webbs (1920) and Hobsbawm (1964), provided valuable frameworks for examining the experiences and status of workers in the nineteenth century. However, the present text tends to support some of the more recent revisions of earlier ideas about the nature of the labour aristocracy. Of the newer work on the subject, R. Q. Gray's *The Aristocracy of Labour in Nineteenth Century Britain c 1848–1900* (1981) is valuable in pointing to the major themes and areas of research identified by the labour aristocracy debate. Problems of the language used to describe occupational status, the sexual divisions of labour and the men's ability to control entry to the trade are all particularly relevant to printing. The work of Savage and Miles, *The Re-making of the British Working Class* (1994), and F. M. L. Thompson's *The Rise of Respectable Society* (1988) are referred to in relation to the assessment of social status and mobility, although the findings of Savage and Miles do not entirely match the results of the study undertaken in Chapter Three of this work.

At a theoretical level the model proposed by Bergquist has particular relevance to this study. Bergquist, in discussing 'new labour history', suggests four interrelated and mutually reinforcing challenges for the labour historian today: control, gender, globalization and post-modernism.[32] Bergquist argues that workers' protests in the nineteenth century represented resistance to proletarianism and loss of control, rather than being a consequence of it. This thesis appears to be borne out by this study, which demonstrates that compositors, without extremes of protest, retained a measure of control in the workplace.

Lummis, in his book *The Labour Aristocracy* (1994), challenges Hobsbawm's framework and is especially critical of the failure to address questions of women's work and consumption. In proposing an alternative model, Lummis starts with the premise that, for the nineteenth-century worker, the first requirement was to gain food, shelter and a degree of security in order to survive: workers adopted strategies to ensure their own future in the light of changes brought about by the dynamics of capitalism.[33] Instead of using a hierarchical model to study the labour aristocrat, Lummis proposes that the experience of workers is better seen as a continuum, allowing for movement as occupational conditions changed. Rather than skilled or unskilled, Lummis describes men as 'company men' or 'associated men' to denote security and insecurity. This notion of 'associated' men is relevant to the printing trade, a trade that relied a great deal on skilled, but casual, labour.

Lummis maintains that a worker's social relations and responsibility at work were balanced with the demands of employers who were anxious to instil in their workers appropriate industrial attitudes. Without any significant social mobility, men were resigned to working a lifetime in the same job and therefore submitted to the collective needs of fellow workers. This appears to have been the case in printing, where collective needs were expressed through the maintenance of 'custom and practice' and chapel rules, occupational solidarity being more important than class loyalty. While acknowledging that theoretically the capitalist system exploited workers to the maximum, this study shows that individual firms did not always behave in this way, choosing not to exercise their power in a free market for labour.

Source material relating to issues of gender is fully discussed at the beginning of Chapter Four. Three relatively recent works by female historians (Reynolds, Cockburn and Baron) provide excellent insights into the male-dominated trade of printing. In addition, Ramsay MacDonald's report *Women in the Printing Trades* (1904) and the many articles in the late nineteenth-century trade press dealing with the employment of women in the trade constitute valuable primary source material.

In the period under consideration the Typographical Association fluctuated between traditional craft unionism and 'new unionism'. This raises questions about the extent to which the union leadership represented the views of its rank-and-file membership, touching on the support for the rank-and-file ideas of Price, Burgess et al. and the criticism of this notion by Zeitlin.

Finally, Alan Kidd's *Manchester* and Ian Harford's work on the Manchester Ship Canal Movement offer valuable insights into the working of local politics in the city that are particularly relevant to this study because leaders of the two main printing unions played important political roles. H. Slatter, General Secretary of the Typographical Association, and G. Kelley of the Lithographic Printers helped in mobilizing the moral and financial support of trade unionists for the ship canal scheme. In doing so both collaborated closely with some of the leading employers in the city.

Primary sources

It is perhaps a bold claim, but there is probably more primary source material relating to printing than to any other trade or profession. Printing has been carried on in Europe for more than 500 years, and because of its long history and importance to civilization there has been a continuous interest in printing and the products of the press. Because of the nature of these products (books, newspapers, official documents, ephemera), there exists a unique record of output, every item of printing providing some information about who produced it, by what means, and for what purpose. Bigmore and Wyman's encyclopaedic *A Bibliography of Printing* (1880, reprinted 1969) describes in detail hundreds of books and monographs relating to the trade, including details of Parliamentary Papers relevant to printing.

Many texts have been written about the art of printing, one of the earliest being Joseph Moxon's *Mechanick Exercises on the Whole Art of Printing* (1683–4). Moxon, hydrographer to Charles II and Fellow of the Royal Society, used his experience as a master printer not only to give a detailed account of punch-cutting type and founding, but also to paint a graphic picture of working conditions in the trade. He describes the ancient customs and practices of the printing-house, in particular the chapel and the duties of the master printer. *Mechanick Exercises* provides valuable information about traditions in pre-industrial printing, allowing comparisons to be made with the commercial printing offices of the nineteenth century. Two later texts carry on the tradition of Moxon: William Savage's *A Dictionary of the Art of Printing* (1841) and John Southward's *Modern Printing: A handbook of the principles and practice of typography and the auxiliary arts* (1882) both provide important contemporary detail about the trade.

Compositors were literate craftsmen well able to express themselves. So it is not surprising that the trade has been well served with an excellent range of trade periodicals providing a constant source of reference. Two in particular, the *British Printer* and the *British and Colonial Printer*, reported extensively on apprenticeships, the employment of women and the provision of trade classes. The *Monotype Recorder* and the *Linotype and Printing Machine Record*, house publications of the rival suppliers of composing machines, offer excellent documentary evidence of the technical and social implications of introducing typesetting machinery. During the 1930s the *Monotype Recorder* ran a number of first-hand accounts from men who had worked in the trade during the 1870s and 1880s.

Literature produced by the trade societies has been used extensively in this work. The *Compositors' Chronicle* (1840–43), *Typographical Societies' Circular* (1852–75), *The Provincial Typographical Circular* (1875–7) and the *Typographical Circular* (1877 onwards) provide a continuous record of trade-society activity. Although essentially the voices of the executive committee, these journals do contain valuable detail on the results of ballots, reports on conferences and matters of general concern to the trade. Rather more modest but still a valuable source is the Federation of Master Printers' *Members' Circular*. Published monthly from 1892, the *Circular* has proved a good source of information on the attitudes and concerns of the employers. The considerable number of company histories (Wymans, Hazells, Tillotsons, Deanprint) provide a further source of information and while these are not impartial, they do furnish interesting detail, particularly in respect of family dynasties.

A number of Parliamentary Papers are used in this work. *The Royal Commission on Rules and Organisation of Trade Unions* (1867) and the *Factory and Workshops Acts Commission* (1875) both proved valuable for evidence of working conditions, particularly relating to the employment of women and children. The Reports of Inspectors of Factories during the last quarter of the nineteenth century have also been useful in assessing working conditions in the trade.

Finally, mention must be made of the extensive trade-society records of the Typographical Association and the records of the Manchester Typographical Society. Comprising minute books, membership records, account books and correspondence, these trace the history of the compositors' trade societies over a period of nearly 150 years.

Principal conclusions

The long tradition of the compositor as 'a better sort of workman', the standard of education and skill required, the close association with the power of the press and early formation of trade societies all suggest that the compositor should be included in any study of the aristocracy of labour.

The skilled work of typesetting was closed to those who had not served a seven-year apprenticeship, ensuring that the trade remained sectional and secretive. Compositors displayed great continuity of custom and practice throughout the period under discussion, effectively resisting any dilution of labour through the employment of women and semi-skilled men. By 1900, techniques of hand composition of type, of proofing, reading and correcting text, had changed little since the fifteenth century. Ancient trade customs of the wayzgoose, initiation ceremonies and the imposition of fines for compositors who contravened chapel rules ensured a high degree of control in the workplace through the chapel and its officials. Although master printers were excluded from membership of the chapel, the responsibilities of the chapel extended to preserving the interests of the employer. Compositors, for example, were fined by the chapel for neglect of work. Tradition, cohesion and stability in the composing room clearly contrast with other sections of the trade, where men had constantly to learn to operate new machines, accept semi-skilled and female labour and form new trade societies.

It is understandable, then, that compositors displayed a great deal of craft exclusiveness in their efforts to regulate the workings of their own craft.[34] However, this kind of continuity in trade practice cannot be interpreted as power to influence change in a wider context. As Marx observed, 'the distinction between skilled and unskilled labour rests in part on pure illusion, or, to say the least, on distinctions which have long since ceased to be real, and survive only by virtue of traditional convention'.[35]

If the work of the compositor was characterized by its continuity, it was also strongly marked by change, both threatened and real. For the first time some compositors worked for powerful capitalist employers in relatively large establishments, a situation that meant less independence in the workplace but often better conditions provided by a paternalistic employer. Neither was the chapel completely immune from change. Gradually, from 1870 onwards, trade union branches and the Typographical Association executive increasingly took over functions that had previously been left to the independence of the chapel, leading, at the end of the period under discussion, to national negotiations on pay and conditions.

Printers displayed a well-established trade consciousness long before industrialization. It can be argued that the printer was a member of an elite 'aristocracy of labour' in the early nineteenth century but progressively lost status, so that by the beginning of the twentieth century the compositor was no longer part of the aristocracy of labour. Although machine compositors on national newspapers were among the highest-paid manual workers, their relative position had declined. Unlike some trades, where the introduction of machinery displaced traditional skills, technical progress in printing created new job hierarchies. While compositors resisted unskilled labour in the composing room, new, more demanding skills were required of the compositor employed on machine composition. News, book and general jobbing compositors were all paid on different scales and experienced varied working conditions, while at the same time the new trades of lithography and photo-engraving introduced other highly paid workers into the trade.

Some evidence suggests that by 1900 there was a shift in emphasis from the individual status of printers towards greater working-class consciousness. Nevertheless, many compositors still viewed themselves as belonging to a trade distinct from other working-class occupations.

Notes

1. Letterpress printing has largely been superseded by the lithographic process and very few firms now use 'hot-metal' setting.
2. *The Concise Oxford Dictionary of Quotations* 55:5 (Oxford: Oxford University Press, 1964).
3. For example, engraver, lithographer, reader, machine printer, stereotyper.
4. Musson, A. E., *The Typographical Association* (Oxford: Oxford University Press, 1954), p. 155.
5. *Print in Britain*, Vol. 10, No. 3, July 1962.
6. Hobsbawm, E. J., *Labouring Men: studies in the history of labour* (London: Weidenfeld & Nicolson, 1968), p. 280.
7. Musson, A. E., *Trade Union and Social History* (London, 1974), p. 2.
8. Child, J., *Industrial Relations in the British Printing Industry* (London: Allen & Unwin, 1967), p. 123.
9. Webb, S. and Webb, B., *Industrial Democracy* (London: Allen & Unwin, 1920 edition), p. 468.
10. Lipset, M., Trow, M. and Coleman J., *Union Democracy; the internal politics of the International Typographic Union* (New York: Free Press, 1968), p. 28.
11. Best, G., *Mid-Victorian Britain, 1851–75* (London: Weidenfeld & Nicolson, 1971), p. 19.
12. Ibid., p. 29.
13. Kirk, N., *Labour and Society in Britain and the USA*, Vol. 1 (Aldershot: Scolar Press, 1994), p. 20.
14. Musson, *Typographical Association*.
15. Kirk, *Labour and Society*, Vol. 2, p. 107.

16. Clegg, H. A., Fox, A. and Thompson, A. F., *A History of British Trade Unions since 1889*, Vol. 1 (Oxford: Clarendon Press, 1985), p. 204.
17. Harrison, R. and Zeitlin, J., *Divisions of Labour* (Brighton: Harvester, 1985), p. viii.
18. Musson, *Trade Union and Social History*, p. 2.
19. Ibid.
20. Moxon, J., *Mechanick Exercises on the whole Art of Printing* (1683; reprinted London: Oxford University Press, 1962).
21. MacDonald, J. R. (ed.), *Women in the Printing Trades: a sociological study* (London: WIC, 1904).
22. Knott, D., 'The study of English provincial printing', *Journal of the Printing Historical Society*, No. 24 (1995), p. 5.
23. Howe, E. (ed.), *The London Compositor, 1785–1900* (London: Bibliographical Society, 1947), p. 10.
24. *Printing history*, 'Journal of the American Printing History Association, Vol. VI, No. 2 (1984).
25. Best, *Mid-Victorian Britain*, p. 114.
26. Lummis, T., *The Labour Aristocracy, 1851–1914* (Aldershot: Scolar Press, 1994), p. 97.
27. Zeitlin, J., 'Craft regulation and the division of labour: engineers and compositors in Britain, 1890–1914', Unpublished Ph.D. thesis, University of Warwick, 1981.
28. 'A British printers' chapel in the nineteenth century', *Journal of the Printing Historical Society*, No. 24 (1995), p. 107.
29. Musson, *Typographical Association*, and Howe, *The London Compositor.*
30. Musson, *Typographical Association*, preface.
31. Lipset et al., *Union Democracy.*
32. Bergquist, C., 'Labour history and its challenges', *American Historical Review*, Vol. 98, No. 3 (June 1993), p. 757.
33. Lummis, *Labour Aristocracy*, p. 25.
34. Musson, *Typographical Association*, p. 70.
35. Burnett, J. (ed.), *Useful Toil: autobiographies of working people from the 1820s to the 1920s* (London: Allen Lane, 1974), p. 81.

CHAPTER TWO

The nature and development of the printing trade

Overview

The primary purpose of this chapter is to present the essential background and context in which to consider the position of the skilled compositor in the developing hierarchy of nineteenth-century industrial workers. The aim is to provide a sound underpinning for the analysis to be made in Chapter Three and at the same time to note any indicators which might elucidate issues central to the debate.

Although this study concentrates on one particular printing craftsman, the compositor, an overview of the trade generally will demonstrate how the experience of the compositor differed from that of other printing craft workers, for example machine printers and lithographers. Isolating the role of one tradesman in this way still necessitates frequent reference to the trade as a whole, as the compositor, although an autonomous worker, only dealt with one part of the printing process.

The status and working conditions of the compositor will be examined to illuminate the more general statements made by economic historians when they refer to 'printers'. To discuss 'printers' without acknowledging wide differentials in education, skill, earnings, class of work undertaken and regularity of employment gives an inaccurate and misleading picture. In order to draw meaningful conclusions about the status of the compositor we must therefore look in some detail at the experience of the compositor in the workplace, at specific times and in particular places. Levels of skill and earnings of compositors varied greatly and often depended on the type of work undertaken and the location of the particular firm. Even greater differences are exposed if comparisons are made between compositors and other skilled printing workers, for example engravers, lithographic printers and readers. Geographical location is also important: the experience of compositors in London and Manchester was quite different to that of compositors in country towns where many worked in non-society offices and received similar wages to workers in trades other than printing.

Functional and structural aspects of the trade are explored through the recurring key themes of continuity, change and regulation. An examination of the trade reveals long continuity of custom and practice, and it will be argued that this had a significant bearing on the compositor's strong craft consciousness. Technological change in printing was variable and patchy; working methods of the compositor at the beginning of the twentieth century were virtually the same as those of the fifteenth century. In contrast, other sectors of the trade used sophisticated machines, automating what had been handcraft work for four hundred years.

Following a brief description of the nature of printing, this chapter emphasizes the importance of the trade within the Victorian economy. It is above all necessary to stress the diversity of printing, which was both a service and production industry as well as a craft, and, for some, a medium for artistic expression. Particular and unique aspects of the trade are recognized. The eclectic nature of printing, informed by, for example, literature, art and science, contributed, at least in part, to the compositor's reputation as an 'aristocrat of labour', a label that will be considered more fully in Chapter Three.

Low demand from commerce and high levels of illiteracy among the general population meant that expansion in printing was controlled and slow; the trade escaped the sudden industrialization experienced in engineering and textiles. In the early years of printing, a substantial amount of capital was required to underwrite the cost of producing a book, inevitably leading printers to seek patronage from the institutions of church and state and from wealthy individuals.

From the late eighteenth century onwards, the printing trade increasingly provided a service for industry and commerce, and must be judged in the context of growing industrial capitalism, a somewhat alien situation for a craft that had for 300 years experienced patronage and protection.[1] Protection and control, then, were not new to printing. By the beginning of the nineteenth century this trade had experienced 350 years of guild and state regulation, controls which were to be replaced in part by trade-society regulation and the power of large employers of labour as printing adapted to the industrial capitalist mode of production. What was new was the way in which labour was subordinated to the will of capital, through what Neville Kirk describes as integrated systems of production and distribution.[2] These factors are briefly considered in order to draw attention to influences, both within and outside the trade, that had some bearing on the autonomy of the skilled craftsman. Events in the nineteenth century, especially the large-scale production of newspapers, books and periodicals, provide a key to some of the issues that still have a bearing on the trade as printing completes the transition from a craft to a modern service industry.[3]

The work of the compositor needed physical strength combined with good hand-and-eye co-ordination and a high standard of literacy, qualities that set the compositor apart from most other manual workers. Compositors took some responsibility for interpreting copy, necessitating knowledge of spelling and grammar; and the close tolerances involved in typesetting demanded some expertise in arithmetic. Foreign-language setting, music printing and algebra made even greater demands on the compositor and the frequent changes in typographic fashions always provided a severe artistic challenge.

Issues of change and control are examined by looking at three aspects of the trade: the chapel; apprenticeship; and the mechanization of typesetting. The ancient workplace organization of the chapel, originally made up of all persons working in a printing office, including the master, gradually changed to represent a single trade, eventually becoming the focus of trade-society organization. Serving as a vehicle for the collective views of the occupational community, the chapel displays remarkable continuity in its history. Exclusiveness, secrecy and respect for tradition within the chapel all played some part in constructing a view of the compositor as 'a better sort of workman'.

The ever-present question of apprenticeship as a means to control the labour supply and as a way of passing on trade knowledge and traditions is explored. Insistence on a lengthy apprenticeship set the compositor apart from most other trades, where a relaxation of apprenticeship conditions resulted in a degree of dilution of labour.

Finally, attention is directed towards the mechanization of typesetting, which serves to illustrate the challenge faced by compositors in adapting to new ways of working through the introduction of the 'machine compositor'. Although it was introduced in the 1880s, the Linotype did not come into widespread use until 1914 and even then the majority of compositors were engaged in hand setting of type. By 1900, hand typesetting, unchanged since the fifteenth century, was still being used alongside systems of paper-tape-controlled typesetting (Monotype) which anticipated the 1960s computer. Unlike the handloom weavers and framework knitters, who were disadvantaged through the introduction of machinery, compositors were not undervalued by this innovation. On the contrary, because greater knowledge and skill were needed to operate composing machines, the social standing of these men resembled that of those in today's silicon industries. Overall, compositors successfully accommodated the new machines while still retaining a measure of control in the workplace.

The nature of printing

Printing, the art and craft of taking impressions by means of a block or stamp, has many interpretations and applications. Traditionally, 'printing' has been understood as the production of multiple copies of an image on paper or cloth through the application of pressure, by hand or machine, to an inked surface. This definition was entirely appropriate until the nineteenth century, when photographic methods of printing were introduced which relied on the action of light rather than pressure to transfer an image.[4] More recent developments in electrostatic, ink-jet and laser systems have extended the meaning of the term, so it should be stated from the outset that, in this study, the former, traditional meaning of 'printing' applies.

Four separate, and usually unconnected, processes fall within this conventional definition of printing. The first is intaglio, which involves printing from a recessed image engraved or etched into a flat metal plate. Developed in the sixteenth century, this method of printing has been favoured by artists for the reproduction of illustrations although its commercial applications were not developed until the advent of the modern gravure process in 1895. The second process, planographic (printing from a flat plate), was invented in the late eighteenth century and developed commercially by the mid-nineteenth century as lithography. The third process, seriography or silk-screen printing, involves the use of stencils. Commercially of lesser importance than the other processes, silk-screen printing is used mainly for posters and point-of-sale materials.

Finally, there is relief or letterpress printing, the oldest form of printing, which includes printing from woodcuts and wood engravings but, more importantly, printing from movable type. It is this process that forms the focus of the present study and it should be noted from the outset that the craftsman compositor, the subject of this work, was concerned only with letterpress printing. Because the first three processes mentioned above were applied essentially to illustrative media, they had little direct impact on the work of the compositor except in the sense that over time other skilled workers were introduced into the trade, increasing the possibilities for inter-craft rivalry and dispute.

Letterpress printing involves two distinct stages: first, the collection and assembly by the compositor of single letters to form words, sentences and pages; and second, the inking and taking of impressions from the type by the printer. Until the late eighteenth century the roles of the compositor and printer were, at least to some extent, interchangeable, each man having the necessary skills to undertake both tasks. However, by the beginning of the nineteenth century two developments threatened the dual role of the printer: the replacement of the wooden hand press by the powered press and the changing nature of the kinds of printing demanded.

There is some dispute as to who was the inventor of letterpress printing, but most scholars credit Johann Gutenberg, together with Peter Schoeffer and Johannes Fust, as the individuals who in 1446 perfected printing from movable type. It is clear that the Chinese practised a form of relief printing many centuries before its introduction into Europe. It is appropriate therefore to point out that the present discussion concerns printing in the Western World. Gutenberg worked in Mainz, Germany and his skill in applying the techniques of his trade as a goldsmith to the engraving of punches and the provision of adjustable moulds to cast single letters is universally recognized.

The development of printing relied on the adoption of existing materials and techniques. Papermaking, for example, was an essential contributory technology to the success of printing. Before its introduction into Europe in the fourteenth century, books had been produced using parchment (stretched sheepskin) or vellum (stretched calfskin), both materials being prohibitively expensive. Additionally the early printers developed suitable ink, probably based on Flemish artists' ink, that would dry rapidly. A wooden wine or clothes press was adapted to apply pressure to the inked surface of the type and a suitable alloy that would reproduce the fine detail of the letters had to be manufactured.[5]

The growth and structure of the trade

It is worth reviewing the beginnings of printing in order to try to explain why the compositor has often been cited as an aristocrat of labour for two main reasons: first, to show the importance and high profile of the products of the printing press to every kind of human development; and second, to demonstrate and emphasize the part played by tradition in this long-established trade.

Introduced during a period of renaissance and reformation, it is not surprising that the art of printing spread rapidly. Within 30 years of its introduction presses were established in more than one hundred European cities and by 1500 this number had doubled. William Caxton introduced the craft of printing into England in 1476, some 20 years after its dispersion through southern Europe. Expansion of printing in England was, however, slow: the trade remained severely restricted by state regulation and in 1557 the Stationers' Company was granted a charter allowing monopolistic control and extensive regulatory powers. No one was permitted to practise 'the art or mistery [sic] of printing' except members of the guild or persons licensed by the Stationers' Company.

During the first hundred years of printing there was little differentiation between the functions of editor, publisher and printer, but by 1550 printing had become an established trade requiring foresight, planning and capital. In 1586 a decree by the Star Chamber brought an end to provincial printing in England and, with the exception of Oxford and Cambridge, presses were confined to London and could not exceed 21 in number. Restrictions of this kind served to control the output of political and heretical writings. Over the next century the imposed decrees lapsed as the Star Chamber was abolished and for a short period the printing trade flourished, only to be curbed by the Licensing Act of 1662, when half the printing houses in England were closed down.

Control by the state and the church was not unique to Britain: all over Europe freedom to publish was controlled. In France, before the Revolutionary and Napoleonic Wars of the late eighteenth century, the number of printing offices was strictly limited and all had to be officially sanctioned and sworn in.

For two centuries after its introduction, the printing trade in England changed little until state control began to decline. After 1688 the Licensing Act was allowed to lapse permanently, giving the printing trade freedom to develop in the provinces, although there was a legal requirement for printers to register.[6] This did not mean that printers were free to print what they liked. Legislation remained to prevent the publication of printed matter of a seditious or treasonable nature. In the eighteenth century laws were even passed against printing and publishing advertising material relating to horse racing in an attempt to restrict interest in the sport (Geo. II, Act. 13). By 1800 there was some relaxation of government intervention and the Stationers' Company had lost its power, becoming little more than a society of employers in printing, bookselling and the stationery trades.

Printing was essentially a controlled and conservative trade, whose restricted progress was not only reflected in the small number of firms in England but also in the limited demand for printed matter in the pre-industrial age. The figures in Table 2.1 represent an estimate of the number of printing offices in England, although because there were at least some unregistered presses, the actual number of presses was probably greater than the table suggests.

Table 2.1   Total number of printing offices in England, 1525–1855

1525	1550	1583	1637	1649	1661	1668	1724	1785	1808	1826	1855
10	30	21	20	60	70	35	75	124	216	323	423

Sources: compiled from various sources, including Cannon, Thomas and Musson (see Bibliography).

Art preservative of all arts

Some indication of the status of printing can be determined by the assertion that this was the art that preserved all other arts: the importance of what was printed both in terms of the content and appearance had at least some bearing on how the printer was judged in society. In the first years of printing the main requirement had been for devotional works (Latin missals, breviaries, psalters and bibles) and classical texts with an average run of 200 copies. By 1500, leaflets containing details of books to be published, stock lists of books, letters of indulgence, grammars and dictionaries were common. During the sixteenth century religious books and medical treatises and herbals, together with books containing home remedies, were produced, as were pamphlets, playing cards and broadsheets.

Many factors contributed to the changes in printing, notably increased industrial and commercial activity which created new demands for printed material; the growth of new wealth and the influence of the industrial classes; the new spirit of capitalism, individualism and the move towards *laissez-faire*. By 1800, with increased commercial activity, there was a well-established demand for forms, stationery, handbills, posters, legal documents, school-books and newspapers.[7] The introduction of the penny post in 1840, allowing cheap and efficient delivery of mail, encouraged the development of direct mail advertising: the number of letters posted rose from 76 million in 1839 to 640 million by 1865. From this time elaborate coloured labels and wrappers were produced as manufacturers took precautions to protect their products against counterfeiting and to establish brand recognition. Decorative printing was especially popular in the nineteenth century, allowing the skill and artistry of the compositor to be seen by a wide public. Style, consistency in spelling and typography all became matters for public interest and comment. The trade societies' own membership cards bore testimony to the great skill and artistic endeavour involved in nineteenth-century printing.

Perhaps the largest area of growth was in popular literature. Aimed specifically at the working classes, broadsides (single sheets printed on one side), chapbooks and cheap pamphlets were produced in large quantities. Execution broadsides were especially popular: illustrated with crude woodcuts and providing details of executions, these often sold between one and two million copies. In the post-Chartist era the move away from agitation and protest towards greater respectability, prudence and financial stability opened up new opportunities for the publication of popular literature. Emphasis was placed on working-class respectability through hard work, thrift, temperance and education – a message that was delivered by the many periodicals of the time. For example, John Cassell, who started off as a temperance reformer, produced the popular *Workingman's Friend* (1852) and Cassell's *Popular Educator* (1852).

The Society for the Diffusion of Useful Knowledge (SDUK) published the popular weekly and *The Penny Cyclopaedia*. With a circulation of 200,000 per issue, the *Penny Magazine* provided clear simple instruction on every subject that would benefit the working man and effectively argued that trade unions, by calling strikes, spread desolation and despair. Although the SDUK ceased in 1847, its influence lasted for many more years.

Technical developments in printing

Improved engineering techniques, the invention of duplicate plates (stereotypes) and the introduction of machine-made paper (1798) all enhanced the possibilities for industrialization of this old-established handcraft.[8] However, it is important to stress that small-scale craft printers coexisted alongside large printers throughout the period under discussion, as they still do today.

Early illustrations of printing offices show no mechanical aids other than the heavy wooden press used by Gutenberg, a press that remained in use until 1800. Capable of printing 250 sheets per hour, the press was slow and extremely labour-intensive. The paper was first damped, then the pressman inked the type, next a boy laid the paper on the press before the pressman pulled down the screw which applied the pressure, and finally a boy took the printed sheet off the press. In this way, using hand-made papers, hand-cast type and the wooden press, printing could be truly described as a handicraft.

From 1800, however, developments in machinery design were numerous, rapid and sustained throughout the period covered by this study. In 1800 Earl Stanhope produced the first iron press, which required less physical strength to operate and allowed output to increase considerably. This was followed in 1810 by the application of steam to a new kind of power-driven cylinder press; by 1814 *The Times* newspaper was printed on a powered press designed by Fredrich Koenig.[9] Koenig's press increased the speed of production to 1100 sheets per hour; by 1828 *The Times* was printing 4000 sheets per hour on Applegarth's revolving press, representing a sixteen-fold increase in output over the hand press.[10] While the printing trade generally escaped Luddite attention and *The Times* did not employ trade-society labour, the power press was installed in secret in case its introduction provoked violent actions by the hand-press men.[11]

The introduction of the power press demanded greater skill of the operative and, more importantly, constant attention during a print run, making it impractical for the new 'machine printer' to spend time setting type. For the first time in the history of printing there was a clear division of labour based on increased specialization and providing opportunities for the employment of unskilled and semi-skilled labour in the pressroom. Competition and rivalry soon developed between compositors and pressmen due to differing wage rates and the fact that in the early years of the century compositors supervised the work of the pressmen. A further consequence of mechanization was the introduction of a growing number of service trades. Before 1800, printers were almost entirely independent of other trades: from casting type to mixing ink nearly all the work was carried out within the confines of the 'closed shop'. More complex equipment involved other workers such as printers' engineers, joiners, smiths and roller makers, a development that further reduced the exclusiveness of the trade.

There is no evidence that printers mounted any concerted opposition to mechanization, although the action of *The Times* in secretly installing a power press does suggest that this was a possibility. Only in the case of the introduction of the stereotype as a duplicate printing surface is there evidence of opposition, where the men saw the process as 'exceedingly inimical to their interests'.[12] Initially developed by William Ged of Edinburgh around 1740, the purpose of the stereotype was to provide duplicate plates of the composed pages in order to print the text on two or more machines simultaneously. Ged was engaged by the University of Cambridge to print bibles and prayer books but it is claimed that his efforts were sabotaged by compositors and pressmen who, before the final cast was taken, made changes to the final proofs, resulting in errors in the finished plates. The process, which involved taking a plaster mould of each page and then filling the mould with molten metal to form a duplicate of the original page, did not become commercially viable until after 1800, but its impact on larger printers was significant.

Stereotyping allowed a single job to be printed on a number of presses and permitted the type to be distributed and reused; a duplicate plate was retained in case the work should be reprinted at a later date. The introduction of the stereotype opened up the possibility of great economic advantages for printers and publishers alike, allowing greater flexibility and savings while reducing the time taken to have a publication printed and on sale. It was especially difficult for publishers to calculate the precise demand for a particular publication; overprinting meant that books and periodicals that did not sell became expensive waste paper. Equally, it was uneconomic to print too few copies and then to be faced with a reprint, especially if the original type had been broken down and distributed back to the type cases.

Stereotypes were important for technical reasons too. If original illustrations in the form of woodcuts and engravings were printed from directly, the lines became damaged by the continual movement and pressure of the press, especially during long runs of printed work. Providing duplicate plates overcame this problem. The *Penny Magazine*, for example, which had a circulation of 160,000, had six duplicate plates cast so that the work could be produced on more than one machine; this also allowed for the substitution of plates that became worn during printing.

Just as paper was an essential element in the success of printing in the fifteenth century, the mechanization of paper manufacture was vital to the mechanization of printing. Hand-made paper was expensive and unavailable in the quantities required for the long print runs now required. When the first efficient papermaking machines were introduced into England in 1803, production capacity increased by a factor of ten over hand-made paper.[13] Capacity increased from 11,000 tons in 1800 to 100,000 tons in 1860 and by 1900 this had reached 652,000 tons.[14] By 1824 the price of paper had fallen by 25 per cent and by 1843 by almost one-half, a trend which continued until 1900 when some papers cost as little as 1*d*. per lb. Improvements in inks and varnishes followed. With the discovery of the first coal-tar dyes, new finer-texture pigments became available, allowing better printability and a wider choice of inks.

The consequences of change

The introduction of the power press meant that an important part of the printing process changed from being labour-intensive to being capital-intensive. Rather than the £10 paid previously for a wooden hand press, the new, expensive machinery meant investment on a large scale. Many printers were forced to seek financial aid from outside the trade and to take steps to ensure adequate returns on capital. In the early years of the nineteenth century the proprietors of *The Times* newspaper, for example, risked large sums of money in supporting and subsidizing mechanical developments in printing. Not only were the technical advances in printing extensive, but the whole scale of production changed because this trade benefited more than most from economies of scale. Mechanized presses needed large volumes of work of the same kind to ensure economic production. Typesetting by hand and the cutting of illustrations were the most expensive part of the process but, once done, an infinite number of copies could be printed off: the greater the number, the less the finished work cost per copy.

The availability of cheap printed matter played an important part in the development of widespread literacy but, in turn, for printers and publishers to benefit from economies of scale, they needed a large literate population. In 1840 it is estimated that out of a population of 18 million, between two-thirds and three-quarters could read, providing market conditions whereby long print runs increased. For example, circulation of the *Penny Magazine* (1832–45) reached 200,000 and both *Reynolds News* and *Lloyds Weekly* broke through the 100,000 circulation barrier in 1856.[15] One consequence of producing periodicals on this scale was that the whole publication had to be brought out on a pre-announced date, demanding accurate planning. By the middle of the nineteenth century the repeal of the 'taxes on knowledge', the Advertisement tax (1853), the Newspaper Stamp (1855) and the Paper tax (1860), led to an increase in demand for printing and a reduction in cost.[16] During the third quarter of the century, the three Education Acts (1870, 1876 and 1880) resulted in increased demands for schoolbooks and eventually created a new class of reader who provided a market for cheap books, popular newspapers and periodicals.

Circulation figures increased to such an extent that, in 1893, when *Pearson's Weekly* ran a 'missing word competition', circulation reached one million copies and the work had to be shared between six printers.[17] Production on this scale needed sound financial backing – a point illustrated at the time of the Great Exhibition when William Clowes and Son, in conjunction with the paper company Spicer Brothers, won the contract for the exhibition catalogue. The 500,000 catalogues produced used 50 tons of type, 30,000 reams of paper and three tons of ink.[18] In addition to the printing, the firm took responsibility for compiling the list of 20,000 exhibits and translating the work into French and German.

It would be misleading, of course, not to mention the risks in this expanding and competitive business. In 1827, during a recession in publishing, six London publishers went bankrupt in one week alone, leaving William Clowes with debts of £25,000.[19] It was especially difficult for small printers to obtain the right balance of work to keep men busy. Printers who did not have a local newspaper to produce were particularly vulnerable to shortages of work. On the other hand small jobs were important to printers because they gave a rapid return on investment compared to books, which were costly, often took a long time to produce and did not always sell. Even some larger firms had trouble making profits through general printing. Raymond Brown, author of *The Story of Balding and Mansell 1892–1992*, estimates that in its 100-year history the jobbing part of the business rarely made a profit.[20]

Size of the trade

Table 2.2 shows that, compared with textiles, engineering and building, printing was still a relatively small industry in 1851.

Table 2.2   Numbers employed in selected industries, 1851 (000s)

Engineering	Textiles	Building	Printing
536	661	496	62

Source: British Labour Statistics, *Historical Abstract 1886–1968* (HMSO, 1970), p. 195.

Even in the later period of our study, development of the trade was on a modest scale. Growth in printing between 1891 and 1911 was a moderate 15.7 per cent, compared with 119.0 per cent in chemicals, 120 per cent in vehicles and 84.0 per cent in food processing.[21]

Not only were the total numbers employed in printing significantly smaller than in engineering, textiles and building, but the industry was made up mainly of small firms. No printing office compared in size or scale to the shipbuilding or engineering firms of, for example, Tyneside, where in 1880 Swan Hunters employed between 6000 and 7000 men and Palmers of Jarrow employed 8000 men.[22] Nevertheless, over a sixty-year period there was a fivefold increase in the numbers employed (Table 2.3). Although the building industry was much larger than the printing industry, the structure of firms was similar. For example, of the 1726 building firms in the north-west of England, 1174 firms employed 10 workers or fewer and only 9 firms employed more than 100.[23]

Table 2.3   Numbers employed in printing, books and stationery, 1851 and 1911 (000s)

Year	Males	Females	Total
1851	62	16	78
1911	253	153	397

Source: Musson, A. E., *The Growth of British Industry*, p. 140

It will be argued that the relatively small size of printing firms had a significant bearing on the course of industrial relations. Many printing companies were small family concerns where the employer would be in direct daily contact with perhaps two or three workers. In these circumstances the social and economic interests of the employees would be seen as the same as those of the owner of a small printing office, providing little incentive for collective action. Employers of this kind would themselves have served their time in the trade and evidence suggests that craft or sectional interests were of paramount importance, often taking precedence over class and political consciousness. Working conditions in many of these small establishments would have been variable, allowing few opportunities for advancement and little in the way of welfare benefits. On the other hand, for many the informality and shared experience of working in a family concern would have outweighed the benefits of working for a large employer.

A further characteristic of an industry composed of small firms appears to be that firms were economically vulnerable, many remaining in business only a short time, others merging or taken over by larger firms. In Manchester, for example, of the 50 printing firms in existence in 1836 only 21 were in business seven years later and only six of these original 21 firms were listed in *Kelly's Directory* of 1891.

Not all printing offices remained small; consequently in firms employing large numbers of workers there was greater opportunity for workers in specific trades acting collectively with the benefit of strong society leadership. On the other hand, conformity to standard working practices through regulation of time and conduct at work meant some loss of control by the men of how work was organized. The need to employ managers and foremen to control large-scale production widened and emphasized the social and economic gulf between employees and employers. Loss of some autonomy in the workplace, however, must be offset against the advantages gained. Working in custom-built factories, which were generally better lit, heated and ventilated, and had improved sanitary arrangements, represented a better working environment. Also provident, sick and welfare funds were more likely to be provided in larger firms, giving a degree of social security.[24]

Specialization

Inevitably the introduction of the power press and the stereotype led to a degree of specialization among printers, partly because presses were designed to take a specific sheet size with a particular kind of work in mind. Specialization in printing began towards the end of the eighteenth century. Some firms concentrated on book production, others on newspapers or general printing, and in firms that produced more than one class of work it was usual to use separate companionships for each class of work (see p. 39). This almost amounted to a number of small firms operating under one roof, as men were paid on different scales according to the work undertaken.

By the mid-nineteenth specialization had increased greatly. The firm of William Clowes and Sons is perhaps typical of the larger firm. Started as a one-man business in 1803, by 1840 the firm employed 600 men specializing in Stationery Office contracts, particularly security printing, legal work and foreign-language texts. It also produced railway timetables, periodicals and posters, and William Clowes, the proprietor, extended the scope of the business by opening a military bookshop in London selling maps and military stationery.

Partly because of language differences, imports and exports of printed matter were not on the same scale as in some industries, although there is evidence that printers and publishers took advantage of any opportunities for international trade. For the European market English printers sold stereos of woodcut illustrations in France and Germany. According to the *Printers' Register* of February 1868, the illustrations in *Harpers' Bazaar* were casts from engravings made and used in Germany. It was also reported that woodcuts used in London and Paris fashion journals appeared a month earlier in the *Victoria Magazin* published in Berlin. Apparently these were sent to different countries together with the translated original text. Books and other publications produced in large quantities had to be sold, and English printers and publishers identified opportunities to maximize capital with remarkable speed. The publishers of the *Penny Magazine* quickly found a way to avoid the 33 per cent import tariff imposed by the American government on all foreign publications by despatching stereotypes of the pages of the magazine to a New York bookseller. The bookseller then arranged for the magazine to be produced using local labour and materials, thus avoiding the tax and allowing the magazine to go on sale at 2 cents per copy rather than 3 cents. Other firms met the particular demands of the trade. *Wood's Typographic Advertiser*, started in 1862, quickly reached a circulation of 4500 copies. The firm specialized in 'stock cuts' (duplicate illustrations) of royal events, religious images and suchlike so that printers had ready-made images to use when appropriate.

Moves towards industrialization had other consequences in that new markets for printed matter brought competing and conflicting interests to the fore. Not only was there competition on the basis of price but also through new machinery, new products and new business methods, all aspects of printing becoming subject to control from outside the workshop. Availability of finance, paved roads, fast coaches, and eventually the railways allowed publishers to organize and control markets, enabling production, within certain limits, to expand its own markets. Because publishers acquired copyright over an author's work, texts were treated like commodities that could be bought and sold in the marketplace, writers becoming subject to control like others employed in industrial production.[25] Publishing became a profession, but printing remained a trade; the printer received a bare 10 per cent of the price of a book which sold at 200 per cent over cost.[26] As John Johnson, Printer to the Oxford University Press, pointed out, 'the "mechanick" printer, unless he was also a bookseller, was a subservient man of low degree'.[27] This was not a new situation, as early as the mid-seventeenth century printers complained that 'the reason no good printing is seen in England is that we are oppressed by the stationers, who pay starving prices for the work – the remedy being to honour printers as they do in foreign countries'.[28]

Increased demand for printed matter and the subsequent technical developments in production were just part of the whole transformation affecting nineteenth-century printing and publishing. Feltes, in his Marxist analysis of nineteenth-century publishing, argues that diversity of format (monthly part publication, three-volume books, bi-monthlies) represented the beginning of a capitalist mode of production, citing the Chapman and Hall edition of *Pickwick Papers* (1836) as the first example of commodity publishing.[29] Long works were 'parcelled up' by publishers and given out to several printing houses. 'Clique' or class journals met the needs of definable groups of potential subscribers and allowed proprietors to control text and images, Feltes even identifies an upper- and middle-class orthodoxy in typography, where the 'tight packing' of type was reminiscent of *The Times*.[30] Another example of the book as a commodity was Mudie's 'select library'. Mudie bought up large quantities of books from publishers at advantageous prices, giving him a great deal of power within the trade and with the general public. He charged a guinea per year to borrowers, encouraging them to borrow rather than buy, and he produced lists advertising 'new and choice books', clearly a forerunner of the twentieth-century book club and best-sellers' list. One particular strategy used by Mudie to maximize his profits and keep prices high was to insist that publishers produce triple-deckers, that is one novel produced as three separate books.[31]

Improvements in the technology of printing lowered production costs and resulted in greater profits for those who were prepared to speculate in periodical publishing, advertising and book production. While production workers in printing often experienced relatively stable industrial relations with their immediate employers, they were caught up in a wider, more intense struggle for control of publishing and the press. Authors, for example, were subject to exploitation and to protect their interests founded the Society of Authors (1884), a society that William Heinemann described as 'a trade union more complete, more dangerous to the employer, more determined in its demands than any of the other unions ... '.[32] Even the artist was no longer in direct control of his work. New methods of reproducing illustrations meant that the final result was subject to selection and manipulation, for example by editors of such publications as the *The Graphic* and *The Illustrated London News*.

Many other developments affected the working lives of printers. To some extent, the invention of the typewriter demystified the compositor's craft. From 1850, when the electric telegraph was introduced, news, announcements and topical stories all became wares that were sold in the marketplace by 'intelligence agencies'. These changes represented specific and fundamental forms of control over the labour process, which further reduced the power of the individual to determine the nature of what was produced.

Printing in the Manchester region

It is appropriate at this juncture to look at some aspects of the printing trade in the Manchester region. Printers tended to be isolated and dispersed in the community, resulting in less social cohesion compared with workers in larger

Table 2.4 Numbers employed in printing in Cheshire, Lancashire and London, 1841–1911

	Cheshire		Lancashire		London	
Year	Male	Female	Male	Female	Male	Female
1841	536	20	4,432	375	12,428	1,801
1851	608	48	5,382	833	21,474	4,893
1861	782	79	8,313	1,668	30,752	7301
1871	1,113	156	11,711	3,303	40,225	9,862
1881	1,324	360	15,497	5,890	48,355	17,607
1891	2,075	643	21,007	8,948	60,929	26,354
1901	3,107	1,443	25,725	13,057	63,566	33,369
1911	4,253	2,789	29,548	17,493	65,395	37,979

Note: As well as general printing trades, these figures include bill posting, stationers and those engaged in paper manufacture.

Source: Lee, C. H., *British Regional Employment Statistics 1841–1971* (Cambridge University Press, 1979).

industries who may have come together outside working hours through social and recreational activities organized by the employers. In Manchester a number of printers were situated close to each other, for example around the Deansgate and Market Street areas, but because these firms were mostly small, this did not amount to a community of printers.

As the figures in Table 2.4 show, London remained the largest centre for the trade; nevertheless substantial numbers were employed in Cheshire and Lancashire.

Examination of the various estimates of the size of the Manchester printing trade in respect of both the number of offices and the number of men employed shows significant discrepancies. In the *Report on Printers' Strikes and Trade Unions*, prepared for the National Association for the Promotion of Social Science in 1860, the Secretary of the Typographical Association reported the following figures for Manchester:

Number of Offices (fair)	56
Number of Offices (unfair)	3
Number in the Society	370
Non-society men	6
Men not working or casually employed	110

Musson estimates the actual number of offices in 1853 as 70, rising to over 150 in 1893.[33] Based on figures provided by the trade union, both these estimates appear greatly to underestimate the actual numbers employed as well as the number of offices. Examination of trade directories of the period reveals the figures shown in Table 2.5.

Table 2.5   Number of printing offices in Manchester, 1836–1900

1836	*1843*	*1891*	*1900*
50*	101*	208*	312**

*   Including lithographic printers.
**   Letterpress only.

Sources: *Slater's Directory* (1836, 1843 and 1900); *Kelly's Directory* (1891).

The apparent understatement by the Typographical Association of the numbers employed in the Manchester printing industry may be of some significance. Assuming that the trade society had accurate figures on its own membership (from subscriptions paid and voting lists), the conclusion must be drawn that there were a substantial number of non-society offices. A further indication of the inaccuracy of these figures is the claim that in Manchester there were only six non-society men.[34] If this were the case, it would mean that 98 per cent of printers in the city were members of the union, a figure that greatly exceeds Musson's generous claim that two-thirds of printers were members of trade societies.

Printing occupied a strategic place in the Victorian economy in that it met the needs for advertising and publicity materials essential to expanding industry and commerce.[35] In the Manchester region, the growth and importance of the printing industry were due in part to the success of the engineering and textile industries, with many small printing firms catering for the specific needs of the different trades. In the case of textiles the demand for pattern cards and multi-coloured labels was so great that these items became a speciality of the Manchester printing trade. Each bale of cloth exported had three labels, one giving a description of the cloth, another stating the manufacturer's details and the third being a brightly coloured picture to appeal to those in the country to which the cloth was exported who could not read.[36]

Literacy of the general public was important to the development of the increasingly complex society and a number of Manchester printers have specialized in the production of schoolbooks and other educational materials.

Often printers were associated with the stationery trades, manufacturing and supplying account books and forms that were in constant demand by the large number of commercial undertakings in Manchester. Specialist printers catered for particular needs: for example the firm of Theil and Tangye specialized in typesetting in German, French, Italian and Spanish, while other firms catered for the needs of the insurance industry and the legal profession. Additionally, Manchester had a suitable infrastructure to support the growth of the printing trade. For example, 44 per cent of the English papermaking firms were located in Lancashire and numerous manufacturers of printing machinery and sundry items such as inks, rollers and type metal were located in Manchester.[37]

The city was never, however, a centre of book production, as the large book houses tended to be located in London or Edinburgh or in country towns where wage rates were lower. Technological impacts on the trade were most significant in the newspaper and periodical trade. From the early eighteenth century through to the present time, Manchester has been second only to London as a major centre of newspaper production. It is estimated that more than 300 newspapers have been produced in the city, from Whitworth's *Manchester Gazette* (later the *Manchester Magazine*), founded in 1730, to the *Manchester Guardian*, founded as a weekly in 1821 and becoming a daily in 1855.[38] Newspaper production on this scale had a significant bearing on the power and influence of trade union activity in the general printing industry. Newspapers relied on taking on operatives who had been trained as craftsmen in jobbing offices and who also provided the pool of casual labour necessary for the economical production of newspapers. Newspaper compositors were paid higher rates than compositors working in jobbing offices, allowing something of an elite to develop within the trade. Higher wage rates were possible because the high price paid for advertising space was out of proportion to the cost of production.

An additional dimension in the industrial relations of the printing trade was the political tendency of the newspapers themselves. Many regional newspapers were started or bought by local industrialists or by political parties. The *Stockport Advertiser*, in its first edition of 22 January 1822, made its political stance clear:

> it is essential that the politic of the paper be known to expose the fierce inroads of revolutionists and anarchists ... the dangerous class of people who, under pressure of a wild and theoretical and impractical reform are too often attempting our admirable constitution.[39]

Swain and Co., proprietors of the *Stockport Advertiser*, was formed and sponsored by the Conservative and Unionist Associations of Stockport and the neighbouring parliamentary constituencies of East and mid-Cheshire and South Manchester. Few newspapers were truly independent: in Manchester, for instance, the *Courier* and the *Manchester Evening Mail* were Conservative papers and the *Manchester Guardian* Liberal.[40] While it is not suggested that the actions of the proprietors were always politically motivated, the printing unions often had to negotiate with astute, ideologically committed, employers.

The printing office

From this general survey it is now appropriate to look in some detail at the internal organization of the printing office in order to understand something of the culture of work experienced by the compositor.

The majority of compositors specialized as book hands, newspaper hands or jobbing compositors, reflecting the different kinds of knowledge and skill needed for various classes of work. In larger firms, work was divided up into separate departments, resulting in a hierarchy of men of the same trade, who belonged to different chapels and who were paid according to different scales within the one firm. In the composing room, the word 'job' had the specific meaning of a piece of work that could be worked as a single sheet, for example fly-bills, trade cards and bill-heads. A 'job' was undertaken by one compositor, who, from about 1850, became known as a specialist art compositor in recognition of work that had been done by one man from start to finish with skill and a certain amount of freedom for creative interpretation.[41] The work of this independent craftsman contrasted sharply with that of compositors employed on book, periodical or newspaper work, who normally worked as part of a close-knit team but often carried out repetitive tasks day in day out.

Reproduced with permission of the V&A Picture Library, London

Figure 2.1 Part of the manuscript of *Dombey and Son* (1848) by Charles Dickens

Compositors had the difficult task of deciphering illegible copy while working at speed. Clearly men working with this kind of copy needed some literary ability and a great deal of patience. It is recorded that when proofed, the average of errors per page was between one and two.

Within the composing room work was organized in one of two ways. A companionship, usually referred to as a 'ship' consisting of six or seven men, took copy and their instructions from an overseer appointed by the master printer. Alternatively a form of subcontracting was organized where a similar number of men worked under a 'clicker', a man who was not paid by the master printer but by the men themselves. When a compositor had set his take of copy, he made this up into pages and any lines left over were passed on to the man setting the next page, a credit or debit record being kept for each man. Men were paid either on 'time', whereby each man shared equally in the payment, or on 'line', whereby each man was paid according to the number of lines set. Work could be held 'on the shelf'; that is, men built up credits allowing them to take time off when work was slack. The system of organizing workers into subgroups gave the men a good deal of control over precisely how the work should be carried out and encouraged men to maximize piecework payments. When working on the 'piece', large amounts of continuous text had to be parcelled out to a ship, and it was the clicker's job to distribute the copy, maintain consistency of style and account for the 'bill' charged by the ship. In the ship system of working, 'lean' and 'fat' copy could be evenly distributed through the ship. Lean referred to difficult copy that was slow to set and usually involved small type sizes, accents or foreign languages. Fat referred to easy text setting, often with many blank spaces, that could be accomplished with speed.

The clicker was not a foreman. In some cases he was appointed by the overseer, but more commonly by the men, who could remove him if he acted unfairly.[42] This form of subcontracting laid emphasis not on the individual craftsman but on the subgroup of workers who had to contribute to the team effort and were ultimately responsible for the level of earnings of the whole ship. In some ways the existence of companionships did little to strengthen trade union organization within the works, often lessening the tendency to take collective action at chapel level in favour of the short-term good of the ship.

In some of the larger firms a structure of three classes of ship operated: the first-class ship took on all the prestigious work, the second-class ship the medium-quality work and the third-class ship, often made up of casual hands, performed the inferior jobs such as carrying out authors' corrections. In this kind of firm men were paid according to different scales and experienced varying working conditions. Divisions of this kind increased over time as technological changes served to widen the gulf between the skills needed to undertake different kinds of work.[43]

Rivalry, too, existed between firms, usually based on the quality of work produced and the varying wage rates paid in each town. Divisions of labour also meant that the all-round knowledge possessed by many printers in the past was lost, as the training given to apprentices was directed to a firm's specialized needs. Wide variations in the skill levels of compositors were acknowledged, both by trade unions and employers, with some men only useful when setting reprint copy while others were able to work with difficult hand-written manuscripts, correcting spelling and punctuation, and using accented letters.[44]

The chapel

Since the early sixteenth century through to the present time craftsmen printers have exercised a degree of control in the workplace through the chapel, a democratic workplace institution legislating on a wide range of matters including aspects of production and the conduct of chapel members.[45] The origins of the term 'chapel' to describe the workmen in a printing office are somewhat obscure. It may have been that the title was conferred on the printing office by a high-ranking churchman, although a common explanation is that the title was adopted when William Caxton set up a press in the precincts of Westminster Abbey, but as the term was also common in France this explanation seems unlikely.

There can be little doubt about the practical and symbolic significance of the chapel. Because of the importance of printing to society, it was even suggested that chapels should be entitled to the same privileges of toleration, indulgence and support as that afforded to churches. The *Gentleman's Magazine* claimed 'that the printing office was such a sacred institution that reverence is due to it, likening the press to the sacred vessels and the printers to priests'.

It is worth noting that strictly the term chapel only applied to the formal meetings of the journeymen compositors, although many writers use the term loosely to include all men eligible to attend such a meeting. Excluding the master printer, apprentices and the correctors (who were selected by the master printer), membership of the chapel was compulsory and members elected the chapel officials: the father of the chapel (FOC) and the clerk of the chapel, both of whom had clearly defined responsibilities. Chapel officials received some remuneration for their responsibilities from chapel funds. In 1900 the normal payment to the FOC was £2 a year and £3 to the clerk. Men attending trade-society meetings at night also received a small payment. The position of the FOC was not the same as that of a shop steward in other trades. He had greater independence and power and was less answerable to the branch of the trade society. In practice what gave the FOC power over both the society and the employer was that he had a good deal of discretion about the extent to which society rules were applied in a particular firm.

The chapel had both disciplinary and benevolent purposes. One important function of the chapel was to maintain secrecy and mystery concerning the art of printing. The aim was to repel 'foreigners', that is all those who had not completed a seven-year apprenticeship. Sonenscher discusses the function of mystery in the workplace in relation to the history of the *compagnonnages* of eighteenth-century France.[46] The *devoir*, described as an informal, clandestine association of workers, was characterized by the pattern of association by initiation. Gradual erosion of legal provisions protecting the trade and the diffusion of a relatively limited range of skills are two reasons why workers in some trades strove to maintain internal solidarity. Symbolically created inequalities between groups of workmen served to make what in fact were similar routine tasks appear different.

Although Sonenscher maintains that there was no equivalent in England to the ritual and mythology of the French *compagnonnages*, there are some aspects of the behaviour of printers in England that show these characteristics.[47] Entry to the chapel through the payment of a 'benvenue' (a corruption of the French *bienvenue* or welcome) and the system of solacing workmen for minor misdemeanours in the printing office both served to maintain and preserve the distinctive nature of the trade. Group and class identities were partly shaped by the experience of work.

In the composing room initiation ceremonies were carried out when a new apprentice started work, serving to emphasize from the beginning the importance of the trade and signify that the boy was joining a privileged group of skilled artisans. The apprentice, carrying a wooden sword, headed a procession of the 'chapellonians' who walked round the room three times. The boy then kneeled before the FOC who exhorted him to be observant of his business, and not to betray the secrets of the workmen, an instruction written into boys' indentures. Finally the boy was 'christened' and given a title, usually a Duke or Lord of some nearby district.[48]

Not only did the chapel exercise positive methods of ensuring cohesion through chapel rituals, communal drinking and the wayzgoose, but negative sanctions were used against men offending the chapel in some way. Fines, 'sending to Coventry', and making it impossible for compositors to carry out their work were all used to ensure that chapel rules were obeyed, a common strategy being to keep men short of materials to work with.[49] Every chapel was said to be haunted by an imaginary spirit named 'Ralph', who could be blamed for the misfortunes that befell chapel members who broke the rules. Compositors who failed to observe the customs of the trade found that their type cases had been mixed by the chapel 'ghost', a task easy to accomplish but extremely difficult to rectify, making composition impossible.[50] 'Pied' cases needed to be cleaned, that is all type removed, sorted and redistributed, which took many hours for cases containing thousands of characters.[51] As a last resort the offending member of the chapel was 'smoked out', all chapel members surrounding his frame with lighted brimstone matches and singing a 'doleful ditty'.[52]

On a small scale these actions might mean that a compositor lost piece-work time but sometimes they resulted in a major confrontation, with both employers and men prepared to defend their rights in court. 'Jerrying' (loud singing, cheering or clapping) was another strategy open to the compositors to show their feelings on particular occasions. It is recorded that the custom of 'jerrying' is as old as the trade itself, and the events which give rise to it as various as the jobs a printer has to undertake.[53] 'Jerrying' was used in re-sponse to agreeable announcements, but it was more often used in a satirical or ironical manner. During a dispute over 'jerrying' at the *Evening Star* office in Ashton-under-Lyne in February 1878, the office was closed to society compositors because the firm refused to pay wages owing to piece hands.[54] When non-society men were engaged, however, it was alleged that many of the type cases were in a state of 'pie', resulting in delays in getting the paper to press. The chapel members made counter-claims that the cases had been pied by the proprietor as an excuse to sack society men and engage non-society men. In the ensuing county court action against the Typographical Society members, the judge pointed out that 'jerrying' was a grave offence, to which the men replied that it was their ancient right.[55]

The idea of ancient rights recurs constantly, the compositors keeping their old craft rules in place perhaps longer than any other workers. Printing was a trade very much influenced by past customs and practices and the institution of the chapel maintained remarkable continuity of function that carried over into the industrial age.[56] As one nineteenth-century commentator pointed out, 'Caxton or DeWorde would find only a slight difference in the modus oper-andi of the modern compositor, although they might mourn his fall in social rank'.[57]

Many of the customs mentioned in nineteenth-century chapel rules were the same as those recorded by Moxon in the late seventeenth century. The 1875 chapel rules of Wyman and Son, London's oldest printers, were said to be:

> the results of the practical experience of several generations of work-men and exemplify the regulations deemed necessary in a large office for the maintenance of discipline and the protection of the interests of the men as between themselves.[58]

Many chapel rules did in fact serve the interests of the master printer, while other rules were for the benefit of men engaged on piecework. Chapel rules from 1734 laid down regulations relating to hoarding sorts (letters) and similar practices that could slow down other compositors.[59] Calling chapel meetings resulted in loss of men's time, so a balance was sought between collecting fines and losing money. Any member calling a chapel meeting had to deposit the sum of 1s. with the FOC, the purpose being to deter frivolous calls for meetings that would result in men losing money unnecessarily. The Manchester Society, for example, insisted on a strict code of conduct from members attending chapel meetings, and the records provide ample evidence that men were frequently fined the relatively large sum of 10s. for behaving in a 'shameful manner'. Disputes in the chapel were settled by a majority vote on the basis that the chapel 'cannot err', but chapel meetings were treated seriously.

Chapel rules covered fighting, abusive language, drunkenness, leaving candles burning, dropping type and many minor misdemeanours of a technical nature. Penalties for breach of these rules and customs was in printer's language called a 'solace'. Before 1700 some physical punishments were administered, but because of claims that some had died on these occasions the practice fell into disuse. It was replaced by fines, the proceeds of which were used to buy drink for the chapel members. In the case of men who did not pay, chapel rules gave authority to the master 'on due and satisfactory proof' to stop the money out of the wages of the offending person.[60] Other rules were light-hearted and somewhat arbitrary; for example, men were fined if they mentioned spending chapel funds before Saturday night, for singing in the chapel and for saluting a woman in the chapel.

In addition to solaces, money for the chapel funds was raised in other ways. New entrants into the chapel were required to pay half a crown and when a journeyman married or his wife gave birth, the man was required to pay the same amount. An apprentice paid into chapel funds on becoming bound and again on achieving status as a journeyman. Fees paid by the apprentice to the chapel were levied because the chapel did not share in the premium paid to the employer.

Some indication of the way craft traditions operated can be gleaned from the way language was used to reinforce exclusiveness and to aid solidarity in the workplace. Often the terms used in the composing room were of ancient and obscure origins, ensuring that strong links with the past were maintained; some nineteenth-century historians attributed these terms to the educated workmen of the first English printing houses.

Such terms as 'chapel', 'father of the chapel' and 'font', which have persisted to the present day, demonstrate references to the early connection between the church and the craft. The type size great primer, for example, originated from Primavarins, the prayers to the Virgin Mary, and the type sizes brevier and canon referred to the part of the Mass that was printed in a larger type in the missal. In the press room under-inked areas on a printed sheet were called 'friars' and the over-inked sections 'monks'. The term 'pie', used to describe type that becomes mixed, is said to have originated in the pre-Reformation days of great confusion. Other words used in the printing office were of French origin, for example benvenue, minion, nonpareil and reiteration can all be traced back to the French journeymen who worked in London in the sixteenth century. Moxon described benvenue as 'being so constant a custom is still lookt [sic] upon by all workmen as the undoubted right of the chapel'.[61]

Technical terms of the trade were freely adapted to social banter; for example a compositor who was diligent was said to 'have his nose in the cap e box'.[62] A 'darkie' or 'ghoster' referred to a man who seized every opportunity to work long periods of overtime and a 'foreigner' was a man who had not served the full apprenticeship or who did not belong to the union. Later the word foreigner was also used to describe a job carried out without the knowledge of the employer.

Not only does this use of language show continuity over a period of 400 years, but these terms took time to learn, which meant that bogus workmen would quickly be discovered if they managed to infiltrate the chapel. Another ancient tradition, which served to differentiate 'true printers' from outsiders, was the singing, on special chapel occasions, of Cuz's anthem. Persisting until the late nineteenth century, this song involved chanting first the consonant, then the vowel, and afterwards both together followed by the syllables joined: ba-ba, be-be, bi-bi, babebi, bobo, babebibo and so on through the alphabet. Because this was difficult for outsiders to learn, it would soon have been clear if men had not served their time in the trade.

Social unity within chapels was especially important, as printers – unlike miners and textile operatives, who lived in close-knit communities – had fewer opportunities for association outside the workplace. Like the tradition of singing Cuz's anthem, organizing the wayzgoose around St Bartholomew-tide also served to reinforce cohesion in the workplace and to emphasize separation of outsiders.[63] Dating from the seventeenth century, the annual wayzgoose marked St Bartholomew's Day, the point in the calendar when printers traditionally renewed the paper windows, after which journeymen were permitted to work with the aid of candlelight. Originally taking the form of a dinner provided by the master printer, after which the men retired to a tavern, the wayzgoose by the late nineteenth century had become an annual day out followed by a social gathering in an alehouse; this tradition carryied on well into the twentieth century. In the USA printers gathered to celebrate the ex-printer Benjamin Franklin's achievements, and judged their prospects against those of Franklin's, a man who had himself experienced the chapel traditions when he worked in London. The close connection between leisure and work provided by chapel activities helped to reinforce the social solidarity of chapel members. Some recreation within the context of the workplace was understandable, given the long hours spent at work. Often these events emphasized exclusiveness, separate events being held for compositors and machine printers and for news and jobbing sections. In 1887 the *Manchester Courier and Evening Mail* news chapel held their wayzgoose at Alderley Edge, where they participated in organized sports, including long jump, 100-yard races and throwing competitions before dinner in the evening. On the same day, the jobbing chapel of the firm went on a ramble to Kinder Scout.[64] In the same year Blacklock's compositors' chapel spent the day visiting the stately house at Chatsworth.

Social events were not just held by individual chapels; sometimes the whole membership of a local society got together socially. In 1892, when the Ashton-under-Lyne branch of the Typographical Association held its annual wayzgoose the branch contributed 5*s*. for each of its 120 members attending. This provoked a bitter row, the branch being accused of 'stealing funds to provide a cheap spree with cheap beer', an accusation firmly rebuffed by the branch committee, which maintained it was up to the membership how to spend its own money.[65]

In addition to the wayzgoose organized by the chapel, employers kept the tradition of putting on a social event for their staff and, if the popularity of these social gatherings is anything to go by, relations between employees and their employers were evidently often cordial. It is recorded that in February 1879 the employees of Richard Johnson, the Manchester printer, enjoyed their annual meal at Goslings Restaurant, where 'the tables were weighted as ever with fruit, nuts, wine and beer'. Employees were given a half-day holiday for this event and this time presented Mr Johnson with a beautifully bound set of the works of Scott and Tennyson.[66] Records show that most printing firms mounted such celebrations at least once a year.

Chapel functions were clearly occasions for relaxation and merrymaking, but by the last quarter of the century there were some critics who objected to the heavy drinking, especially temperance and teetotal reformers from dissenting religious groups.[67] Clearly unimpressed by any notion of the compositor as a better sort of workman, temperance reformers claimed that 'when the tailors and compositors sign the pledge, ninety out of every hundred break it – they don't have the slightest notion of what honour is'.

Objections were made by those who disapproved of the 'depraved happenings' on moral grounds, while others objected to touting suppliers for money. It had been the tradition to bolster chapel funds through collecting money from firms who supplied type, paper and ink – a practice that could be seen as corrupt, with an implied threat of blackmail. By 1900 a number of suppliers took a stand against this practice. John Kidd and Co., a major supplier of inks, issued a notice stating 'we will not give, or permit to be given to ... chapel money, wayzgoose subscriptions or Christmas boxes'.[68]

The trade press often condemned the wayzgoose as a nuisance and a waste of money, and many trade union leaders and employers took the view that the profession was brought into disrepute by this undignified behaviour.[69] Although the *Typographical Circular* regularly reported details of the annual chapel outings, it rather contradictorily attacked the idea of the wayzgoose, claiming that 'it is often a prelude to the seven deadly sins ... a meal of six or seven courses is unsuited to a working man especially when flooded with the worst sort of drink'. It was pointed out that this objection was because the 'untimely spoken drunken printer is seen by the general public'. The anonymous writer in the *Circular* suggested that the half-sovereign spent on the celebration could be saved and perhaps an alternative would be for 'the men to worship together when the bells ring out on a Sunday morning'.

Despite the objections of some moral reformers, drink played an important part in the working life of the compositor for a number of reasons. Its nutrient and thirst-quenching properties were important to men who had to work long hours in the hot dusty atmosphere of the composing room, some men complaining that there was nothing more disgusting than a 'dry' chapel.[70] Possibly originating in pre-industrial habits brought in from the countryside, communal drinking practices provided a tangible social bond among workers, and the insistence by compositors that this was a 'tradition' appears to have been a defence of customary ways of doing things, providing a warning to those who wished to bring about change.

Elaborate rules were drawn up as to how money to buy beer should be raised and on what occasions it should be ordered. The radical campaigner Francis Place noted in 1833, 'in every printing office there is a bottle of rum, the men served themselves, keeping a score against themselves'. Taverns were used as 'call houses' where printers met the local society secretary to receive assistance in finding lodgings and seek news of any available work; the same taverns served as post offices and banks. The chapel never assembled without the fee of one gallon of porter, and combinations of three or four chapels would meet, traditionally on a Saturday night, to drink from the chapel funds and organize friendly societies. In Manchester, 4d. out of the monthly subscription of 1s. 6d. was spent on drink. 'Wet rent' was paid to the publican; that is, a guarantee was given that a certain quantity of liquor would be consumed in exchange for the free use of a room. However, as early as 1843 the Manchester printers voted to do away with 'wet rent' and instead pay the landlord £2.[71]

Many observers objected to the unwholesome, dishevelled 'pot man' selling ale in the workshops. Gradually, with the development of industrial capitalism, larger employers saw the use of alcohol as a question of discipline; its over-use resulted in inefficiency, accidents and insubordination. In 1892, for example, R. & J. Sharpe, the Manchester colour printers, gave evidence to the Parliamentary Commission that 'there was great irregularity through drunkenness'.[72]

A number of trade union leaders also saw drink as an unnecessary distraction that impeded the development of working-class respectability.[73] The Manchester Society eventually abandoned the tavern for meetings and instead opened their own premises, The Typographical Institute, 10a Pall Mall. These offices served as a call house, accommodation being provided in lodging houses rather than taverns.

Opposition to drink by employers was, however, tempered by the fact that this was a trade that relied heavily on casual labour, and employers were anxious not to antagonize prospective workers by placing a total ban on alcohol.[74] As one compositor recorded:

plenty is heard of the compositor who drinks less and receives more wages, but we have not noticed a word about the army of compositors, generally older men, who eat considerably less than they did under the old regime.[75]

The tradition of printers taking a drink during working hours continued into the late twentieth century, when public houses in the vicinity of newspaper offices were granted special licences to allow shift workers to have a drink in the early hours of the morning.

Within the workplace other customs served to confirm membership of the trade in quite specific ways, contributing to the formation of group and class identity.[76] Playing quadrats was popular with compositors. This was a game in which five or seven 'em quadrats' (spaces) were shaken like dice on to the stone, the highest number of 'nicks up' (a groove along one side) thrown after three throws being the winner.[77] Quadrats was a game played exclusively by compositors; they were the only members of the trade having ready access to the 'quads' required. The game was also played by American compositors, where the custom was to play for alcoholic drinks.

Another habit common in printing offices was the taking of snuff. Just as Lancashire mill workers masticated tealeaves and agricultural labourers chewed split peas, printers took snuff. Surprisingly, perhaps, many nineteenth-century printing offices did not allow compositors to smoke while working, and taking snuff provided an alternative. The practice involved elaborate and friendly gestures and these were incorporated into the chapel customs; for example, when an apprentice was released from his indentures the occasion was marked by the privilege of receiving a pinch of snuff from the FOC. At one of the early meetings of the Manchester Society it was agreed that tobacco be given to those who wanted it, although a small majority rejected a proposal that the society purchase two handsome snuffboxes.

While many of the traditions mentioned so far involved an element of craft exclusiveness, the obsessive concern with secrecy in the trade extended beyond normal trade matters with the formation of secret groups of tradesmen. Known as 'gifts', these groups were called by fanciful names, such as The Lions (1858) or The Pioneers (1874). They were members of the trade society but signed the slate (registered their availability for work) in 'gift' houses, causing general concern in the trade even in the late nineteenth century. Each member was pledged to notify any other member who was out of work where jobs were to be had, excluding those who were not members of the privileged cliques, a practice the trade union found abhorrent and difficult to stamp out.[78] The qualification of a gift man was 'that he shall not be, at the time of joining, [over] 45 years of age'; possibly the reason for this was that the 'gift' provided some sickness and unemployment benefits for its members.

The *Typographical Protection Circular* of 1849 maintained that 'gifts' were effectively a union within a union, describing them as 'the aristocratical few who attempted to monopolise the press work through the creation of miserable monopolies'. Secret groups of this kind did little for cohesion among the members of the London Society of Compositors. London was divided geographically by six or seven gifts with about sixty members each. Giving members a monopoly over vacancies, each man had to swear that he 'shall not acquaint any but his own Gift men where employment is to be obtained', making it almost impossible for provincial journeymen to obtain work in London. Gift members dominated the executive of the London Society of Compositors (LSC) in the 1890s in what amounted to a struggle for power between supporters of 'old' and 'new' unionism.[79] No gifts are known to have existed in the provincial trade represented by the Typographical Association, but the continued existence of such groups in London was a source of friction between the two unions.

In the USA there were secret societies of printers from 1840 until at least 1930, although some of their functions were different from those of the English gifts. Made up of 'hand-picked' men from the local typographical unions, their aim was to keep union control in the hands of those who would 'protect the interests of the union'. Initially called the Order of Faust, the society was subject to frequent name changes to disguise its existence (the Brotherhood, the Caxton League), and displayed many characteristics of Freemasonry, with oaths of secrecy, passwords and special handshakes.[80] In some ways the Order of Faust's actions, in seeking minority control of the union, were similar to those of the gifts in the LSC, although in the American case the purpose was to operate an efficient political machine from within the union rather than act as a protection agency. Both cases, however, represent examples of extreme exclusiveness of some subgroups working in the trade.

Although the chapel served to represent the members of the trade societies in much the same way as the miners' lodge commonly brought together men working in the same pit, it is worth noting that chapels were not simply the forerunner of trade union activities.[81] The early records of the Manchester Society show a concern mainly for relatively minor trade issues rather than wider concerns of working conditions and collective bargaining. Bateman, in his study of Bristol printers' chapels, also found that the established chapel systems were debilitating to the trade unions and needed to be ignored, disciplined and reorganized before they could be useful agents of trade unionism.[82]

Autonomy of the chapel could work in two ways. In a firm where there was a reasonably content group of workers, men were not always prepared to implement branch rules that might have little bearing on their own situation but might risk bringing them into confrontation with an otherwise compliant employer. As Musson concedes, many of the society rules were 'paper rules' only. At other times, when it suited the chapel to confront its employer, it would seek the backing of the branch to support its case. There are numerous examples of problems caused by individual chapels taking up hours of the branch committee's time in discussing in great detail minor points of procedure.

Another reason why the institution of the chapel did not easily become a base for trade unionism was that many of the chapel rules were formulated for the benefit of the employer. Chapel rules that were intended to punish men on behalf of the employer were of little relevance to the main interests of the trade union, and it was unrealistic for the union to attempt to take on the responsibilities of the employers. Nevertheless, this was a craft that, by 1800, had remained largely unchanged for 350 years, and future changes in the role and status of the printing craftsman were much informed by past traditions.

Apprenticeship

Apprenticeships dated from medieval times, having origins in the corporate control exercised by craft guilds.[83] The seven-year apprenticeship existed in the printing trade from the sixteenth century when the Stationers' Company, from its inception in 1557, maintained an almost complete monopoly of control, reinforced by parliamentary licensing acts such as the Star Chamber Decree of 1586.[84] The constant complaint in the nineteenth century of 'illegal men' referred to the 1563 Statute and was applied to men who had not served the full apprenticeship.[85] Usually marked by a formal deed registered at the Guildhall, apprenticeship served three main functions. First, it provided a system to regulate the supply of labour into a particular craft. Second, it specified the necessary time for an adequate degree of craft training, seven years in the case of printing, and third, it granted the man entry as a Freeman of the city, with the right to carry on business there.[86]

For more than 200 years harsh controls were applied to printing, but by 1800 the Licensing Act was allowed to lapse, leaving printing free from the authority of Parliament and the Stationers' Company. One consequence of the decline in the authority of the Stationers' Company was the gradual breakdown of the 'indoor' system, whereby apprentices lived as part of the master's household and received no payment for the duration of their indenture. Until 1800 most apprentices in printing were 'indoor', and although this was clearly a system in decline, as late as 1882 John Southward, the author of *Practical Printing*, recorded that some large printing offices had dwellings attached to the firm where the apprentices lived, supervised by a matron.[87]

The move to the outdoor system of apprenticeship meant that apprentices lived at home or in lodgings and received payment for their work. For the first time journeymen were in a position to influence the number of apprentices entering the trade, although many journeymen were not in favour of the outdoor system on the grounds that apprentices without the strict discipline of living with the master printer were in 'moral danger'. There may have been some truth in this, as in the space of two years, 32 apprentice printers received sentences for crimes committed in London and Surrey. The unease of the journeymen at the change may, however, have been a more general objection to labour becoming a mere market commodity.[88]

With the growth of the trade societies in the early nineteenth century, the regulation of numbers entering the trade became a matter of increasing concern, and records of the early typographical societies show that apprentice ratios were not kept in check without a struggle. In 1799 five committee members of the Society of Journeymen Pressmen were sentenced at Newgate to two years' imprisonment on the charge of 'interfering with the masters as to the number of their apprentices'. One of those charged, N. Lynham, died in gaol.[89]

As early as 1806 journeymen printers addressed a circular to the parents and guardians of prospective apprentices, warning of the consequences of an overstocked labour market:

> We beg leave to inform the Public one of the Resolutions entered into by the Masters is, that they will put one apprentice to every Journeyman; by that means one half of the business will be completely thrown out of work, their trade entirely lost and themselves, together with the unhappy youths, reduced to beggary!!![90]

In the same year the claim was made that every market town in England and Wales took an average of one apprentice and after seven years sent that man to London.[91] In his prize-winning essay written in 1850, 'The disease and the remedy', Edward Edwards, secretary of the London Society of Compositors, argued that the distressed state of the printing trade was due to excessive boy labour and had been so ever since the seventeenth century.[92] In some offices no apprentices were employed; in others the ratio varied from nine men to four boys to equal numbers of journeymen and apprentices.[93]

Musson describes the apparent problem of an excess of apprentices as one of the greatest difficulties facing the Northern Union. However, it would appear to be insecurity on the part of the compositors, who were concerned about the threat of an overstocked labour market, rather than the reality of too many apprentices that caused alarm.[94]

From 1846 the National Association resolved that in book and jobbing offices two apprentices should be allowed, irrespective of the number of journeymen. In larger offices one apprentice was allowed per four men to a maximum of three. In newspaper offices not more than three apprentices were allowed and none were permitted on daily newspapers.[95] Applying this ratio to the returns from local secretaries, it is possible to establish how successful the union was in limiting the supply of labour into the trade through the control of apprentices. Of 61 towns providing full membership details to the secretary of the Provincial Typographical Association in January

1860, 24 had less than their entitlement, 29 had more than their entitlement and 8 had exactly the correct quota.[96] All Scottish towns and the major centres of printing in Ireland (Dublin, Cork and Kilkenny) exceeded the quota allowed, tending to confirm the view that in Scotland and Ireland the trade union was less strong than in the major towns in England, where it would appear that the Provincial Typographical Association exercised greater control.

Of the five major towns listed in Table 2.6, four had fewer than their allotted numbers. Liverpool, which was known to be a centre with strong union support, was 30 apprentices short of its quota and Manchester had only one apprentice more than its allotted number. Considering the 61 towns surveyed, the actual number of apprentices employed totalled 1244, while the agreed ratios would have allowed 1208, giving an excess of 36 apprentices which represented only 2.9 per cent of the total. These figures should be considered in relation to the ratio of apprentices in other trades, for example in calico printing, where Berry and Co. of Lancashire employed 55 apprentices but only 2 journeymen and at Tod and Co., Dumbarton, where there were 60 apprentices and 2 journeymen.[97]

Table 2.6   Number of apprentices employed in five important towns, 1860

Town	Apprentice allocation	Actual no. of apprentices
Manchester	112	113
Sheffield	50	49
Liverpool	83	53
Hull	138	98
York	32	31

Source: Compiled from information in the *Social Science Report on Printers' Strikes* (1860).

The conclusion to be drawn is that, in 1860, in towns with strong union support, there was no great excess of apprentices overall. What the figures do not reveal is the distribution of apprentices between firms and within each branch. As the majority of printing firms were small businesses employing just one journeyman, even keeping to the agreed quotas resulted in a substantial number of apprentices. Taking Stockport as an example, Table 2.7 shows that out of 12 offices represented at the inaugural meeting of the Typographical Society, 8 offices employed only one journeyman. In total 25 journeymen were employed, together with 24 apprentices.

In addition to the structural aspects of the apprenticeship system there were important functional reasons why the system had always been important to

Table 2.7   Numbers employed in Stockport printing firms, 1871

Company	Number of men	Number of apprentices
County News	7	3
County Jobbing	3	2
J. Smith	1	1
Haig	1	1
Froggart and Co.	1	1
Mr May	2	1+1 turnover
Mr Davenport	1	2
Advertiser	5	3
Butterworth	1	2
Dalton	1	1
Dimmock	1	5
Barlow	1	1

Source: Stockport Public Library, ms. SZ 30 (1871).

employers and trade societies. An apprenticeship had to be bought and earned, and was therefore seen as a form of property which conferred rights and a certain minimal standing in the community, especially important in the English hierarchical society of the nineteenth century.[98] Apprentices were only allowed to join the Typographical Association during their last year of apprenticeship – although from 1891 this was extended to their last two years.

Through an apprenticeship boys had invested in a trade, and for a period of seven years had received less than full wages, although for the later years they had done a 'man's work' effectively as cheap labour. Especially important in printing was the right an apprenticeship gave a man to set up on his own account. Typically a boy worked from seven to ten years as an apprentice, followed by a few years as a journeyman and then, if sufficient capital could be acquired, he became a master himself. This was fairly common, as by the nineteenth century only a modest sum of money was needed to buy the equipment to start a small printing office. Charles Mamby Smith, for example, recorded that he spent '£20 on a small iron press, as good as new, large enough for 8 pages on a post sheet, and a further £20 on type, more than enough for the purpose'.[99]

In many cases entry to the trade involved the payment of a premium by the parent or guardian of a boy who became an indentured apprentice. The practice of paying premiums appears to have been normal in London and the Midlands, but was less common in Scotland, Wales and Northern Ireland.[100] Premiums were more common in the case of compositors than any of the other printing trades, although it was common in larger publishing houses,

𝕿𝖍𝖎𝖘 𝕴𝖓𝖉𝖊𝖓𝖙𝖚𝖗𝖊 made the *first* day of *April*

one thousand and nine hundred and *ten*   𝕭𝖊𝖙𝖜𝖊𝖊𝖓

Arthur Culver
hereinafter called the Master of the first part,

John Mills
hereinafter called the Parent, (or Guardian) of the second part and

Henry Mills
hereinafter called the Apprentice of the third part 𝖂𝖎𝖙𝖓𝖊𝖘𝖘𝖊𝖙𝖍 that the
said Apprentice of his own free will and consent and by and with the
consent and approbation of his said Parent (or Guardian) testified by his

executing these presents. 𝕯𝖔𝖙𝖍 put place and bind himself Apprentice
unto the said Master and with him to remain from the day of the date
hereof for the term of *seven* years thence next following and fully to
be complete and ended to be taught and instructed in the art trade and
business of
Letterpress Prnting (Compositor)
𝕬𝖓𝖉 the said apprentice doth hereby covenant promise and agree with
the said Master that he the said Apprentice shall and will at all times
during the said term whenever thereunto required well faithfully and
diligently according to the best of his skill and ability serve the said Master
in the said art trade or business of
Letterpress Printing
and obey his reasonable commands. And shall not nor will at any time or
times during the said term or after the expiration of thereof directly or
indirectly divulge disclose discover or make known any of the secrets
business correspondence or connections of his said Master unto any
person or persons whomsoever. And shall not waste misspend embezzle
purloin damage or destroy any of the moneys goods plans books
documents papers or writings of or belonging to or in the custody or
possession of his said Master or suffer the same to be done by others. And
also shall and will well and faithfully account to his said Master for all
such moneys goods or other things as shall be received by him or
otherwise come into his care or possession during the said term. And will
in all respects behave himself as a good and faithful Apprentice ought to
do during the whole of the said term.

Figure 2.2 Copy of an indenture

where premiums varied between £200 and £500.[101] In the case of printing, premiums were mostly charged by smaller firms, and there is some evidence to suggest that firms found this a lucrative source of income.[102] In 1892 Henry Slatter, president of the Typographical Association, reported the case of one Lincolnshire printer who employed eight apprentices but only one journeyman and had taken a fee of £30 for each apprentice.[103]

Clearly apprenticeships were of value. In a letter sent to Francis Place, it was claimed that 'at Strahans, apprentices are taken there as current cash or according to Masonic rule, to bring things upon the square'.[104] There are some instances where a relatively high premium was paid by some parents who wished their sons to be taught 'all aspects of the trade' so that the boy might eventually become a master himself. In 1779, for example, William Clowes, who later founded the firm of the same name, was apprenticed at the age of ten to Joseph Seagrave of Chichester, for the sum of £30.[105] In some cases the attitude of certain apprentices who had paid high premiums was less than subservient, the boys expecting to be treated as one of the family.

According to W. E. Adams, who was apprenticed to the *Cheltenham Journal*, indentures (see p. 54) drawn up by a lawyer were a one-sided agreement with needlessly heavy legal expenses including a £1 stamp. The premium in Adams's case amounted to working without wages for one year and for the remaining six years for very little pay.[106] Indentures did not always specify the work to be carried out and often left out important questions relating to time off to attend trade classes and the requirement to work overtime. George Jones, who became an apprentice in 1899 at the Stockport firm of Deans, earned 6s. a week in his first year, rising to 14s. in his fifth year. But because his mother had to pay a fidelity bond of £100, for most of his apprenticeship he was just getting the money his mother had paid. Indentures signed by Jones on starting work stipulated that, during his apprenticeship, he must not marry, play cards or dice, enter pubs or playhouses, buy or sell, be absent from work and that he must keep his master's secrets and obey his lawful commands.[107] The practice of charging premiums gradually declined during the nineteenth century but as late as 1927, 3 per cent of printing apprentices were required to pay premiums varying from £10 to £100.

While not all apprentices paid premiums, all those undertaking a formal apprenticeship were required to sign indentures, a legal document setting out the terms of the apprenticeship. Legal indentures were important documents that had to be shown by men seeking work in order to prove they were *bona fide* tradesmen. Clearly skill was seen as an exclusive property which needed to protected, men being judged honourable or dishonourable depending on whether or not they were in possession of indentures.[108]

An indenture of 1865 relating to an apprentice lithographic printer was drawn up by a solicitor and sealed with a 2s. 6d. stamp. In this example the responsibilities of both parties were stated:

... doth bind himself as an apprentice and shall and will diligently serve the said John Snow in the trade of lithographic printer ... and not do any hurt or damage to his said master – shall not spoil or waste, purloin or embezzle money or property. Shall not absent himself and with demeanor, conduct himself as faithful and sober apprentice.

For his part the employer agreed to:

provide sufficient meat and drink, washing and lodgings and suitable and proper apparel and also physic and surgical aid in case of illness or accident.

Wages of 6s. per week were to be paid, rising by a shilling each year to reach 12s. in the final year, provided 'he shall strike off and finish not less than 300 pulls in black quarter double crown or 250 in bronze ink on each and every day'. Like the wages, the number of prints to be taken increased until the final year when the boy was required to print 450 copies each day.

Legal rights relating to apprenticeships were not just on the side of the employer; apprentices had rights too, and on occasion were prepared to take action if their interests were overlooked. In one instance, when an apprentice summoned his employer for 'refusing to teach him the trade and business of a compositor, according to the terms of the apprenticeship', the court ordered the employers to fulfil the contract and to 'find two sureties in £5 each for the due of carrying out the same'.[109] Disputes also arose between firms as any printer employing an apprentice indentured to another firm was guilty of 'harbouring another man's servant'.

Primary source material from the nineteenth century provides ample evidence that all parties treated the whole question of apprenticeship in the printing trade as a serious matter. By common law an employer could engage any number of apprentices, but in practice many firms agreed with the policy of the trade societies that an excess of apprentices would result in a pool of poorly trained men. Many 'respectable' employers expressed their disapproval of small offices taking on excess apprentices because it lowered the quality of craftsmanship and increased the chances of their competitors having a source of cheap labour.

In 1850 the trade society pledged to assist the 'honourable and respectable' masters to restrict the number of apprentices. From the union's point of view the question of apprentice quotas posed a dilemma, in that attempts to enforce unrealistic quotas hindered the growth of the society and led firms either to ignore the restrictions or become non-society.

A further difficulty arose because of the multiplicity of small non-society offices where the Typographical Association had no influence.[110] Many firms remained in business only a short time, resulting in large numbers of partially trained boys legitimately seeking work as 'turnovers', leaving the unions powerless to enforce agreed quotas. Turnovers, known in America as 'two-thirds men', were usually 'runaway' apprentices who after two or three years' experience in the trade sought work at a higher wage with another employer. Turnovers, unless re-bound to a new employer by means of a legal agreement, were not permitted to join the trade society, the great fear being that the trade might be swamped with partly trained men.

It was not just over the question of controlling apprentices that the societies took a firm line; the typographical societies were determined at all costs to keep the trade free of those who were not fully entitled to membership. For instance, men who owned any printing equipment themselves were barred from membership of the society, as were members of other branches who were in arrears. Often men from outside the trade attempted to join the society; the branch minutes record numerous examples where the committee was offered bribes to issue membership documents to individuals who were not entitled to work in the trade. Even in legitimate cases the Manchester Society often refused membership, and when they did allow a man to join they often charged the relatively high entry fee of £5.

No doubt the compositors' concern was increased by what they had witnessed in machine printing, where it was more difficult to control apprenticeships rigidly because unbound boys and girls were employed to feed and take off paper from the machines. Here boys and girls were paid so little that it was cheaper to employ them than to fit automatic feed and delivery systems.

One of the objections to an excess number of apprentices was related to the notion of what constituted boy's work and what was men's work, the men arguing that if too many apprentices were employed there would be insufficient low-level work to keep them occupied. In Stockport, for example, the Society men grumbled that the apprentices were given men's work, that is, the most remunerative work for men engaged on piecework. In 1882, the Typographical Association came into dispute with Waterlows, who 'employed boys on men's work, refusing to apprentice them'.[111] Too many boys entering the trade may have meant that apprentices became cheap labour, as happened in engineering, threatening the union's long-term prospects as well as the immediate power to bargain.[112]

While 'printers' devils' were described as 'definitely subordinate with outward appearances of grubby urchins, shabbily attired', there appears to have been a measure of agreement between employers and men on what constituted appropriate behaviour of the apprentices who worked in this respectable trade. As John Southward pointed out in 1872, 'discipline, obedience and courtesy are required … indolence and shiftlessness having no place in a printing office'.[113] Master printers had several options regarding punishing apprentices in order to enforce obedience, including corporal punishment, although the more usual way was to bring the apprentice before a magistrate. One reason for this recourse to law was that unless there was a specific clause in the indenture covering misconduct, an apprentice could not be legally dismissed, even for gross misconduct or theft. Often cases arose from what was described as 'larking' or causing wilful damage. At Bow Street Police Court in 1873 an apprentice compositor who had damaged type to the value of 5s. was sentenced to prison, with hard labour, for six weeks.[114] About the same time a machine apprentice received a prison sentence for placing a bolt in a machine to get a 'mike' (a rest from work).[115] In many cases apprentices were brought before the court for 'absenting themselves from work' and causing expense and inconvenience to the employer. At Westminster Police Court in 1874, a boy who had served two and a half years of his apprenticeship was fined £5 or one month's imprisonment when he went absent from work for a month. Shortage of money to support themselves was frequently given as the reason why apprentices went absent, but this left the courts unimpressed, taking the view that 'it was the responsibility of the boy's guardian who was party to the indentures and therefore covenanted to support him'. Even when the apprentice reached 21, the youth's father was still liable if his son terminated his employment.

High spirits and practical jokes were common in the printing office, and boys sought every opportunity to get their own back on unpopular journeymen. As Samuel Ralphs of the *Stockport Advertiser* recalled, boys put a pinch of gunpowder in the tobacco boxes, filled coat pockets with coals and produced a dead rat wrapped in newspaper.[116] Generally, though, if a boy was co-operative, dependable and truthful, there would be journeymen who took an interest in his well-being.

Employers, too, took a responsible attitude to apprenticeships, usually marking the completion of an apprenticeship in an appropriate way. When William Mackay finished his apprenticeship in 1882, it is reported that the *Manchester Evening News* gave a dinner for 40 at the Hope and Anchor Inn to celebrate the occasion. The *Typographical Circular* contains many reports of such celebrations, usually involving the presentation of an illuminated address and speeches offering 'fatherly advice' to the new journeyman.

It is important to note that in a long-established trade such as printing, ideas of using the power of craft exclusiveness were not restricted to any one party. Sometimes employers and craftsmen united in their opposition to measures which damaged the trade in any way, and at other times the idea of craft custom brought employers and craftsmen into conflict. As Kirk observed in relation to the cotton industry, relations between workers and employers exhibited a variety of complex and often contradictory features.[117]

By the last quarter of the nineteenth century the Typographical Association recognized that serving a seven-year apprenticeship was not itself an adequate guarantee that a boy would make a good compositor. Society rules were amended to allow any boy staying on at a technical school beyond the age of 14 still to take up indentures. Anxious that the trade should not be undervalued by poor craftsmanship, the association advocated that before starting work in the trade the applicant should undertake tests of skill to ensure that eventually he would take pride in a high standard of craftsmanship.[118] Interestingly, this idea was taken up eighty years later when apprentice selection tests were introduced.

C. T. Jacobi, a director of the Chiswick Press and author of a number of books on the trade, in an address to the Master Printers' Federation in 1901, pointed out that work had become so specialized or monopolized by different firms that apprentices were not getting all-round training. Concerns were expressed by employers about the poor performance of apprentice compositors in the preliminary City and Guilds examinations because, it was suggested, the 'class of lad generally apprenticed in the case room has deteriorated, whilst machine apprentices were better educated and intelligent than formerly'.[119] In part this was a concern about the quality of future overseers and managers, but it was also recognition that with the introduction of mechanical typesetting the trade was changing, or, as one master printer put it, 'now the brain has to do what was formerly done by hand'.[120]

From 1880, renewed attempts were made to control of the number of apprentices and ensure proper training was given; however, this depended mainly on the strength of the local unions, unlike the situation in some other countries, where there was government intervention.[121] The trade societies in Britain did discuss asking for parliamentary intervention to ensure that apprentices were properly taught the craft, but eventually abandoned the idea because any third-party intervention was deemed unacceptable. In contrast, Germany, a country producing excellent-quality printing, had stringent laws to ensure that boys were only trained by an acknowledged master of the craft. In the USA, government schools provided facilities for supplementary training of printers' apprentices and insisted on formal apprenticeship agreements in which the unions took a prominent part.[122] Larger firms in England had organized systems of training and were more likely, after 1890, to support apprentices who attended trade classes. One Fleet Street printer, for example, provided comprehensive training for all apprentices, including 'a whole course in printing, together with music, arts lectures and cricket'. While welcoming this approach, the Typographical Association expressed concern that this 'might be too much mothering'.[123]

In discussing apprenticeships in engineering, Lummis argues that the experience was such a varied one that it is not appropriate to use the condition of apprenticeship as one of the criteria for identifying the existence of a labour aristocracy. This view misses the crucial point that apprenticeship was not simply about training; it provided a licence to work in the trade for the next fifty years. Completion of a seven-year apprenticeship did not guarantee that the boy became a skilled worker, but it must be borne in mind that a compositor on completing his apprenticeship would probably have extended his knowledge through moving to other offices.

It is not possible to agree with either Lummis or More when they claim that there was nothing to separate non-apprenticed trades from apprenticed trades in terms of skill.[124] Skill was not entirely socially constructed. A great deal of printing, especially after 1850, demanded high levels of skill and creative effort from the compositor, in part as a result of a revival in fine printing and the influence of the Arts and Crafts Movement. Foreign-language setting, music printing and mathematical texts all required highly skilled men who would have gained experience after serving their apprenticeship.

Apprentices usually started work as copyholders (reading the copy out loud for the proofreader to check), and then, after a few months, became errand boys of the 'ship'. Boys intended as apprentices had to be bound within three months of starting work, but in less reputable offices they were often allowed to do typesetting for a prolonged period before signing indentures, effectively extending the period of apprenticeship beyond the specified seven years. If, eventually, they became fast at typesetting, they could work on reduced piece-rates.[125] Boys in smaller jobbing offices were likely to gain experience on a variety of work, but firms of this kind did not have the facilities to provide a comprehensive training. Samuel Ralphs, apprenticed at the *Stockport Advertiser* in 1855 when he was 13 years old, worked from 7.00 a.m. to 7.00 p.m. except on publishing days, when he worked until 10.30 p.m. His duties included carrying water, lighting fires, running errands and pumping water into the drain. On publication day he assisted the pressman in taking proofs from the hand press.

The conclusion must be drawn that, in spite of many difficulties, the trade unions representing compositors were largely successful in controlling entry to the trade, the seven-year apprenticeship remaining in force until after the Second World War. Unlike the building and engineering trades, no unskilled or semi-skilled labour was used in the composing room, and most hand setting of type remained unchanged in the period 1850 to 1914. Possibly the seven-year apprenticeship was longer than strictly necessary; nevertheless it represented a common experience that all compositors had gone through. Undoubtedly there was some affection in the trade for this experience, which helped to set the men apart from others.

The introduction of mechanical composition

After the introduction of the power press in the early nineteenth century, the urgent problem facing the printing trade was how to speed up the composition of type. Demand for printing increased throughout the nineteenth century, both in terms of the number of publications and the quantities required. To a large extent the technical advances in the pressroom met this latter demand, with faster-running machinery capacity growing ten-fold between 1850 and

1900, mainly due to the introduction of web presses in 1880.[126] The crucial problem was matching and planning the speed of hand composition to the greatly increased demand and throughput, especially in book and newspaper production, where speed was essential.

Increased pressure in the composing room was met by expanding the labour force and through greater specialization in the composing room in an attempt to take advantage of faster speeds in the pressroom; however, setting type by hand remained a slow, laborious process. An experienced compositor, working without interruption, might set in the region of 1000 ens of copy in an hour (1000 letters and spaces representing approximately 170 words). On the assumption that the average English word contains five letters plus one space, it is possible to estimate the length of time to set a book or newspaper. The *Penny Magazine*, for example, describing the production of the *Report of Commissioners of Factories Inquiry* in 1833, pointed out:

> The volume contained 1200 folio pages with 1,296,000 words. A good compositor can pickup [set] about 15,000 letters a day so it would take one compositor 460 days to produce this text. In fact the Report was ordered by the House of Commons on 28 June and was laid complete upon the table of the House on 10 July, less than a fortnight.[127]

This kind of demand put pressure on men to work fast. It is little wonder that at Cassells the composing room was known as the 'stone yard', a reference to prisoners serving hard labour by breaking stones. Compositors worked 54 hours a week, each setting 54,000 ens per week, a near impossible target to meet, because the rate paid for composition included the cost of distributing the type after printing. Not only was the composition of text a slow, tedious process; the absence of typesetting machines meant that type for hand composition was expensive and often scarce, so that men lost time due to an inadequate supply of type.

So important was speed and accuracy in typesetting that competitions were held to find the fastest typesetter. In the USA, where national typesetting tournaments were held, professionals toured the country doing nothing else but compete for money, a sport that appears to have appealed to male competitiveness, and a facet of the work the compositors were not prepared to have challenged by women. Sponsored by the International Typographic Union, which codified the rules, 24-hour endurance races were held to see who could set the most copy with the fewest mistakes. After a time, the union realized the folly of demonstrating to employers how fast men could work and instead of speed competitions they organized events centred on typographic quality.[128] In Britain, the Typographical Association quickly realized that participation in speed competitions could be detrimental to the long-term interests of its members, and actively discouraged such events.

Two approaches to the process of mechanization in the composing room were tried. First a machine was developed that assembled pre-cast type into words and sentences, and then after use the type was redistributed and the machine was reloaded with type. The second approach used machines that both cast and assembled type.

The first practical type-assembly machine was produced in 1840 by James Young and Adrien Delcambre, and was capable of outputting 6000 ens per hour, six times the speed of hand setting. Development was slow and no English composing machines were exhibited at the Great Exhibition of 1851. By 1857 Robert Hattersley brought out an improved version of the Delcambre–Young machine, which produced 7500 ens per hour.[129] The introduction of the typewriter in 1867 gave added impetus to the search for a mechanical means of setting type, and it was thought that it might have been possible to use the typewriter to impress letters or to find a means of transferring an image – an idea that anticipated the use of the IBM typewriter 100 years later.

By 1875 Hooker's electric typesetting machine appeared. Steam-driven by a belt and shaft, an electrical circuit activated a striker, which released a piece of type, which then dropped into a line. Although these early machines speeded up the typesetting process, they suffered the serious limitation that after use the type needed to be redistributed by hand and the machine refilled, conditions which gave rise to the possibility of employing cheap labour in the form of boys and girls. By 1880 this limitation had been overcome by the introduction of the Thorne machine, which could both set and distribute type. For a short period the Thorne machine proved popular with newspaper offices, including the *Manchester Guardian*, where, in 1882, it is claimed that this machine produced 11,700 ens in one hour, ten times the speed of hand setting.[130]

By 1889, 32 different composing machines had come on to the market. Thirteen or 14 of these had already become things of the past, 7 or 8 were available, and 14 or 15 were looming in the future.[131] By this date, however, most of the problems associated with the earlier typesetting machines had been solved with the introduction of Mergenthaler's Linotype. The Linotype was both a typesetting machine and a typecasting machine, producing slugs of metal containing whole lines of type on one machine, a system especially suited to the needs of newspaper production, where speed of handling was particularly important. Crucially, the Linotype produced new type each time, without the need for distribution, the used lines being melted down after use.

In relation to the composing machine, the Typographical Association stopped short of outright opposition to its introduction but instead opted for a policy that maintained the *status quo*, demanding that all machines be operated by time-served compositors.[132] In 1878 the association carried out a full ballot of its members to ascertain their views on eleven questions relating to the introduction of mechanical composition. The response to this opportunity to express opinions on such an important issue was surprising in two ways: very few members voted; and of those that did, many voted in a contradictory way. Additionally, problems arose because the majority of those taking part voted for all propositions on the ballot paper, regardless of the fact that some propositions were the direct opposites and negatives of others. Ten branches sent in no returns whatsoever and 22 branches failed to comply with the executive instructions that voting papers should be scrutinized by branch officers.

A subsequent report in the *Circular* condemned the apathy of members in not 'interesting themselves enough in this important issue', claiming that it was impossible to ascertain the will of the membership. In response, a number of rank-and-file members expressed anger at the way the executive had handled the ballot by even suggesting that boys and girls might be used for distribution on the new composing machines. These were important issues at the time, as it was thought that the trade may have been opened up to child labour and to men who had not served their time.

The clear message from those voting in the ballot was that there was little outright opposition to the introduction of mechanical composition. What appears to have happened is that many members of the union were prepared to let the executive committee make decisions, although in the end they were unhappy with the result. It would seem that members of the union were not keen to be proactive on this issue but were prepared to take a 'wait and see' attitude, at least until some real danger became apparent. The fear was that outright opposition to mechanical composition might well encourage employers to employ non-union labour.

Table 2.8 illustrates the rather erratic and contradictory voting patterns of the membership. Voting against any rule being introduced (motion 2) and then voting in favour of restrictions about who should be allowed to operate the machines represented a contradiction. Opposition to the use of unbound boys comes through clearly, but having already agreed that no rules be adopted, the executive is left with the dilemma: does the discretion given to the executive under motion 2 allow them to set aside motion 9?

The adoption of the second proposition, 'that members do not wish any rule be adopted at present', was interpreted as an expression of confidence in the executive, allowing it to deal with each case as it came up. In reality, many members probably felt that rules relating to mechanical composition were unnecessary because, in the short term, its introduction posed little threat.

With one exception, branches in the Manchester region followed the national voting patterns, the exception being the motion relating to piecework, where it appears that members were unhappy about banning piecework. A possible explanation was the existence of a fairly high number of newspaper compositors in the region who were reluctant to turn down the chance of higher wages through piecework. On motion 2, while the region voted in favour of no rules being needed, a substantial minority voted against this,

Table 2.8   Results of a ballot of members of the Typographical Association
regarding mechanical composition, 1878

| Proposition | Manchester area* | | Nationally | |
	For	Against	For	Against
1. No opposition be made to mec. comp.	503	7	2,291	40
2. That no rules be adopted relating to mec. comp.	291	147	1,614	513
3. Standard stab wages be paid to machine operators	407	30	1,773	293
4. No piece work be permitted	152	216	622	1,192
5. It be optional for employers to work piece or stab	205	203	1,101	830
6. No piece work until a scale be agreed upon	323	77	1,500	417
7. If piece worked, hand piece rates to be changed	160	216	758	1,066
8. If worked on piece, rates to be fixed by EC	369	61	1,860	199
9. Distribution be confined to journeymen	380	99	1,645	504
10. Unbound boys or girls be allowed to distribute	148	318	724	1,322
11. That a rate be fixed to include distribution	253	98	1,286	483

*   Manchester area taken as Ashton, Bolton, Chester, Hyde, Macclesfield, Manchester, Oldham, Rochdale and Stockport.

Source: *Typographical Association Circular*, June 1878.

suggesting that members in the region were not keen to leave the issue to the executive. The apathy shown by many compositors in respect of mechanization is understandable because in 1878 very few machines were in use, and the vast majority of compositors worked in small jobbing offices where the new machines would have had little direct impact on their way of working.

Although the introduction of the Linotype had an important bearing on the position of the compositor, it must be stressed that mechanization in the composing room was a gradual process, taking place over a period of 40 years. Only firms having appropriate work adopted mechanical typesetting and it is estimated that, even by 1914, only 10 per cent of firms had installed the machinery.[133] It is impossible to determine precisely the extent of the impact of the Linotype on the number of compositors employed, as demand for printing was increasing and a number of compositors retrained to become machine operators. It has even been suggested that because machines reduced the cost of typesetting and increased the speed of production, publications became larger and cheaper, creating more work for hand compositors. Loss of jobs in composing could be estimated at around 4 per cent given that between 1891 and 1911 the number of compositors remained static while there was a 4.5 per cent increase in labour in other sectors of the trade.[134]

Table 2.9 shows that in Manchester, the *Manchester Evening News* introduced eight Linotypes and retained all 46 compositors, but at the *Courier* office, where 12 machines were installed, 55 compositors lost their jobs. It would appear that in total 84 hand compositors lost their jobs across the seven firms listed, suggesting at least some short-term instability in employment with the introduction of composing machines. David Preece, in his study of the introduction of mechanical composition in Bradford, found that a number of older hand compositors who had spent their working lives in reasonable security, were laid off and finished their careers as casual hands doing seasonal work.[135]

Table 2.9 Number of Linotypes in use in Manchester and the effect on hand compositors, 1893–94

Company	No. of machines	No. of compositors before	No. of compositors after
Courier	12	75	20
Guardian	14	79	72
Sporting Chronicle	6	28	20
Evening Mail	6	25	11
Evening News	8	46	46
Guardian jobbing	4	88	88
Percy Bros.	3	–	–

Source: Executive Committee of the Typographical Association, extracted from information in Howe, *The London Compositor*, p. 498.

Another view suggests that the introduction of the Linotype actually prevented an influx of cheap juvenile labour, as without the increased speed of the machines it might have been necessary to bring in cheap labour to cope with the growing demand for hand-set typematter.[136] Faced with the possibility of the introduction of cheap labour and the large-scale displacement of its members, the Typographical Association opted for a policy of control rather than outright opposition to mechanical composition.[137]

Marking the start of collective bargaining, the union recognized that it was advantageous to negotiate nationally, claiming, 'it is better to get this matter of the new rules settled between the national bodies rather than cause fifty or a hundred little difficulties, by negotiating at branch level'.[138] In 1898 a national agreement was reached between the Linotype Users' Association and the executive of the Typographical Association on conditions for

Linotype operators, allowing for an increase of 12 per cent on existing stab rates, all skilled operators to be association members.[139] This action by the executive greatly angered members of the union, who were disappointed at the small differential in rates between hand compositors and composing machine operators, taking the view that the executive had exceeded its powers. For many members the actions of the executive confirmed the view that the society was not being run in a democratic way, many branches protesting that the leadership of the association had acted at variance with trade union principles.[140] Members' suspicions that the executive had given in too readily to the Linotype Users' Association were further reinforced when it was disclosed how rapidly the net profits of the Linotype Company had grown. From £9583 in 1893, profits rose quickly to £162,882 in 1897.[141]

Collective agreements did not of course solve the many problems that arose through the adoption of machines in this long-established craft. Relations between employers and craftsmen were changing as employers sought ways to maximize output from expensive machines through the implementation of complex piece- and task-work systems, examples of what Kirk identifies as Taylorite management control techniques.[142] The control that the chapel had over the distribution of work was challenged as employers introduced systematic work-measurement strategies. Clocks were installed on Linotypes to record the number of ens set, providing employers with accurate information about output and enabling them to foster competition between operators. In some firms it became the practice to post output figures for each man above the machines.

The anxiety felt by some society men that unskilled labour might be introduced to operate machines proved to be unfounded. In the USA unskilled men were tried out as Linotype operators for a short time but the results proved unsatisfactory. It quickly became apparent that greater skill and accuracy were required of the Linotype operator. Errors by the operator resulted in rekeying and recasting the whole line. Even a comma missed out meant the line had to be reset, although in practice mistakes were often allowed to stand in order to save time making corrections, a custom that gave the Linotype something of a reputation for producing poor-quality work.

Other difficulties arose because of the unreliability of the machines, which needed constant attention. Breakdowns of the intricate parts were frequent, leaving a significant gap between expectation and performance.[143] Another problem with the Linotype was that it was possible to run out of matrices in much the same way that hand compositors ran out of type, which resulted in delays. Health suffered too, because the machine used molten lead alloy that was heated by gas jets, resulting in many complaints that there was a strong smell of gas in the composing room.

Compositors showed some initial concern that they would become mere line assemblers and that employers might think that they would be able to set type with both hands. To a large extent this fear proved unfounded because responsibility for daily servicing and minor repairs rested with the operator, further extending the specialist knowledge required by the compositor and reducing the disruptive potential of the machinery. This view was confirmed by the machinery manufacturers, who pointed out that it was more beneficial for men to do their own repairs because if outside experts were brought in to make mechanical adjustments, this would reflect on the competence of the operators.

The irregular nature of demand for printing and the high initial cost of the machines meant that the Linotype was only viable in relatively large firms where there was a steady flow of work.[144] Some indication of the complexity and cost of mechanical typesetting can be ascertained from the fact that in 1898 when P. T. Dodge, president of Mergenthaler Linotype Corporation, presented the original Paige typesetting machine to the Science Museum at Cornell University, the machine had absorbed nearly two million dollars of capital in the manufacture of its 19,000 parts.[145]

For reasons connected with printing quality there were limitations on the class of work the Linotype could be used for. It was particularly appropriate for newspaper and book production, but for higher-quality work and more complex setting Monotype was more suitable. An advantage unique to Monotype was the facility to store paper tapes in case of a reprint rather than tying up capital in keeping type standing, an attractive proposition for any firm.

Introduced slightly later than the Linotype, the Monotype system of mechanical typesetting was brought out in 1897. Monotype was invented by Talbot Lanston of Washington, a well-known statistician and inventor of the calculating machine. Lanston, who had no technical knowledge of printing, took 12 years to perfect the system, which comprised two separate machines, a keyboard (or perforator) for punching a paper tape and a casting machine that was controlled by the tape. Monotype differed from the Linotype in two important ways; it was suitable for a wide variety of work; and it needed two operators – a skilled compositor to key in the text and a caster attendant, usually a mechanic or stereotyper.

Early claims that the Monotype represented a revolution in printing were somewhat overstated, as was the claim made in the *Pall Mall Gazette* of 10 July 1897 that 'the caster minder can easily attend 10 machines all running at once'. In practice one man could look after only two machines. Others forecast the demise of the compositor, the *Daily Journal* warning: 'the Monotype working in such a manner, as to threaten with extinction a body of operatives that is second to none in point of character and intelligence – the compositor'.

The division of labour through the employment of caster attendants represents the first incursion of semi-skilled men into the previously skilled domain of typesetting. Generally the Monotype machine was welcomed by hand compositors who trained on the machines because the work was technically challenging and working conditions cleaner and more comfortable. There appears to have been little friction between hand compositors, machine compositors and proofreaders, possibly because there were opportunities for time-served men to retrain, and in any case, men thought of themselves first and foremost as compositors. Nevertheless the creation of a new category of compositor, the Monotype operator, resulted in still another stage in a growing hierarchy of men within one trade.[146]

As with the Linotype, firms were fairly slow to adopt the new system, and by 1900 there were only 22 Monotype machines installed in Britain. At £600 for the machine plus £20 for each set of matrices, cost obviously precluded many firms from investing in Monotype, especially in view of the fact that there was always a surplus of hand labour. Some employers themselves were cautious, with the Monotype Corporation reporting 'an order was cancelled when the printer ascertained that the machine was not run on treadle power, the printer declaring he would not place himself at the mercy of any steam or electric power company'.[147]

Specialized mechanization of this kind introduced another interested party into the increasingly complex field of industrial relations: the machinery manufacturers. Keen to promote their own systems, manufacturers had to strike a balance between coercion and confrontation in their dealings with the trade unions. Robert Hattersley, for example, considered legal action against the Typographical Association, blaming the union for lack of progress in selling the machine to the trade. When the Linotype was first introduced into Manchester, the Linotype Company wrote to the Manchester Typographical Society offering to train compositors on the new machines for a few hours each day. The firm did, however, make it clear to the union that if they did not co-operate, the company would 'train men from anywhere'.

The Manchester branch did agree to co-operate but on condition that only society members would be trained, although the union was less than pleased when the Linotype Company used the results of the speed trials in their publicity literature.[148] Linotype, in particular, took steps to cultivate labour leaders, organizing formal tours of the works and recreational facilities, followed by elaborate hospitality.

The Monotype Corporation had considerable direct influence on the trade. The original board of directors of Monotype was described by the *Westminster Gazette* as 'men of the highest honour and social standing'. All the board were connected to the printing and publishing trade and included C. A. Pearson, of *Pearson's Weekly* fame, a pioneer of popular literature and later to found the *Daily Express*, William Heinemann, publisher, W. O. Morrison of Morrison and Gibb (the Edinburgh printers) and J. F. Wilson, a director of Cassells and author of *Sixty Years in Fleet Street*. Later, H. C. Crust, editor of the *Pall Mall Gazette*, Lord Asquith and Harold Macmillan (later Prime Minister) also became directors.

Especially in the case of Monotype, better-educated and -trained operators were required to deal with the mathematical and technical aspects of the system. The Monotype Company offered operators works training and competitive examinations on what was quite complex machinery. Offering prize scholarships for operatives to attend courses at their London offices, Monotype frequently appealed directly to compositors, bypassing employers and trade unions in their determination to establish a pool of skilled operators. The company provided incentives in the form of gold medal awards to operators who could maintain a speed of 15,000 ens per hour for four consecutive hours. Courses were described as 'post-graduate', serving to further emphasize status differences between hand compositors and the new machine operators.

Establishing user groups of operatives and supporting technical college courses were all part of Monotype's strategy to build up loyalty and pride in operators, essential if the company were to further its commercial aims and avoid conflict within the trade. A Monotype Users' Association was formed, primarily intended to exchange technical information but clearly encouraging bonding between men who had the same specialized interests. In the USA, the International Typographical Union (ITU) took a much more proactive stance, setting up schools to train their members in mechanical composition. Not only did the union have a good deal of influence on training, but there is also evidence that the Monotype Club, a nominally apolitical subcraft organization, was active in promoting its candidates for union office.[149]

Both the Linotype and Monotype companies successfully gained the support of 'machine' compositors and in doing so helped create an elite of workers within the trade. In many ways the competition between the two main providers of mechanical typesetting machines benefited the trade in that standards of typography were constantly rising and both firms contributed equipment and expertise to technical education.

Of the two main systems of typesetting, Monotype probably had a greater direct impact on the status of the compositor because the underlying feeling was that the separation of mental and manual tasks must be a good thing. The Monotype took away from the keyboard operator the need to bother about type in a direct sense, a feature that could not be claimed for the Linotype, where the operator served the dual roles of keyboard operator and mechanic. Compositors operating the Monotype keyboard usually worked in an office environment; this was a 'clean job', allowing operators to go to work in good clothes, further adding to the prestige of working with complex and quite sophisticated equipment. As the *Daily Mail* of 2 August 1897 reported, under a headline reading 'demon machine eats paper and lays type', the workings of the Monotype were described as 'an achievement beyond human understanding'. The *Star* of 9 July 1897 optimistically claimed 'the time has arrived when the journalist may write his articles in hot type'. In the same month *Press News* enthusiastically forecast the economy represented 'by a system where editors, authors and writers do their own composition or where keyboard operators are also stenographers'.

Conclusions

What emerges from this brief consideration of the development of the printing trade, especially with reference to the period 1850–1914, is a complex picture which both confirms and contradicts the notion that the compositor could be considered a part of an 'aristocracy of labour'. The possession of a trade and the independence of labour also led to endemic sectionalism among skilled workers.[150]

Compositors displayed remarkable adherence to ancient craft practices and traditions while at the same time accommodating modern industrial techniques. Apprenticeship, as Zeitlin points out, was the crucial context in which craft values were passed on to the next generation, that is the reproduction of the craft itself.[151] Shared values and experiences and the binding together of craftsmen for self-protection strengthened notions of craft pride.

Throughout the period the seven-year apprenticeship was maintained as the only legitimate way into the trade and all attempts by employers to introduce unskilled labour were repelled. Likewise, the chapel still played an important functional role in the organization of day-to-day work in the printing office, stressing exclusiveness and separation from other parts of the trade.

Mechanization came to the composing room 75 years later than it did to press work, and by this time the Typographical Association had developed from a small trade society into a successful trade union well able to negotiate nationally. While adopting a cautious and conservative stance that stressed conciliation rather than conflict with employers, the Typographical Association was able to safeguard the working conditions of its members.

At the same time, evidence suggests that the image of a free, independent craftsman with high status in the community was under threat. The development of industrial capitalism resulted in the involvement of large publishers and newspaper proprietors with the power to switch production to centres that gave cost advantages. Scientific management techniques implemented by managers and foremen replaced many of the functions of the chapel and the FOC. Specialization increased, together with pay differentials, leaving large numbers of compositors working in small jobbing offices on relatively low pay, a situation that makes it difficult to justify their inclusion in any elite group of workers.

In the following chapter an attempt will be made to consider these issues in more detail in order to assess the validity of claims that compositors formed an elite group of workers who remained aloof from the vast majority of the working class.

Notes

1. For example the Oxford University Press in England, the House of Elsevier in Holland and the Imprimerie Royale in France.
2. Kirk, N., *Labour and Society in Britain and the USA*, Vol. 2 (Aldershot: Scolar Press, 1994), p. 3.
3. Musson, A. E., *The Typographical Association* (Oxford: Oxford University Press, 1954), p. 1.
4. See, for example, the OED definition, which includes calico printing and photographic printing.
5. Wiesner-Hanks, M., *The world of the renaissance print shop*, Dept. of History, University of Wisconsin-Milwaukee (Internet).
6. Cannon, I. C., 'Social situation of skilled workers; London compositors', unpublished Ph.D. thesis (University of London, 1961), p. 12.
7. For examples of printing 1850–80, see Bigmore, E. C. and Wyman, C. W. H., *A Bibliography of Printing* (London: Holland Press, 1978).
8. Stereotyping is a system of taking a mould from the forme of type and casting a duplicate plate in order to run the same work on a number of presses.
9. Ryder, J., *Printing for Pleasure* (London: EUP, 1957), p. 21.
10. Ibid.
11. Steinberg, S. H., *Five Hundred Years of Printing* (London: Penguin, 1974), p. 277.
12. Bigmore and Wyman, *A Bibliography*, p. 83.
13. Steinberg, *Five Hundred Years of Printing*, p. 138.
14. Ibid.
15. Curran, J. and Seaton, J., *Power without Responsibility* (London: Routledge, 1992), p. 15.
16. Ibid., p. 30.
17. *British Printer*, January 1893.
18. Clowes, W. B., *Family Business 1803–1953* (London: Clowes, 1953), p. 45.
19. Ibid.
20. Printing Historical Society, *Bulletin*, No. 39.
21. Stearns, P. N., *Lives of Labour: work in a maturing industrial society* (London: Croom Helm, 1975), p. 158.
22. McClelland, K., 'Time to work, time to live: some aspects of work and the re-formation of class in Britain, 1850–1880', in Joyce, P. (ed.), *The Historical Meanings of Work* (Cambridge: Cambridge University Press, 1987), p. 180.
23. Duffy, P., 'Conflict and continuity in the Manchester building trades, 1833 to 1870', unpublished M.A. dissertation (Manchester Polytechnic, 1990) , p. 3.
24. See, for example, Keefe, H. J., *A Century in Print 1839–1939* (London: Hazell, Watson & Viney, 1939).
25. Feltes, N., *Modes of Production of Victorian Novels* (Chicago: Chicago University Press, 1986), p. 9.
26. Ibid., p. 28.

27. Johnson, J., *The printer, his Customers and his Men* (London: Dent, 1933), p. 25.
28. Bigmore and Wyman, *A Bibliography*, p. 83.
29. Feltes, *Modes of Production*, p. 4.
30. Ibid., p. 61.
31. Landow, G. P., *Mudie's Select Library and the Form of Victorian Fiction: Literature, history and culture in the age of Victoria* (Brown University, 1999). Internet: Victorian Web.
32. Heinemann, J. W., *Heinemann: a century of publishing* (London: Heinemann, 1990), p. 92.
33. Musson, *The Typographical Association*, p. 80.
34. Crompton, J. W., *Report on Printers' Strikes and Trade Unions since January 1845*, The National Association for the Promotion of Social Science (London,1860).
35. Zeitlin, J. H., 'Craft regulation and the division of labour: Engineers and compositors in Britain, 1890–1914', unpublished Ph.D. thesis (University of Warwick, 1981), p. 3.
36. See, for example, the work published in *The Printers' Specimen Exchange* (1880–95).
37. *Papermakers' Directory* (London, 1903).
38. Timperley, C. H., *Encyclopaedia of Literary and Typographic Anecdote*, Vol. II (New York and London: Garland, 1977).
39. Astle, W. (ed.), *History of Stockport* (York: Scholar, 1971), p. 52.
40. Cook, C. and Keith, B., *British Historical Facts 1830–1900* (London: Macmillan, 1975).
41. *Monotype Recorder*, Vol. XL, No. 2 (1954), p. 1.
42. Southward, J., *Practical Printing* (London: Raithby Lawrence, 1882), p. 280.
43. *Monotype Recorder*, Vol. XL, No. 2 (1954), p. 2.
44. Savage, W., *Dictionary of the Art of Printing* (London, 1841; reprinted New York: Franklin, 1964).
45. Child, J., *Industrial Relations in the British Printing Industry* (London: Allen & Unwin, 1967), p. 39.
46. Sonenscher, M., 'Mythical work: workshop production and the compagonnages of 18th century France', in Joyce, *Historical Meanings of Work*, p. 31.
47. Thompson, F. M. L., *The Rise of Respectable Society* (London: Fontana, 1988), p. 246.
48. Wallis, L. W., 'A most venerable institution – the Chapel', *Print in Britain*, Vol. 8 (1960/61), p. 292.
49. *Monotype Recorder*, Vol. XXXII, No. 33 (1933), p. 17.
50. Rule, J., 'The property of skill in the period of manufacture' in Joyce, *Historical Meanings of Work*, p. 112.
51. Type cases were used to contain the letters, numerals, spaces and sorts. The upper case contained 98 boxes and the lower case 53. If the letters became mixed up the case was said to be 'pied'.
52. Savage, *Dictionary*, p. 147.
53. *Typographical Association Circular*, No. 305, 1878.
54. Ibid.
55. Ibid.
56. Zeitlin, 'Craft regulation', p. 6.
57. *Notes and Queries*, 2nd series, No. 27, 16 May 1857, p. 393.

58. Chapel Rules, Messrs Wyman and Sons, London 1875 (see Bigmore and Wyman, *Bibliography*, p. 131).
59. Howe, E. (ed.), *The London Compositor, 1785–1900* (London: Bibliographical Society, 1947), p. 29.
60. Moxon, J., *Mechanick Exercises on the Whole Art of Printing* (1683; reprinted London: Oxford University Press, 1962).
61. Ibid., p. 327.
62. Wallis, L. W., *Print in Britain*, Vol. X, No. 9, January 1963, p. 36.
63. The feast day of St Bartholomew was celebrated on 24 August.
64. *Typographical Association Circular*, October 1887.
65. *Typographical Association Circular*, May 1892.
66. *Typographical Association Circular*, February 1874.
67. Thompson, *Rise of Respectable Society*, p. 138.
68. *British Printer*, Vol. XII, 1900.
69. *Monotype Newsletter*, No. 72, 1964.
70. Cunningham, H., *Leisure in the Industrial Revolution 1780–1880* (London: Croom Helm, 1980), p. 68.
71. Leeson, R. A., *Travelling Brothers: the six centuries road from craft fellowship to trade* (London: Allen & Unwin, 1979), p. 147.
72. *Reports from Commissioners, Inspectors and Others*. PP, Vol. 18, Part IV, 1892.
73. Thompson, *Rise of Respectable Society*, p. 318.
74. Roberts, J., 'Drink and industrial discipline in nineteenth century Germany', in Berlanstein, L., *The Industrial Revolution and Work in Nineteenth Century Europe* (London: Routledge, 1992).
75. *Monotype Recorder*, Vol. XXXIX, No. 1, 1949.
76. Thompson, *Rise of Respectable Society*, p. 246.
77. Minutes of the Manchester Typographical Society, 4 April 1826 (ms).
78. McAra, T. W., *Reminiscences of Printing and Fleet Street*, Stationers' Company Craft Lectures (London, 1928).
79. Child, *Industrial Relations*, p. 128.
80. Lipset, M., Trow, M. and Coleman, J., *Union Democracy: the internal politics of the International Typographic Union* (New York: Free Press, 1968), p. 35.
81. Brown, E. H. P., *The Growth of British Industrial Relations* (London: Macmillan, 1959), p. 287.
82. Bateman, D., 'A Bristol printers' chapel in the nineteenth century', *Journal of the Printing Historical Society*, No. 24, 1995.
83. Fox, A., *History and Heritage* (London: Allen & Unwin, 1986), p. 8.
84. Musson, *The Typographical Association*, p. 3.
85. Ibid., p. 46.
86. Child, *Industrial Relations*, p. 28.
87. Southward, *Practical Printing*, p. 810.
88. Child, *Industrial Relations*, p. 66.
89. Bigmore and Wyman, *Bibliography*, p. 2.
90. Howe, *London Compositor*, p. 117.
91. Ibid., p. 120.
92. Bigmore and Wyman, *Bibliography*, p. 194.
93. Crompton, *Report*, p.79.
94. Mussson, *Typographical Association*, p. 42.
95. Crompton, *Report*, p. 79.
96. Ibid., Appendix 1.

97. Ward, J. T. and Fraser W. H., *Workers and Employers: documents on trades unions and industrial relations in Britain since the 18th century* (London: Macmillan, 1980), p. 12.
98. Fox, *History and Heritage*, p. 46.
99. Smith, C. M., *The Working Man's Way in the World* (1857; reprinted London: PHS, 1967), p. 141.
100. *British Printer*, November 1927.
101. Plant, M., *The English Book Trade* (London: Allen & Unwin, 1965), p. 367.
102. According to the *Printers' Register* of 6 February 1868, Mr and Mrs Lavender, who ran a small printing establishment, 'received women on payment of a £5 premium'.
103. *Royal Commission on Labour*, 1892, PP Minute 22808.
104. Howe, *London Compositor*, p. 120.
105. Clowes, *Family Business*, p. 2.
106. Adams, W. E., *Memoirs of a Social Atom* (1903; reprinted New York: Kelly, 1968), p. 85.
107. *History of Deanprint* (Stockport: Deans, 1990), p. 20.
108. Burnett, J. (ed.), *Useful Toil: autobiographies of working people from the 1820s to the 1920s* (London: Allen Lane, 1974), p. 80.
109. Southward, *Practical Printing*, p. 316.
110. Zeitlin, 'Craft regulation', p. 193.
111. *British and Colonial Printer*, January 1882.
112. Ibid.
113. Southward, *Practical Printing*, p. 320.
114. Ibid., p. 316.
115. 'Mike', a slang term for shirking work (OED).
116. Astle, *History of Stockport*, p. 65.
117. Kirk, *Labour and Society*, Vol. 2, p. 68.
118. *Typographical Circular*, No. 320, May 1879.
119. *Federation Circular*, BFMP, June 1905.
120. Ibid.
121. Ibid.
122. *British Printer*, Vol. XL, No. 238, November/December 1927.
123. *Typographical Circular*, February 1882.
124. More, C., *Skill and the Working-class* (London: Croom Helm, 1980), p. 144. See also Lummis, T., *The Labour Aristocracy 1851–1914* (Aldershot: Scolar, 1994), p. 17.
125. McAra, *Reminiscences*.
126. Web presses use a reel of paper in the printing process rather than single sheets, thus eliminating the need for hand feeding and enabling far greater speeds to be attained.
127. *Penny Magazine*, Vol. II, issue 107, October/November 1833.
128. Walker, R., 'A time of giants: speed composition in nineteenth century America', *Printing History*, Journal of the American Printing Historical Association, Vol. XIV, No. 2, 1992, p. 14.
129. Clair, C., *A History of Printing in Britain* (London: Cassell, 1965), p. 221.
130. *British and Colonial Printer*, December 1882.
131. *Monotype Recorder*, Autumn 1949.
132. Zeitlin, 'Craft regulation', p. 202.
133. Berlanstein, L., *Working People of Paris 1871–1914* (Baltimore and London: Johns Hopkins University Press, 1984), p. 79.

134. Preece, D., 'Social aspects and effects of composing machine adoption in the British printing industry', *Journal of the Printing Historical Society*, No. 18 (1983/4), p. 11.
135. Ibid., p. 12.
136. Ibid., p. 13.
137. Cannon, 'Social situation', p. 77.
138. Preece, 'Social aspects', p. 4.
139. Musson, *Typographical Association*, p. 141.
140. Ward and Fraser, *Workers and Employers*, p. 154.
141. Ibid.
142. Kirk, *Labour and Society*, Vol. 2, p. 5.
143. Berlanstein, *Working People of Paris*, p. 35.
144. Ibid., p. 35.
145. *Monotype Recorder*, Vol. XXXIX, No. 1, 1949.
146. *Monotype Recorder*, Spring 1935.
147. *Monotype Newsletter*, No. 36 and *Monotype Recorder*, Vol. XXXIX, No. 1, 1949.
148. *Typographical Association Circular*, No. 705, June 1911.
149. Lipset et al., *Union Democracy*, p. 221.
150. Savage, M. and Miles, A., *The Remaking of the British Working-class 1840–1940* (London: Routledge, 1994), p. 4.
151. Zeitlin, 'Craft regulation', p. 144.

CHAPTER THREE

The status of the compositor in the hierarchy of labour

Overview

Chapter Two examined the experience of skilled compositors in the context of the diverse and evolving printing trade of the latter half of the nineteenth century. It was been demonstrated that ancient customs and practices coexisted with emerging industrial methods, leading to a complex and often contradictory view of a trade that was, at the same time, both a hand craft and a sophisticated modern industry. The conclusion must be that, in respect of both technique and organization, the trade was traditional, cautious and calculating.[1]

Using the general picture outlined as a background, the aim of this chapter is to establish if the compositor did qualify for inclusion in the elite of labour aristocrats. A brief review of the historiography of the subject provides insights into the origins and development of the labour aristocracy thesis, noting some of the strengths and weaknesses of the notion. This is followed by the central core of the chapter, which takes a detailed look at the experience of the compositor and measures this against Hobsbawm's conditions for membership of an elite group.

Origins and meaning of the labour aristocracy thesis

So many debates have taken place on this subject that there is a real danger of losing sight of the real-world experience of workers through over-concentration on theoretical issues. In dealing with a topic that has generated so much argument for over a century, misunderstandings can arise through conflation of arguments about the nature of the labour aristocracy with questions as to why there was such a stratum. From the outset it is important, therefore, to distinguish between the descriptive reality of the labour aristocracy on the one hand and the extensive debate that has surrounded its theorization on the other.

In the nineteenth century there was little essentially new in the structures, stances and occupations of the labour aristocracy, but what was changing was that non-craft groups were taking craft status and styles as their model.[2] In reality, an aristocracy of labour had developed over many centuries from small-scale manufacturing, from which it had drawn its traditions. As the *Weavers' Journal* pointed out in 1835:

> ... many powerful aristocracies exist – namely those trades, who support by internal regulation, a requisite compensation for their toil, who bar the door against every intruder and whose style of living, if frugally managed, is superior to that of the field labourer.[3]

According to Shepherd, the earliest reference to an aristocracy of labour dates from 1835. However, the term did not come into popular use until Engels advanced the idea in 1885, and again in 1892 in the preface to his *Condition of the Working Class in England*.[4] Lenin subsequently developed the idea, claiming that a group of workers had been 'bribed out of imperialist super profits into watchdogs of capitalism, into corrupters of the labour movement'. Lenin argued that England's monopoly position in Victorian world markets had created relatively good conditions of life for the labour aristocracy, who were exposed to the ideas of the ruling class and in turn transmitted these to the wider working-class movement.[5]

Central to the labour aristocracy debate is the notion that a distinct process of 'working class formation' took place in British society between 1840 and 1914. It is claimed that this had major political implications in that a section of the working class was more respectable than other workers, adopting moderate social and political behaviour.[6] Early research in labour history (Webb, Cole et al.) explained the emergence of the labour aristocracy, following the decline of the radical movements in the first half of the nineteenth century, in terms of membership of the 'new model' unions, support for the co-operative movement and the ideals of self-help. According to Hobsbawm, the persistent liberal radicalism of the labour aristocracy is easily understood, as it related to the earlier conservatism of selected groups of workers in 'special circumstances'.[7] This explanation is not fully convincing because it fails to explain why widespread working-class support for the Tory Party extended far beyond the ranks of a minority labour aristocracy.[8] Neither is there any satisfactory explanation of how the views of the labour aristocracy were transmitted to a wider cross-section of the working class.

During the 1950s and 1960s a number of labour historians, including Hobsbawm, developed the Marxist view that the labour aristocracy was determined by its economic base. Hobsbawm turned his attention to the worker's experiences in the workplace and, to a much lesser extent, the home in an attempt to explain the emergence of the labour aristocracy, an approach generally supported in the later work of Foster, Gray and Crossick. According to Hobsbawm, in the early part of the nineteenth century the labour aristocracy was mainly made up of small shopkeepers, superior artisans and some independent masters and foremen. By the end of the century it was reckoned to include commercial travellers, lithographic printers, joiners and cabinetmakers.[9] Precisely how this section of the workforce came to carve out a privileged position for themselves is subject to debate. At least in part this special position may have come from relatively high earnings, sound trade union organization and a degree of control in the workplace, although in the case of commercial travellers and small shopkeepers membership of a trade union would not apply.[10]

Issues of control in the workplace are central to the debate, and the examination of the printing trade that follows provides many examples of control throughout the period under discussion. What does become questionable is to what extent an element of control in the workplace amounted to real power. Compositors retained some say over working conditions through the chapel, but showed few signs of fundamentally challenging the prevailing social order or, for that matter, of supporting the dominant political and economic order. In the case of printing it is often overlooked that much of the control exercised by the chapel was in the collective interests of both the men and the employers. In short, it was often in the employer's interest to allow the chapel a degree of control in order to ensure the smooth running of the printing office. For example, it was the chapel, rather than the master printer, that controlled unruly or inefficient workmen by levying fines.

Identifying the labour aristocrat

No consensus exists as to precisely how a labour aristocrat should be identified; nor is there any agreement as to their numbers. Level of wages, group consciousness, authority and control in the workplace are all recognized as identifying features, but the weighting given to each varies. What is clear is that there were few absolute and permanent divisions between workers. Cole and Postgate offer a model identifying three groups of workers: highly skilled artisans who had served a full apprenticeship in traditional trades like printing, watchmaking and bootmaking; those men who had lesser skills (some metal trades, miners); and finally labourers.[11]

Harrison points to a deficiency in the labour aristocracy debate in that although economic, political and cultural aspects have received attention, the occupational dimension has been neglected; he argues that divisions existed within occupations rather than between occupations.[12] This may well have applied in printing, where there were marked differences between men in the same trade. In the work the compositor did it was common to refer to 'classes of work', a reference to the prestige and skill required in undertaking certain kinds of work. For example, compositors working casually on low-quality jobbing work would have contrasted sharply with an elite of men engaged on, say, a prestigious publication that allowed for great pride in craftsmanship. However, if distinctions are made based on skill, this definition can be seen to be flawed if the economic dimension is also used, as the most skilled men were not always paid the highest wages.[13]

Hobsbawm attaches the greatest importance to the level and regularity of earnings but fails to make it clear whether high earnings were a consequence of belonging to the labour aristocracy or whether earning capacity qualified men to be included in this elite. 'If a compositor did not get a higher wage than, say, a tailor he would regard himself as ill served whatever the relative demand for each on the market.'[14]

In contrast, Penn advocates what he calls the 'militant craftsmen thesis'; that is, at certain times groups of skilled workers took a militant lead. The corollary to this is that with the progressive deskilling of the labour force the trend was towards a homogeneous and relatively quiescent workforce in terms of militant action.[15] Again this notion might apply to some extent in the printing trade but it can be argued that as time went on, more rather than less skill was demanded of many compositors.

Both Gray and Crossick identify a segment of the workforce, generally regarded as skilled, having served an apprenticeship, who were distinct from the rest of the working class and the middle class. Qualification for inclusion includes low rates of marriage into families of other social groups, involvement in trade unions, the co-operative movement and temperance societies.[16] Some historians have criticized this definition because both Gray and Crossick fail to establish what gave the labour aristocrat his skill and high wages. Skill was only important as long as there was a demand for that skill, and in the case of compositors different skills were needed in the later period from those needed in 1850.

Other historians have highlighted the problem in defining skill. Skill could be the ability to do something well, but the Victorians employed the term in more restricted ways, for example distinguishing between strength, diligence and industry on the one hand, and performance of tasks requiring judgement and dexterity on the other. Harrison emphasizes diversity, suggesting that unevenness and complexity were the rule, with great differences in the size of firms, in sectors, and with elaborate segmentation of the product market. This view is particularly appropriate to printing and highlights both strengths and weaknesses of craft regulation. For example, as far as the compositor was concerned, newspaper work demanded only a limited range of skills, and yet men working in this sector received high rates of pay. It was competition among daily newspaper proprietors, together with the perishable nature of the product, rather than skill in the workplace that made employers vulnerable to the power of the chapel.[17]

Lummis, rejecting the hierarchical model implicit in Hobsbawm's thesis, makes the distinction between 'company men', who were comparatively secure workers, and insecure 'sub-aristocrats'. Lummis attaches more importance to security than to level of wages, and cites the example of the Woolwich dockyard where only half the posts were established positions.[18] The Lummis model, which views the labour aristocracy as a continuum rather than a hierarchy, is largely appropriate to printing, but it is necessary to note the widely differing kinds of casual labour in printing. Some skilled casual workers employed by the newspaper industry enjoyed high wages, a degree of welfare provision and security of employment, a situation that contrasted with the instability encountered by many casual tramping printers.

The criteria used to identify the labour aristocrat

While some criticism has been made of the model used by Hobsbawm, most labour historians readily acknowledge his important contribution to the debate. It is entirely appropriate therefore to test the six criteria used by Hobsbawm to identify the aristocrat of labour. Regularity of employment and level of wages, his most important criteria, will be considered separately as the two conditions are not necessarily related. Spasmodic unemployment could, for example, cancel out the benefits of relatively high wages in the short term.

Regularity of employment

Trade-society records, official statistics and the trade press show that, for many compositors, the trade was not especially secure in respect of continuous employment. Throughout the period under consideration the printing trade suffered both seasonal and cyclical unemployment, resulting in at least short periods of unemployment for the majority of compositors. Slow but continuous technological development, particularly the introduction of mechanical composition in the last quarter of the nineteenth century, threatened the jobs of compositors and, although the expansion in demand for printing offset the prospect of mass unemployment, many older men were laid off.[19]

At its quarterly delegate meeting held in August 1895, the London Society of Compositors (LSC) special committee on unemployment identified 12 main causes of unemployment:

1. Excessive overtime
2. Boy labour
3. High-pressure production
4. Influx of labour into London
5. Efflux of work from London
6. Too long a working day
7. Machine labour
8. Female labour

9. The 'grass' system
10. Faulty call book
11. Inefficient training
12. Demoralized residuum

The Typographical Association, representing compositors in the rest of the country, shared the concerns expressed by the London compositors. By far the greatest expenditure of the union was on unemployment relief which took the form of mileage paymenst enabling men to travel in search of work; the amounts paid out give some indication of the instability of the trade (see Table 3.1).

Table 3.1   Amount of money paid in mileage relief by the Typographical Association, 1863–72

Year	No. of members	Estimated income(£)	Mileage relief expenditure (£)
1863	1,940	840	1,165
1864	1,964	810	702
1865	1,992	863	575
1866	2,181	945	669
1867	2,262	980	1,090
1868	2,246	973	875
1869	2,266	981	1,030
1870	2,430	1,053	873
1871	2,687	1,164	684
1872	2,812	1,218	674

Source: Slatter, H., *The Typographical Association: the first fifty years* (1899).

Expressed in terms of weekly subscriptions of members, the average amount paid out in unemployment relief in the period 1863 to 1910 represented 28 weeks' subscriptions per member. In other words, half the union's income was spent on out-of-work payments. In bad years, 1869 for example, the society spent more on mileage relief than its total income. Although there were fluctuations throughout the period, from a low figure of 13 weeks in 1871 to a high figure of 41 weeks during the depression of 1876–80, through the period as a whole the figures indicate considerable distress from unemployment.

To an extent the relatively large sums of money paid out in mileage relief are evidence of the seasonal nature of the industry in the third quarter of the nineteenth century. Seasonal fluctuations in employment were greater in printing than in many trades.[20] Both general printing and the book trades were subject to seasonal changes in demand, with unemployment rising steeply in October, the explanation being 'that the holiday demand was worked out and the Christmas rush had not yet begun'. It should be noted that a great deal of the printing carried out was for commercial firms, and consequently the trade suffered during general trade depressions. Compositors who worked for large firms specializing in legal and government work were especially vulnerable. Both Hansards and Spottiswoodes were dependent on parliamentary sittings and during the long recess, hundreds of compositors were dismissed.[21] Overall, job security in printing was no better than in other trades (see Table 3.2). Apart from shipbuilding and engineering, where unemployment rose to 10 per cent in 1893, printing followed a similar trend to other trades except that in 1894 unemployment reached 5.9 per cent, compared with 4.1 per cent in building and 4.0 per cent in the cabinetmaking and furnishing trades.

Table 3.2   Cyclical fluctuations in unemployment in printing (%), 1887–94

Year	% change
1887	2.9
1888	2.5
1889	2.5
1890	2.1
1891	3.9
1892	4.3
1893	4.0
1894	5.9

Source: 'Persistent distress for want of employment 1889', PP, Vol. 24, 1895–6)

One general factor underlying the cause of unemployment in printing was an overstocked labour market, created partly because of the large number of small firms each training at least one apprentice, who after a seven-year period joined the pool of labour seeking work. Small employers were almost as vulnerable as the journeymen, with many small firms remaining in business for only a short time, again resulting in men seeking work. As the London Society of Compositors pointed out, 'all employment has become uncertain, no situation is permanent'.[22]

Although not as vulnerable to the affects of imports as some trades, from 1855 printing was progressively faced with foreign competition, work printed abroad competing well with English productions. Imports of printing from Germany affected the trade in Manchester rather more than the book trades of London and Edinburgh, although in London alone there were 1000 compositors unemployed in 1895.[23] It was alleged that in Germany convict labour was being used to undercut prices first in the Christmas-card market and then in general colour printing.[24] In July 1900 trade was so poor that in London alone 500 compositors were out of work and by September of that year this number had risen to 1000.[25] In the same year a record number of book contracts were sent from Britain to America.[26] Another factor that did not help the employment situation was the large number of foreign, particularly German tradesmen who were employed in London, especially in chromolithography. Exports of printed material were not high; the Master Printers' Federation blamed high wages, shorter hours and high tariffs in Britain for the impossibility of exporting British printing abroad.

Wage levels

Commentators on the printing trade often assume that because men belonged to long-established trade societies they were in a strong position to maintain wages and fight unemployment.[27] This was not always so. Although the operative printers were relatively well organized early in the nineteenth century, they did little to press wage claims; wages tended to remain static, and there was no general rise in the money wages of compositors between 1810 and 1866.[28] London compositors were better paid than any other group of workers, earning 33*s*. in 1801, increasing to 36*s*. in 1810, but in 1866, when the London compositors presented a memorial to the master printers for an increase in wages, the 1810 scales were still in force.[29]

The disadvantage of the indices listed in Table 3.3 is that they represent average earnings in a normal week irrespective of the hours worked; however, they do indicate that between 1810 and 1830 the earnings of compositors fell while those of the other two trades remained static. By the end of the century both the engineers and the builders had improved their earnings by around 50 per cent, while compositors showed less than a 20 per cent increase.

Often chapels were not strong enough to counter attacks on pay. In one daily newspaper where pay was inadequate, only half the men were in the society, and with a large number of apprentices, the executive decided not to pursue the matter as the chances of success were slight.[30] One reason for the relative decline in the fortunes of compositors was that the prosperity of the Typographical Association varied greatly and in some periods verged on bankruptcy.[31]

A number of historians support their arguments by citing the declared aims of the trade union without examining the reality. For instance McClelland, in discussing distinctions among groups of workers, cites the printers, who did not recognize non-union men in 'times of peace or war'.[32] This was clearly

Table 3.3 Wages and the standard of living, 1810–1900 (indices of average earnings in a normal week, 1891=100)

Year	Compositors	Builders	Engineers
1810	88	71	71
1820	78	71	71
1830	78	71	71
1840	83	75	75
1850	83	73	73
1860	83	76	79
1870	85	84	84
1880	96	96	90
1890	98	100	100
1900	100	111	108

Note: Index numbers allow for the changing importance of the different occupations within each industry.

Source: *British Labour Statistics, Historical Abstract 1886–1968*, HMSO, 1970.

true as an ideal but in practice Typographical Association members worked in mixed offices. In 1867 the executive of the Typographical Association recorded that at the offices of the *Warrington Guardian* there were 14 members, 7 non-members and 15 unbound apprentices, circumstances that left the union with little real power.[33] It must be remembered that non-society men were often those who had been temporarily excluded from the union for non-payment of arrears, therefore non-membership of the society cannot be taken to mean that they were in some way opposed to the union.

Many labour historians cite the printer, or more specifically the compositor, as the archetypal skilled worker, but this generalization disguises great differences in experience between workers and leads to assumptions that are incorrect. In his book *The Typographical Association*, Musson rightly hints at the complexity and diversity of the workplace experience of the compositor, especially after 1850.[34] Persistence of casual and tramp labour, together with a large number of non-society offices, came at a time when real income began an irregular decline. Between 1905 and 1912 the mean percentage increase in rates of wages for printers in 88 towns and cities was 4.1 per cent comparing unfavourably with the years before 1900.[35] Although there had been a rise in real standards of living, reducing the likelihood of general industrial unrest, conditions for many workers in printing fell well short of what could be considered a secure and stable occupation.[36] With growing prosperity, general living expenses increased and men often had to seek work further from home, finding lodgings or using the railways to travel to work.

Hobsbawm, citing the level and regularity of earnings as the main criteria in identifying the labour aristocrat, uses Baxter's figures for 1865 to calculate the size of the aristocracy of labour. He fails to interpret the evidence he himself uses, in that no distinction is made between the individual trades within printing or between the different classes of work undertaken by tradesmen in the same group. Although his table refers to specific trades (see below), Hobsbawm generalizes and assumes that all or most printers belong to the same group when in fact the trades listed formed only a small minority of the trade.

> Trades in 1865 with weekly wage-rates of 40 shillings and above
> Printing:
> Newspaper compositors
> Readers
> Some machine minders and engineers (printers)
> Lithographers – many

> (Leone Levi, *Wages and earnings of the working class* [1867] in
> Hobsbawm, *Labouring Men,* p. 280)

In a table of recognized wage rates produced by the Provincial Typographical Society in 1860, wage rates in different localities show large variations:

Cambridge	27s.–40s.
Oxford	30s.–33s.
Boston	21s.
Wexford	15s.
Macclesfield	24s.
Chester	27s.
Manchester	30s.–40s.
London	33s.–48s.

What the figures show is that a compositor in London may have earned three times the amount earned by a man working in Wexford and twice that of a compositor in Macclesfield. Compositors employed in Oxford and Cambridge earned high wages because of the experience needed to work on the publications produced at the university presses. The relatively high wages paid in Manchester reflect the city's importance commercially and as a centre for newspaper production, contrasting sharply with the rates paid in country towns, for example:

Carlow	18s.
Ayr	20s.
Norwich	21s.
Waterford	15s.

Applying the criterion Hobsbawm used in calculating the size of the labour aristocracy as those workers who earned 28s. or more, it is clear that the majority of compositors would not qualify for inclusion, although the claim is often made that printers were better paid than the mass of unskilled and skilled workers.[37] Caution is needed because of the geographical significance of wage variations, and while wages may have been below the national average, they may have compared favourably with those in towns of a similar size and with wages paid to other trades in the same town.[38] This is the justification used by Hobsbawm, who deliberately neglected regional variations in wages, arguing that workers would still occupy the same relative position to their 'plebeians', other things being equal.[39] Other things were not equal. Printing was a relatively small industry and in towns dominated by large industries, for example engineering or mining, it is probable that wage differentials among trades would have shown up clearly. For this reason, in 1867 the Typographical Association tried unsuccessfully to enforce a national minimum, a wage that was below the rate paid in most large towns.[40]

In Manchester, the wage rates for compositors employed in general printing in the period 1850 to 1914 were very close to the rates paid to two other skilled groups, the engineers and the cabinetmakers (see Table 3.4).

Table 3.4   Wage rates and hours worked in selected years for compositors, fitters and cabinetmakers in Manchester, 1850–1914

	Compositors		Cabinetmakers		Engineers (fitters)	
	Wages (s.)	Hours	Wages (s.)	Hours	Wages (s.)	Hours
1850	30	60	28	60	–	–
1860	30	59	–	–	30	57½
1870	30	55	32	56	32	57½
1880	35	55	35	54	32	54
1886	35	55	35	54	34	54
1890	35	55	35	54	34	54
1900	35	50	36	48	36	53
1906	35	50	38	48	36	53
1914	38.6d.	50	38	48	39	53

Source: *British Labour Statistics, Historical Abstract 1886–1968*, HMSO, 1970.

Towards the end of the century, the increase in collective bargaining resulted in greater uniformity between trades. What the figures appear to indicate is that from 1880 the cabinetmakers had a slight advantage compared with the compositors in that they worked fewer hours. From 1880 to 1906 the compositors received no increase in wages while the other two groups received modest increases; however, what is most significant is that in

Manchester, all three groups received virtually the same wage. What the figures do not indicate is the amount of overtime worked and the regularity of employment. A typical working week would be from 8 a.m. to 7 p.m. Monday to Friday with one-and-a-half hours for meal breaks, and 8 a.m. to 1 p.m. on a Saturday. However, compulsory overtime was common, including all-night working when a job was required in a hurry. In book and periodical houses it was common to operate a system of night and day work, exclusively day work throughout the year being virtually unknown.

Irregularity of employment was a major problem that the trade unions could do little about. In 1914 at the National Labour Press in Manchester, compositors often only worked a two-and-a-half-day week and took Saturday off. However, while the men were laid off some work was carried out by the overseer and when this was reported to the society, the company responded by threatening to dismiss some of the regular staff, leaving the society power-less to act.[41] Interestingly, it was the Typographical Association that started the Labour Press, providing most of the finance.

Not only did wage rates vary between towns but also there were big differentials between offices in the same town. In Manchester during 1854–55, when the *Guardian* and the *Examiner and Times* became dailies, the established rate for news compositors was 40s. per 54-hour week, but it is reported that some compositors on piecework earned as much as 56s. for a 54-hour week.[42] At the same time advertisements appeared for compositors at 'not less than 34s'.

Differentials of this kind can be partially explained by the different classes of work undertaken even within one office. Some men earned good wages by working at speed on straightforward text setting while others undertook work that qualified for extra payments (small type sizes, mathematical texts, and foreign languages). Others might be engaged on work demanding concentra-tion and skill, a factor reflected in the relatively high wages earned by compositors on the university presses of Oxford and Cambridge. In compari-son others would be required to do relatively easy tasks such as setting posters and playbills. Even within general commercial printing the quality of work varied a great deal from crude, simple styles to printers who followed the American trend towards 'artistic' printing, a style that demanded great skill and creative effort on the part of the compositor.[43]

This is not to suggest that high skill levels were always rewarded with high pay and security. If qualification as a member of the labour aristocracy depended on skill and high wages, it would be relatively easy to identify a super aristocracy within the ranks of compositors. Unfortunately this was not the case, as market forces rewarded those employed on work that had a high priority at a particular time. For example, speed of production was often a critical factor in certain classes of printing, allowing printing operatives greater bargaining power when the work had to be produced in a limited time, irrespective of skill requirements. Examples of this kind of work included newspapers, periodicals, legal documents and some official government publications. In the case of newspapers the large amounts of money paid by advertisers allowed the proprietors to pay relatively high wages to their employees.

In the late nineteenth century wage differentials between trades were not the same in all countries. Significantly, German compositors earned less than compositors in England, prompting some English printing firms to contract out foreign-language setting to German firms. In Russia engravers earned a monthly average wage of 72 roubles while compositors earned only half this amount, although this represented twice the wage of spinners and potters. In Spain there was little difference in pay between the compositors, shoemakers and carpenters, all of whom earned in the region of 3 pesetas per day. Scandinavian compositors earned only 3.70 krone compared to the machine printers' 4.70 krone and the 3.80 krone paid to brassworkers.

Piecework

Throughout the period under consideration there was a great deal of controversy over the relative merits of standard weekly wages, known as establishment or 'stab' work, task work and piecework. Arguments for and against the different methods of calculating pay came from both the employers and the employees. The main argument against stab rates was that it allowed idle or incompetent workers to earn the same as skilled conscientious men, which was unfair to both employers and good workmen. The compositors themselves displayed a certain pride in having a trade, often viewing time rates as appropriate for labourers, but not for the independent hardworking craftsman. Complexity of piece scales caused many problems in working out correct rates. In part the reason for this centred on the distribution of 'fat' copy, that is straight typesetting where the compositor was able to reach high speeds, as for example in the composition of a novel set in 9 or 10 point type. 'Lean' copy, on the other hand, involved more intricate setting and often required text to be set in small sizes, which was a much slower process. Higher prices were paid for gazetteers, dictionaries and scientific texts because the number of sorts used meant that they had to be kept in separate boxes, and it took the compositor time to locate them. In many offices materials were in short supply, so that men had to search for type and piece together leads for interlinear spacing. Pieceworking has often carried the blame for the low standards of some nineteenth-century printing, particularly when men working at speed used large spaces between words to increase the number of lines set and save the time-consuming task of splitting words at the ends of lines.

Pressure came from the master printers, who expressed the view that the policy of paying men what it cost to live rather than what they were worth made good men carry the 'dud' on their backs.[44] In countering this argument, the Typographical Association pointed out that no man was forced on to an employer. He could be sacked at any time and employers were using this argument to keep wages at a minimum rather than a maximum level. With piecework each man was paid what he earned according to ability and effort, but sometimes poor workers were transferred on to piecework in order to secure maximum output for minimum wages.[45] Even men who worked fast did not always benefit fully because when one job was finished the men could spend a long time waiting for the next job. During slack times, equipment could be tidied up and standing type distributed, but then the men quickly became bored and were forced to take time off in lieu of overtime rates at another time, a system known as 'time on the shelf'.

As Lummis points out, it is wrong to assume that it was the 'labour aristocrats' who set the pace in piecework and were somehow on the side of the employers.[46] Creating a mixed system of stab and piecework allowed employers to control wages according to the kind of work in hand, switching men between the two methods of calculating pay. Men on time rates, for example, undertook authors' corrections because these were directly chargeable to the publisher. Although the Typographical Association successfully resisted the introduction of task work, that is minimum output from stab hands, the association faced an impossible task in ensuring that the complex piece rates were adhered to. In fact, in many instances chapels took no notice of the resolutions passed at branch meetings unless it suited their purpose.[47]

The element of competition in pieceworking suited many employers because the organization of the 'ship' meant that those workers intent on high earnings took over the organization and distribution of the work.[48] Piecework tended to increase the pace of work, but problems arose as the size of firms increased and a foreman was appointed by the employer rather than the clicker to control the work.[49] By 1880, even readers in many firms were on piecework.[50] Interestingly, in the late nineteenth century when the Oxford University Press was printing one million bibles per year, the work cost more to proofread than to set. It is reported that each new edition was read 20 times and any staff member who found a mistake received one guinea.[51]

News compositors favoured piecework because it ensured high wages, but this often caused disputes between news and jobbing compositors employed in the same firm. Although the union attempted to discourage members from taking casual work, employers frequently engaged casual labour on piecework, and this tended to depress wages.[52] As the Typographical Association's figures show, in periods of good trade, between one-fifth and one-eighth of the union members worked casually and during a slump this number increased to around one-third.[53] Men often worked in more than one office; for example, the Manchester Branch Committee heard the case of Mr Watts, a compositor who was employed on the *Assurance Agents' Chronicle* on a

Monday and Tuesday and was idle on Wednesday and Thursday. On Friday evening and Saturday morning he worked at Chilterns and on the *Umpire* on Saturday night. The committee decided that his actions were not against the society's rules relating to 'smooting' because he did not exceed what amounted to a normal week's work.[54] The branch was less generous, however, in the case of a compositor from the *Guardian* office who worked on the newspaper during the day and returned at night to Oldham where he ran a printing business of his own.

Prospects for social security, unemployment and strike relief

With little or no disposable income, a major concern for virtually all nine-teenth-century workers, skilled and unskilled alike, was to ensure regularity of earnings through continuity of employment. Failure to maintain income resulted in reliance on the parish dole or the workhouse.[55] Highest rates of male pauperism occurred among labourers, general dealers, builders and agricultural workers; nevertheless, an appreciable proportion of skilled trades-men, including compositors, found themselves reliant on poor-law indoor provision. In the case of skilled workers, unemployment relief in the form of money to seek work elsewhere or assistance with emigration provided at least a degree of security that served to protect their status in the community.

For reasons explained in the first part of this chapter, compositors were especially vulnerable to seasonal and cyclical unemployment, presenting the trade societies with considerable difficulties, given that one of their main functions was to protect members from having to sell their labour at a price lower than its 'true' value.[56] This value was defined as the customary rate for the work rather than a rate that reflected changing market values. In the printing trade three measures were used to assist the unemployed in order to discourage them from accepting work paying less than the agreed rate: out-of-work relief, usually in the form of an incentive to travel to another town to seek work; strike or unemployment allowances; and assisted emigration.

Support for men on the road was an essential part of the strategy used by the Typographical Association, as this served to keep men out of unfair offices and faithful to the union. Most trades had a tradition of tramping, although there were exceptions – for example spinners and miners. In the case of printing, since its introduction in the fifteenth century, there had been a custom of men moving from place to place because of their work and it is likely that these men received hospitality on their travels. A form of travel-ling or tramp relief was in operation by the early part of the eighteenth century as the provincial printing trade began to develop, with members of the trade receiving assistance as they travelled in search of work. This infor-mal system pre-dates the formation of the trade's societies.[57] By 1826 there were established typographical societies in the main towns in Britain and an organized system of relief whereby unemployed men or men on strike were issued with a 'ticket' or a 'tramp card' as evidence of their entitlement to relief.

Tramp relief was intended to remove surplus labour from towns that were in recession and to assist members of the trade who were suffering distress. It also served to lessen the chances of men taking work in unfair houses. While tramping resulted in the failure of many strikes because there was always a pool of mobile labour, it could also work to the advantage of the trade societies because it was possible to remove men from a town where a dispute occurred. Men seeking assistance were provided with a ticket or tramp card together with an amount of money to cover travelling expenses, although those returning within a short time were required to reimburse the society. On arrival in a town the tramp needed to present his 'card' to the secretary of the local society who then gave him an allowance to cover the cost of a bed for the night. If work was available locally, the man was expected to take it and reimburse the society; otherwise he had to move on the next morning to reach another town by nightfall, the date and place being recorded on his card.

Relief was given only once in a six-month period, so men on the tramp had to do a 'round' of all the branches. However, some men cheated by not taking the prescribed route between towns and then claiming to have travelled a greater distance than they had. Others claimed to have lost their card in order to conceal how much relief they had received. Eventually, in an effort to make the system less prone to cheating, cards were numbered, making it easier for relieving secretaries to detect false claims.

The Typographical Association spent a great amount of time and effort in administering the tramp system, so it is little wonder that they failed to devote attention to some of the more important issues of the day. Trade-society branches took a very serious view of any men found to be defrauding the system, and if found out, men were summoned for making false claims. One compositor who had only paid into the society £19 in subscriptions was found to have drawn benefits in excess of £75, including a ticket for passage to America. The man was charged at the Mansion House Police Court and ordered to pay back the money or serve two years' hard labour. In another case a member of the Dublin Society named McNarmara was sentenced to six months' hard labour for defrauding the Gloucester Society of 8s. 7d. Even when the amounts involved were as small as 6d. cards were withdrawn and the name of the offending tramp printed in the *Circular* with instructions that no society should relieve him.

The whole question of providing relief for unemployed members divided the trade. In 1839 the Manchester allowance was fixed at 10s. for a single man and 15s. for a married man, the aim being to provide enough money to prevent absolute poverty without attracting undeserving claimants.[58] A move nationally to replace tramp relief in 1846 with a standard 6s. per week for those unemployed was not met with universal acceptance.[59] Many argued that it would put too much strain on union funds, causing subscriptions to rise and subsequent loss of membership. Strong feelings of pride and independence were in evidence, with men arguing that unemployment pay would be subject to fraud, difficult to administer and might encourage men to become lazy and not seek work.[60]

Between 1840 and 1870 a change took place in the attitude of compositors to unemployment. At the 1849 Typographical Conference, the argument was put that tramping was essential because a man with a large family could neither move easily nor emigrate, a contention which assumed that migration was the necessary answer to poor trade.[61] From the union's point of view, tramping served to spread surplus labour and disperse a pool of potentially cheap labour, at the same time meeting the needs of an industry that, to a large extent, was subject to fluctuating and seasonal demand.

Table 3.5   Amounts paid in benefits by the Typographical Association, 1873–98 (£)

	1873	1878	1883	1888	1893	1898
[A] Mileage relief	590	1,243	372	634	561	608
[B] Out-of-work pay	145	1,992	1,535	2,659	4,569	6,925
A as % of B	407	62	24	24	12	9

Source: The Typographical Association (1899).

Although the figures in Table 3.5 show that from 1873 tramp relief was progressively replaced by unemployment pay, it is significant that tramping persisted in the trade for so long. The Typographical Association recognized that the system was out of date, but instead of abolishing tramping it made minor alterations to the rules to make benefits easier to administer. A major difficulty was spreading the burden of tramp relief between societies, and many arguments arose because of the varying levels of relief paid in different towns. One of the problems during the 1850s was that some branches were more or less 'tramp societies', a situation that caused some annoyance to those societies that were intent on upholding trade standards. If tramping helped the trade societies through the need to correspond with each other, it often split the trade through the difficult question of reciprocity, resulting in considerable animosity between towns.

The Manchester Society relieved 110 tramps in 1835 but by 1841 this number had increased to 340.[62] London and Manchester both suffered through an influx of tramping compositors, London because of the relatively high wage rates and Manchester because it was located within reasonable walking distance of the many densely populated towns in Lancashire and Yorkshire. In 1862 the Provincial Typographical Association delegate meeting appointed a committee to frame rules for a national scheme of tramp relief, the objective being to remove the unemployed from large towns.[63] Called the 'Relief of Unemployed Printers' Plan', the aim of the new scheme was to 'impart increased respectability to the profession through the provision of a standard rate of 1d per mile tramped, plus 6d per night "bed money"'.[64] This benefit had to be earned through a two-year (or longer) probation period, during which time men had to pay additional subscriptions, without arrears. In return men could be issued with a 'first-class document' enabling them to claim mileage relief at a standard rate when unemployed. Even this scheme was open to abuse, with men carrying forged documents and providing false mileage claims which the Typographical Association took steps to counter by providing men on the tramp with maps and introducing a rule that required men in work to notify any vacancies. Vacancies had to be entered in a call book that was kept in a public house or the society office.[65]

The value of tramping to the individual varied a great deal. Comparison can be made between J. W. Rounsfell's ordeal as a tramping printer and the experience of Mamby Smith – both men were compositors who wrote biographical accounts of their trade experiences. Rounsfell, walking from town to town in England, suffered great hardship and misery, often living the life of a beggar. Mamby Smith, on the other hand, travelled through Britain to France, accumulating money, learning French and finally working as a tutor before returning to set up a press for a private patron.[66] Although both men were described as compositors, they had little in common. The lifestyle and opinions of Mamby Smith were firmly within the tradition of the 'respectable artisan'. Although suffering from periodic unemployment, he always adhered to 'honest and decent' principles, opposed radical political activities and condemned his tramping work mates as lazy and filthy.[67] What the comparison between Rounsfell and Smith illustrates is the extreme difference between the prosperous journeyman who tended towards conservatism, displaying great pride in his craft, and the generally despised casual tramp worker.[68]

Clearly there were positive aspects to the system of tramping. For some, tramping provided the opportunity to broaden their knowledge and strengthened the sense of a community of printers. Young journeymen were able to extend their experience and improve their craft skills, at the same time forging links with societies in different towns. Tramping was the main way societies kept in touch and it was an important means of transmitting knowledge and information about new techniques and methods of working. Importantly, it allowed men to pass on information about the state of the trade in other towns and to provide insights about particular employers in exchange for informal relief from men in work. For many, tramping provided a degree of independence, relieving the monotony of doing the same kind of work year in year out and allowing men to extend their experience of different classes of work, a custom that remained well into the twentieth century. It would appear that there was some affection for tramping as part of an ancient tradition in the trade and, more importantly, there was still irregularity in employment. Trade depressions between 1873 and 1878, and again from 1893, are reflected in the amount paid out, both in tramp relief and unemployment benefit.

In the USA, where tramping was extensive, it was claimed that 'tramps carried across the continent the craft's lore and tradition, especially the values of independence, respectability and reciprocity. Unlike the tramp's reputation in Britain, in America, tramps represented a superior, independent kind of workman in comparison to regularly employed journeymen. Permanent compositors were said to be 'dictated to by employers, becoming specialised dependant workers simply claiming allegiance to the old craft culture.'[69]

Any advantages gained through tramping must be considered alongside the grave difficulties encountered. The whole system of tramping was based on the assumption that work would be available somewhere, but evidence suggests that often this was not the case. During a recession, moving the unemployed around the country, especially in summer when there was no work to be had, was a waste of time and a severe drain on union funds.

A 'round' of all the branches by a compositor during the 1850s resulted in a trip of 2800 miles.[70] Possibly an extreme case, but it is recorded that a compositor drew a London card on 1 March 1848, returning just under a year later. He had tramped to Brighton and around the south coast to Bristol, then via Birmingham, Liverpool and Carlisle to Edinburgh, to Stranraer, Belfast, Dublin and 19 Irish towns, returning to London via Liverpool, Yorkshire and Cambridge. Gaining relief in 70 towns, he found work in only three.[71] W. E. Adams, a compositor who worked on the socialist weekly, the *English Republic*, until it failed in 1855, tramped the 273 miles from the Lake District to London and found:

> not an odd job anywhere, nor any relief either except a shilling at Birmingham. In Macclesfield even industrious men were having difficulty in obtaining bread ... it was the winter of the Crimean war.[72]

Adams was not a member of the union because at that time there was no branch in Coniston where he worked, or in his home town of Cheltenham. However, it is clear, that he was in sympathy with the ideals of the trade unions, having worked on the *English Republic* 'not to make money but to serve a cause'.[73]

Tramping involved great hardship, with men being away from home, walking long distances and becoming degraded and demoralized through living in cheap lodging houses. The amount of money spent out of society sick funds on 'bad feet, swelled legs and surfeits of colds' provides some indication of what conditions on the road were like.[74] Genuine unemployed tradesmen suffered from lack of food and anxiety about the family left behind. Adams describes having to share beds with dirty, coarse and vulgar men and frequently witnessing drunkenness, fighting and bad language.[75] As late as 1899, John Southward, the author of many textbooks on the trade, observed that 'the general public recognized the tramp printer, identifying him with dissoluteness, improvidence and vagrancy', adding, 'the moral character had been improved by the stringent rules laid down by the Typographical Association'.[76]

Many employers were reluctant to employ tramps, and evidence given to the Royal Commission on Labour (1892) described printers in 'call houses' as 'intemperate, indolent and incompetent.'[77] It is of course a mistake to generalize and assume that all compositors on the tramp were bad workmen, because men took to tramping for different reasons. Some were single men, who did not qualify for static unemployment pay. Others, for personal reasons, preferred an unsettled life. Wanderlust, loss of pride through drink, resentment of authority, unhappy marriage and inability to cope with life were all given as reasons for the frequency of tramping in printing.[78] One explanation why some men were accused of being professional roadsters was that employers usually operated a policy of 'last in, first out', so that when work ran out, casual men were the first to be dismissed.[79] Some men did not make any serious attempt to find work, presenting false cards, working in unfair offices and harassing men in work for donations, perhaps the 'lazy and filthy vagabonds' described by Mamby Smith.

During the first half of the nineteenth century tramp relief was a necessary evil, being the only alternative to the workhouse or parish dole. Tramping probably peaked in 1879 when tramping printers were paid for 336,000 miles, but it did not finally end until 1913. From 1887 limited out-of-work benefits were introduced, supported especially by Manchester compositors, who argued that this would enable members to stay in various towns to await work, keep them and their families together and prevent members becoming 'vagabondized by hawking their labour around the country'.[80]

The Typographical Association adopted a policy of sanctioning a strike only as a last resort. The association frequently refused members' requests for strike action, taking the view that it would be 'hazardous at a time when press and public opinion were against trades unions to initiate a strike'. When a strike did take place it would appear that men were well compensated. Allowances for men called out on strike took various forms: a lump sum, a weekly allowance or a 'backed' or 'double' tramp card. Usually strike payments amounted to more than out-of-work relief and just less than stab rate, as payments had to be large enough to ensure that men left their work during a strike and did not drift into unfair offices. From the point of view of the trade union, the availability of such a mobile workforce ruined many strikes, as it appeared that there were always some men prepared, out of desperation, to take the place of those on strike.

From the 1840s, emigration was advocated by all the printing-trade societies as a means of dispersing excess labour, the Provincial Typographical Association claiming in 1849 that money spent on emigration was more worthwhile than strikes, which were a costly waste when there was a 'superabundance of hands'.[81] In a sense emigration was just an extension of the tramp system, sending men to other countries rather than other towns. Elaborate schemes were set up to aid those tradesmen who were prepared to go to America, Canada and Australia, but these provoked little response.[82] Emigration grants proved to be an expensive and ineffective way of dealing with the excess of labour, society members being unwilling to contribute even 1*d*. a week towards sending men abroad. From the 1850s there was a change of policy by the Typographical Association, which began actively to discourage emigration. In part this was a response to opposition by American and colonial trade societies which were against any influx of workers from overseas, fearing the effect this might have on wages. The wages of compositors in America were higher than those of their counterparts in Britain and it was a third cheaper to live, a situation the American unions were anxious not to disrupt.[83]

Printers were not always prepared, or possibly able, to help their less fortunate colleagues. In 1827 the Manchester Society turned down pleas for assistance from the London compositors 'because too many of our own men being out of work'. At a later time, when the Manchester Society held urgent meetings to discuss aid to the unemployed, members voted by a majority of 220 against paying a levy of 6*d*. a week.

The prospects for compositors of increased social security in the period under consideration did not rest entirely in the hands of the trade societies. Paternalism on the part of employers was of increasing importance, with the provision of benefits in exchange for workers' loyalty being quite widespread in the printing trade. In part the provision of such benefits arose because of the desire of many firms to attract the best workers. As early as 1820, William Clowes provided a benevolent fund for his workers. Every man contributed 2*d*. per week and the firm provided a funeral benefit of £5.[84] At Cassells, where workers were provided with a choice of full meals with tea and coffee, the firm received praise from the Typographical Association, which commented, 'a good deal of intemperance which unfavourably characterises some printers ... employers should provide facilities for men to eat as a Christian ought to eat'.[85] The benefits provided by the London printers Hazell, Watson & Viney furnish an example of what the larger company offered. From 1870, the firm ran a savings bank for its employees with more than one-third of the workforce saving on a regular basis. The same company operated a thrift fund to provide low-cost loans and, from 1874, a voluntary

sick fund in which half the employees took part. Employees were also encouraged to purchase shares in the firm, a scheme which effectively provided
insurance against financial hardship, with more than 600 employees taking
advantage of it.[86] There can be little doubt that schemes like the one offered
by Hazells ensured a degree of stability among the workforce. By introducing
workers to a form of popular capitalism, the employers reinforced ideas of
common interests and pride in the firm. Employees who owned a 'stake in
the firm' were less likely to take disruptive action, while others who had
taken out loans from the company were not able to easily change jobs.
Middle-class initiatives stressing mental and moral improvement served to
encourage respectability and responsible citizenship.

In the latter half of the period under consideration a number of Manchester
employers provided welfare benefits. The Co-operative Printing Society offered numerous benefits, including some housing to its employees, although
not on the scale of the firm of Paul Dupont in Paris, which provided subsi-
dized housing, profit-sharing, pensions and medical treatment for its 550
workers.[87] From 1893, John Heywood, the Manchester printer and publisher,
provided any employee with 25 years' service who retired through ill-health
a pension of half-pay.[88] Another Manchester printer, R. & J. Sharp, invested
£750 in shares, the profits being distributed among their long-serving workers. In addition to benefits provided by employers, many of the larger chapels
provided members with sickness benefits, the *Manchester Guardian* chapel,
for instance, ran a successful sick fund from 1850.

Welfare benefits were not only provided by trade unions and employers.
Numerous charities, friendly societies, religious groups, building societies
and clubs also provided a network of support, usually of the self-help kind. In
1861 the government established the Post Office Savings Bank to provide
small-scale safe banking, seeking to encourage saving among the working
class, apparently successfully, as by 1869 there were 1.5 million depositors.[89]
Friendly societies experienced rapid growth and by 1874 it is estimated that
four million workers were members, thus providing sickness, accident or
burial benefits for over eight million dependants. This was of course in
addition to commercial provision on a massive scale by such companies as
the Prudential and the Co-operative Insurance Society.

From 1880, the Typographical Association, further adding to the social
benefits available to skilled men, introduced a voluntary superannuation
scheme with the following scale of benefits:

Years of membership	Weekly pension
20	6s.
25	7s.
30	8s.
40	10s.

The provision of these pension benefits proved a popular move, certainly helping further to distinguish the skilled worker from the casual labourer. The strenuous efforts made by the Typographical Association to assist its members in maintaining some dignity in times of unemployment and on retirement clearly demonstrate that, compared with the mass of unskilled and unorganized workers, the compositor fared relatively well in terms of social security. In this respect it can be argued that the compositor qualified for inclusion as a part of an 'aristocracy of labour'. Risks of unemployment changed little during the period 1850 to 1914, but the compositor was better able to cope with distress in the later period. In 1850 the Typographical Association had a membership of 600, but by 1914 this had grown to 23,000, affording greater power to influence events in the trade, wider control of branches and the provision of a well-organized system of benefits.

During the same period social conditions generally improved, especially in the fields of housing, public health and education, changes that tended to benefit the 'respectable artisan class' and provide opportunities for better standards of social security.

Conditions at work

The third criterion used by Hobsbawm in judging a worker's position in the hierarchy of labour was his conditions at work, including the way he was treated by foremen and masters.[90] Two immediate difficulties are apparent in considering working conditions. First, the period under consideration was one of change in both the size and structure of the printing trade, and second, compositors were found in two very different types of employment – surviving small-scale crafts and large-scale industrial production.[91] In printing, the introduction of factory methods over a long period, alongside pre-industrial methods, meant that the overall social impact was more diverse and complex than the sudden creation of a factory proletariat.[92]

Hobsbawm repeats the view that printers belonged to a trade little affected by the Industrial Revolution except in the materials and power applied to the processes, and that the position of craftsmen was unaffected or even strengthened during this period.[93] This view implies a degree of control by workers over the process of industrialization in printing and forms an integral component of the argument supporting the notion of the printer as a labour aristocrat. It is necessary to consider the validity of this claim.

A major weakness in Hobsbawm's argument arises because he interprets the retention of some craft practices as synonymous with lack of change. Many changes took place in the nineteenth-century printing industry, both in the function and structure of the trade. For the first time there was a division of labour between the compositor and printer, bringing with it opportunities for dissent between the two groups. The compositor believed he was a superior worker to the machine printer who had only to 'watch a machine', a notion that was partly confirmed by the fact that compositors in the early years of the century were frequently placed in charge of the machine printers.

Mechanization was not simply the application of power to existing processes; it was the vehicle for the changes that transformed a small, craft-based trade into a major industry. Printing, which in the eighteenth century had been dominated by small-scale London bookseller/printers, became a capital-intensive industry catering for the needs of the developing industrialized society of the nineteenth century. Much of the control exercised by craftsmen through the chapel in earlier times was transferred to large employers of labour who were intent on maximizing profits.

The complex picture of a trade displaying continuity of craft practices alongside advanced industrial methods was further complicated by those who expressed a romantic idealism, seeing printing as a craft or calling. In part, the latter view amounted to a spirited defence of craft values at a time when Victorian enthusiasm for literature and science bred contempt for those concerned with humble crafts.[94] G. W. Jones, the founder of the *British Printer*, saw printing as:

> a true calling rising to the height of supremest service, whether employer, workman or apprentice, above all we are printers, a relationship no trade union or masters federation can destroy.[95]

The view was that the first duty of the craftsman was to protect the standards of the craft tradition. Echoing William Morris and the Arts and Crafts Movement, Jones argued that craft values were never more necessary because of modern influences. He stated: 'it is our job to maintain the rich traditions of our craft in the expression of beauty and service through interest in our job, love of our calling and mastery of our craft'. What Morris did in setting up his Kelmscott Press was to deny the commercial efficiencies of the division of labour and the advantages to be gained by using machines, producing limited editions that only wealthy connoisseurs could afford.

Sentiments such as these reflect another dimension to the idea of a labour aristocracy, this time coming from the employers. Recalling a golden age of the past through the mastery of the trade and ideals of craft tradition would have had little appeal to the vast majority of compositors who were employed in unhealthy workshops on tedious, repetitive typesetting, paid by the piece and suffering from frequent periods of unemployment. As one printer, recalling the 1840s, pointed out:

> the life of a printer, as a general rule is a monotonous round of drudgery affording little scope for adventure or interesting experience. There were no established holidays and men could be called on to work from 6.00a.m. till 10.00p.m ... the workshops having small windows and scanty sanitary accommodation.[96]

As for mastery of the craft, this was an unrealistic hope as the developments in mechanical typesetting resulted in a degree of specialization that prevented any individual from gaining complete mastery of the trade. For the first time in the long history of printing, the work of the compositor was divided to create specialisms, increasing the opportunities for conflict between men in the same trade.

Formal attempts were made to bridge the ideological gap between commercial printing and printing as a craft through the formation of the British Typographia. Started in 1887, this society was formed for the mutual improvement of its members through the exchange of ideas and discussion of trade topics. The British Typographia had aims similar to those of the Federation of Master Printers and its governing council was comprised mainly of master printers, but did include C. J. Drummond, Secretary of the London Society of Compositors. The *British Printer* became the official organ of the British Typographia and when the society closed in 1900 its high ideals were carried on through articles in the *British Printer*.[97]

From 1850 there are many signs of increasing levels of craft consciousness, but little evidence of radical tendencies within the trade. Absence of militancy and strong occupational comradeship suggests that compositors were not prepared to jeopardize their jobs. Trade and trade society publications alike tended to put emphasis on individual progress, improvement and the development of skills rather than on the wider issues of redistribution of wealth and inequalities in society. There was a conscious recognition that the aesthetics of the printed image, typefaces, illustrations and the layout of the printed page were a branch of applied art – a view that helped bolster the image of the compositor as a better sort of workman. As early as 1868 lengthy articles were appearing in the trade press drawing attention to the unnecessary movements practised by compositors, describing these as ridiculous, purposeless and time-wasting. Advising men to 'stand perfectly upright, soldier-like, knee joints together, the upper part of the body erect, not curved', reflects the beginnings of scientific management, where people from outside the trade passed judgement on how the independent craftsman did his job. The *Typographical Circular* carried reprints of Christian Social Union articles stressing the responsibilities of union members, the general tone being one of deference and courteous regard for employers. Respectability at any cost was the recurring theme, with strong indications that this was an 'aristocratic trade' that should be distanced from the mass of trade unionism.

By the late nineteenth century compositors had moderated their drinking habits and the tavern played a lesser role in the affairs of the union. Opposition was increasingly expressed within the trade to the use of the 'cheerless and forbidding' tavern as a calling house and arguments were put forward for the provision of 'private rooms furnished with books, newspapers and parliamentary papers'. One reason given for this stress on respectability was that it would 'show the manner in which the general trade conducts its business, its temperate tone, its non-antagonistic approach, its elevation in the social scale'. A second reason given suggests that improved behaviour would gain the respect of employers 'and dispel the odium, which has always rested on the words trades unions'.[98]

In considering a trade with long continuity in craft terminology, it is possible to recognize the significance of change when it did occur, as language provides some clues as to the perceived status of men in the trade. From the late nineteenth century printing houses gradually became known as 'works', reflecting the move away from a craft carried out within the master's house to custom-built factories. Even so, the term 'printing office' was preferred to 'printing works'. Status distinctions were reflected in descriptions of the trade as a 'calling' or 'profession' rather than a 'craft' or 'trade'. When compositors petitioned for a wage increase in 1874 they referred to the trade as 'our profession'.[99]

By the end of the nineteenth century, partly as a consequence of specialization and the introduction of new trades (for example caster operators and photoengravers), there was a growing awareness of occupational status within printing and a tendency for compositors to close ranks. As an employee of Cassells recalled, 'a compositor thought himself several notches above the machine printer, and the clerical worker, even though taking considerably less money, looked on himself as being greatly superior to those on the mechanical side of printing'.[100] It is recorded that status differences between sections of the trade were so great that men who came into daily contact at work would often look the other way when they passed in the street.[101] Men had a clear perception of their own standing, tending to associate with others of similar status, and thus avoiding any impression that they accepted a lower position. St John Heinemann, describing relations between office staff and compositors, explained:

> the office staff believed at the beginning that they were better educated, better dressed and superior in all ways. But it transpired that the printers had a high opinion of themselves, especially the compositors who had a well-deserved pride in their work as craftsmen.[102]

Any acknowledgement of the status of the compositor by Heinemann needs to be judged alongside his obvious dislike of trade union representatives. Describing an experience in negotiating at the Windmill Press, he commented: 'three revolting creatures appeared to represent the men, most unworthy specimens of the working-class, one fat podgy creature, another a horrid little adenoidal Hebrew'.[103]

Sharp occupational and status differences between sections of the workforce were made obvious by dress. The *Penny Magazine* claimed that the compositors were:

cleanly, well dressed, intelligent looking active artisans not much think-
ing about the matters of the world they have in hand but properly intent
on picking up as many letters in the hour as may be compatible with
following their copy correctly.[104]

Until at least 1900, it was common for clickers and older compositors to
wear top hats while machine-room hands dressed in corduroys with a silk
handkerchief tied in a knot with the ends brought round the braces.[105] Certainly, visual evidence from the late nineteenth century supports this view,
showing compositors in a large book house dressed formally with stiff white
collars, black cravats, ties and waistcoats. At the Greystoke Press in 1880,
compositors were described as 'top hatted, frock coated gentlemen'.[106] For
many years the *Typographical Circular* carried only one advertisement and
that was for 'Everclean Linon Collars' which were described as 'ink-proof
and can be wiped clean'. The formal dress of the compositors meant that
these men experienced difficulties in buying workmen's tickets on the railways, as the railway companies appeared to assume that only navvies,
bricklayers' labourers and men who wore filthy clothes travelled by workmen's tickets. Only the efforts of the Workers' Trains Association brought
about an end to this absurd restriction.[107] Not only did compositors pride
themselves on their appearance, but they also maintained high standards in
their dealings with each other, invariably alluding to each other as gentlemen.
Some hint of how compositors perceived themselves is provided by evidence
of genuine companionship with a strict code of craft manners: for example,
never to speak to a man during his tea break and to show respect for another
man's tools.[108]

From the third quarter of the nineteenth century many of the larger printing
firms displayed a more enlightened and considerate approach to their employees, which tended to encourage and reinforce the workers' own perception
of status. Charles Wyman, in evidence to the Commission of 1875, claimed
that 'the atmosphere of a printing office is more the atmosphere of a school
than is the case in many trades. They are surrounded by printed paper and by
that which is more or less of an improving nature and intellectual character.'

When William Spottiswoode (1825–83), the Eton- and Oxford-educated
son of the founder of Eyre and Spottiswoode, took charge of the family firm
in 1850, he immediately reduced the hours worked and provided educational
facilities for all apprentices, including evening classes and annual examinations. Spottiswoode appointed a schoolmaster and a chaplain, and in 1853
started a choral society and a rowing club. Additionally, the firm provided
food for all employees at very moderate prices.[109] Conditions such as these
represented a considerable improvement in working conditions, although
employers expected in return an acquiescent workforce.

With a surplus of labour in the trade, discipline in many firms was quite
harsh – a situation the trade societies could do little about. At the *Daily*

Citizen office in Manchester men were warned not to talk while working and when a compositor named Steen asked another man for the loan of some apostrophes, both men were dismissed.[110]

Recreational activities of printers in the late nineteenth century tend to reflect respectable middle-class values. In 1897, typical of many of the larger printers, the *Morning Post* had a golf society, a rowing club and a cricket team. The Manchester newspapers had a cricket league in which each office entered a team, and the Typographical Association also had teams for bowling and cricket. In Scotland it was reported that, by 1894, printers had taken up photography, music and played golf and soccer.[111]

The changing social aspirations of compositors were often matched by improved physical working conditions, especially in the case of medium- and large-sized offices. Before 1875, few if any buildings were constructed as printing offices, but were usually converted dwellings with small windows and scanty sanitary accommodation.[112] In 1843, Charles Dickens, in his capacity as chairman of the Printers' Pension Corporation, pointed out two major health problems encountered by compositors:

> Immured as he is, in a close confined place of business, from an early to a late hour, and frequently throughout the night, breathing little else than a tainted atmosphere, it is no wonder that he displays a cadaverous countenance and emaciated appearance.[113]

Dickens also drew attention to the frequent loss of sight in older compositors and the deterioration of sight in men before the age of manhood. It would appear that thirty years later the situation was little improved, as the Inspector of Factories pointed out in 1875:

> small printers are a poor and sickly class given to intoxicating drinks. Many of their workshops are in outhouses, badly ventilated and in the vicinity of the opening of sewers, and other objectionable places. Their hours are unreasonable and frequently all night.
> (Report of the Inspector of Factories, 31 October 1875, p.110)

G. P. Reveirs, recalling his apprenticeship in the late nineteenth century, described how printers worked in old houses converted by knocking down partitions between rooms and cutting openings in the walls dividing houses; as a result rooms were close, dark and stuffy.[114] The same writer related how in the firm he worked in, there was only one w.c. for 40 compositors and one lead sink to wash in, a description confirmed by many other biographical accounts of nineteenth-century printers. Conditions tended to be cramped and unhygienic, with poor ventilation because many of the buildings were old.[115] According to Charles Wyman, employers just left it to the compositors to organize their own ventilation. Samuel Ralphs described the composing room at the *Stockport Advertiser* as 'a room about 20 feet square and partly underground ... it was dark and dismal'. The reading closets were said to be the worst feature of many offices. Heat in printing shops was very great, as compositors used at least two gas jets and presses were steam-driven. It was recorded that 'Phthhisis decimates [sic] the badly ventilated workplaces of the compositors.'[116] With the introduction of the Linotype and Monotype, which used gas to heat the type metal, the problem of fumes in the workplace increased.

The Factory Acts Extension Act 1867 brought printing offices into the system of inspection and although there were many abuses of the Act, it did lead to improvements in general working conditions.[117] During the last quarter of the century many new buildings were erected or converted to house book and newspaper firms and these offered better working conditions through the provision of large working spaces with better ventilation and sanitary arrangements.

Examination of the mortality figures for different trades provides some clues as to the effects of the working environment on health (see Table 3.6). Taking the adjusted figures for England and Wales for 1900–1902, printers came close to the average with 994 deaths, suggesting, perhaps surprisingly, that working in printing was less healthy than working in coalmining, bricklaying and tanning. At 45 to 55 the mortality rate was almost twice that of agricultural labourers. Plumbers, potters and general labourers, however, appear to have worked in conditions more detrimental to health.

Death at a young age was a common occurrence and clearly there is no simple cause and effect relationship between mortality rates and occupations; differences occur for many reasons. The physique of the men entering a particular occupation would vary; living conditions, lifestyle and diet would play a part, as would level of income.[118] Another factor may have been fitness, as, with the exception of occasional lifting, printers did not benefit from physical exercise and fresh air that some trades experienced at work.

Conditions within the workplace were an important factor, and the conclusion must be that printing was not a particularly healthy occupation. One possible explanation is that printers, like plumbers and lead miners, suffered from the poisonous effects of working with lead, continuous contact with lead bringing on saturnine poisoning. A study of hospital statistics carried out in Leipzig in 1871 showed that out of 1600 printers treated, 77 per cent were injured through exposure to lead. The consequences of lead poisoning were obvious when men didn't take basic hygiene seriously. When Frank Kirkland, a 17-year-old apprentice compositor from Derby, died of lead poisoning, his father, also a compositor, told the coroner that his son had been warned many times about eating food at work with dirty hands.

It has been estimated that among compositors 70 per cent of deaths in 1870 occurred because of diseases of the chest, prompting Dr Wyntor to recommend that compositors grow moustaches and beards as they were 'natural respirators'.[119] Compositors also suffered from 'dropped hand', paralysis of

Table 3.6   Occupational mortality rates in England and Wales, 1900–1902

Relative number of deaths occurring within a year from all causes, including accident, in a group of fixed size and age composition, when it is made up wholly of men at work in or retired from the occupation shown.

Clergy	524	Printers	994
Gardeners	563	Tailors	1,027
Farmers	596	Plumbers, painters, glaziers	1,114
Railway workers	610	Cotton manufacture	1,114
Butchers	1,148	Farm labourers	621
Coach, cab, omnibus	1,157	Schoolmasters	665
Civil servants	723	Hairdressers	1,196
Grocers	729	Lead miners	1,206
Lawyers	750	Coalheavers	1,221
Tanners	774	Glass manufacture	1,260
Carpenters and joiners	820	Chimney sweeps	1,343
Gas works service	878	Brewers	1,393
Coal miners	885	Dock labourers	1,481
Bricklayers and masons	906	Potters and earthenware	1,493
Domestic indoor servants	927	Blacksmiths and strikers	937
Seamen and merchant service	1,646	Physicians and surgeons	952
Innkeepers and publicans	1,781	Wool and worsted manuf.	984
Tin miners	2,131	Commercial travellers	988
General labourers	2,235		
		All occupations together	1,000

Source: Supplement to the 65th Annual Report of the Registrar-General, Part II Reprinted in Brown, *The Growth of British Industrial Relations*, p. 35.

the extensor muscles of the wrist, perhaps a precursor of the present-day repetitive strain injury.

In spite of improvements in general working conditions, many printing firms suffered through the maintenance of low-priced contract work and severe competition. R. Hazell (of Hazell, Watson & Viney), describing conditions at the turn of the century, pointed out that there was plenty of keen craftsmanship but seldom a scientific approach to technical problems.[120] Most printed matter was of an urgent nature and men had to concentrate while working at high speeds, which frequently caused stress. W. E. Adams, who worked as a compositor in a Manchester jobbing office in 1855, attributed his own good health to the lack of stress in that particular firm and the excellent air in the Isle of Wight where he was brought up.[121] The general view was that if printing was unhealthy, there were many trades even more unhealthy.

Increasingly, firms kept type stored in the hope of reprint orders, resulting in shortages of spacing materials and type and encouraging compositors to hide scarce materials away. This led to tensions between men working together on the same work. Often the old type sizes brevier and long primer were in use at the same time as the newer standardized point system, although the two were incompatible. This constituted a serious situation for men on piecework and was an inefficient way to run a business. Other firms were reluctant to invest in new equipment. During the 1890s, when the circulation of *The Times* fell, most of the equipment and machinery in use was more than 40 years old, but there was no justification for spending large sums at a time when there was competition from 172 daily newspapers in Britain.[122]

A poor working environment often meant unsafe working conditions and although it was not as dangerous as some trades, printing was not without its hazards. Printing machines had fast-revolving cylinders driven by cogs and moving belts which sometimes broke, causing injury. In 1895 at the Oxford University Press, a boy of 14 had to have both legs amputated after being caught in a Wharfedale machine. Two years later a 'lumbering litho stone' killed another boy.[123] Lithographic stones, like formes of type, were heavy and consequently the source of many injuries. With the introduction of mechanical composition both the Linotype and Monotype machines involved casting type with molten metal, with the risk of causing severe burns through splashes from hot metal and adding to the polluted atmosphere of the printing office.

Detailed conclusions are provided at the end of this chapter, but it is appropriate to sum up here by drawing attention to the fact that the experiences between workers would have been different both inside and outside work owing to the large number of variables. Focusing on the workplace experience provides few answers about working-class consciousness among printers. The size and structure of the printing trade meant that the kind of occupational solidarity shown by the colliers of Northumberland and Durham or the dockworkers in London and Liverpool was not possible. Working conditions experienced by a newspaper compositor in Manchester and a jobbing compositor in a market town would have been quite different; nevertheless indications are that, generally, many compositors did adopt the mannerisms and behaviour appropriate to membership of an elite group of workers.

Relationship with social strata above and below

Hobsbawm's fourth criterion to identify a labour aristocrat, a worker's relationship with the social strata above and below his own, requires cautious treatment because of the complexity of the issues involved. Wealth, authority, education, lifestyle, culture and political influence all contributed to the complicated mix of attributes determining class. Generalizations relating to whole groups of workers fail to distinguish qualities such as ambition, ability, income and security among men within each trade, factors that are important in determining if a man belonged to a 'super-aristocracy' or to what Lummis calls 'the tail of skilled men', that is, men who suffered insecurity from unemployment and inadequate earnings.[124]

Compositors, it will be argued, were found across the whole spectrum of the working class. During the second half of the nineteenth century subgroups developed within the trade of compositor; some men were trained to do only one class of work, others could carry out a range of work while others became specialized in coping with highly complex setting. Many did suffer insecurity through spasmodic unemployment or inability to work due to sickness or old age, circumstances unlikely to allow upward mobility. In contrast, some compositors were able to earn relatively high wages, working for example on the newspapers, while others were able to set up small businesses, opening up the prospect of acquiring property, wealth and status, circumstances that could lead to geographical, social and occupational mobility.

Throughout the trade literature of the nineteenth century a great deal of nostalgia was expressed among older men for 'the good old days' and while this may partly have represented sentimental illusions it probably indicates some loss of status, feelings of worth and pride in craftsmanship. In the early nineteenth century the Committee of Compositors clearly pleaded for recognition of the status of their work:

> just as the physician and lawyer have a trust reposed in them – such confidence could not be reposed in people of very mean or low condition – just as goldsmiths and jewellers are superior because of the trust they command – so should the compositor who is handling words of equal importance to jewels.[125]

This polite but firm request from the compositors for recognition of their worth did, however, conceal a threat that the confidentiality of work could be breached unless they were paid a wage appropriate to their standing.

Notions of respectability, like relations with other strata, did not depend solely on the occupation of the father. To some degree, formal and informal networks in the neighbourhood provided opportunities for contact with a wider social mix. Religion, for example, offered a meeting place for all classes. Membership of political and philanthropic groups, participation in sport and amateur dramatic societies, all gave opportunities for contact with a wider grouping than that of the workplace.

Study of a specific trade within a particular town overcomes some of the methodological problems inherent in making generalizations at one level, but this approach may suffer from the danger that the trends identified might not be applicable elsewhere. As Gray points out, the separation of artisan elites may be a characteristic of certain localities, while other patterns apply in different places.[126] However, it may be useful to look at the issue of marriage as a vehicle for social mobility. Significance of marriage between various strata may depend on geographical distribution of houses and the range of local occupations. For example, in the case of Stockport, the town chosen to examine marriage patterns, the bulk of the population lived within a three-mile radius of the town centre, with a concentration of workers in the hatting and textile industries. In these circumstances, as Lummis points out in relation to the general picture, widespread inter-class marriage was not possible simply because there were limited numbers of lower middle-class people to marry.[127]

Unlike Bristol, Edinburgh and London, Stockport had no concentration of printers, but there was a reasonable demand for printing as this was a busy industrial town. In 1893, 257 men were employed in the printing trade compared with 4493 in textiles and 2764 in hatting. Although no more than half of the 257 printers would have been compositors, the numbers are deemed adequate to determine any obvious trends in social mobility.

In spite of some limitations in drawing firm conclusions from the evidence, examination of the marriage registers covering Stockport in the period between 1875 and 1915 was carried out in an attempt to answer two questions. Whom did skilled printers marry and what trades did the sons of printers follow? In carrying out this examination other secondary observations were made to facilitate comparisons. A note is made of occupations that were considered 'poor' and a sample of fathers/sons with middle-class occupations is included as it demonstrates a pattern of upward mobility, which contrasts sharply with the experience of skilled printers.

Rather than conducting a full survey of all marriage certificates, the study covers a period of more than 20 years and takes a significant sample from the registers of three of the established churches in the town. Unfortunately, marriage certificates in many cases fail to record the occupation of the bride, a crucial piece of information as the income of the women would be vital in contributing to the economic mobility of the family. Any tendency towards upward mobility may well have been expected to come from women, who had limited opportunities in the labour market, forcing them to rely largely on their husband's income. The limited information relating to the occupations of brides suggests that the marriage partners of skilled compositors were employed in the 'ordinary' working-class occupations common in Stockport (hat trimmer, weaver, dressmaker). There are no instances in which the bride of a printer could not write, although in the case of other workers many instances occur where the brides were unable to sign their names in the registers (cook, charwoman, cotton operative, hatter). Inability of one or more of the parties to sign the marriage register is taken as evidence of low educational standards.

In the absence of occupational information on brides, the social position of marriage partners is taken from the occupational background of the spouses' families, providing what Thompson describes as the most sensitive and acute indicators of community or class feeling in that it demonstrates what each social set finds tolerable (see Table 3.7).

Examination of the social backgrounds of the families into which skilled printers married reveals little to support Hobsbawm's claim that the labour aristocrat merged with the lower middle class. Hobsbawm refers to Clark's description of the latter group as 'the best paid clerks, book keepers and the better sort of working folk'.[129] Gray and Crossick use a similar argument by claiming that a segment of the workforce was generally regarded as skilled, having served an apprenticeship, and was distinct from the rest of the working class through rates of marriage into families of other groups. There is no evidence of what Hobsbawm calls 'shading over' of the aristocracy of labour into other strata, an argument used partly to explain the lack of unity within the labour movement.

Women had some interest in upward mobility in that their future life experiences would have depended on the occupational experience of the men they married. Thompson, in his study of the period 1850–90, found that roughly half of the marriages of sons of skilled workers, in both Kentish London and Edinburgh, were to daughters of skilled workers, providing confirmation of the stability of the habits and attitudes of the labour aristocracy.[130] This pattern is not reflected in Stockport. During the period 1875–1915, less than a quarter of the sons of skilled printers married daughters of similarly skilled workers, a figure which hardly supports the notion of stability within the labour aristocracy. The figure is much lower than the one quoted by Crossick and Miles and by Savage, who found that between 1850 and 1870, roughly two-thirds of all bridegrooms whose fathers were skilled married women from similar family or higher non-manual backgrounds.[131]

One possible explanation for this discrepancy is that it is virtually impossible to count and classify workers accurately as 'aristocrats' or 'sub-aristocrats' because of the vast number of workers who defy classification. From the Stockport sample, railwaymen, seamen and hatters may not qualify as skilled workers yet they could well have enjoyed greater job security and earnings than skilled masons, engineers and printers, who suffered spasmodic unemployment.

Similar difficulties arise in considering the claim by Thompson that 22.3 per cent of the marriages of sons of skilled workers were to daughters of unskilled labourers (in the period 1850–70).[132] In Stockport the figure is 28 per cent but no significance can attached to the 5.7 per cent difference as it is impossible to determine the skill level of those employed, for example, as grinders, gardeners and tripe dressers.

Table 3.7 Printers: sample of occupations of brides, fathers and fathers-in-law at the time of marriage, Stockport, 1875–1915

Groom	Bride	Groom's father	Bride's father
Machine printer	n.s.	Dyer	Joiner
Printer	n.s.	Carter	Butcher
Compositor	n.s.	Gardener	Labourer
Compositor	n.s.	Rope & twine mnf.	Seaman
Printer	Reeler	Printer	Collier
Printer	Jointer	Provision dealer	Hatter
Printer	n.s.	Gardener	Farmer
Machine printer	n.s.	Colour mixer	Pigment grinder
Compositor	n.s.	Tailor	n.s.
Compositor	Weaver	Weaver	Plasterer
Compositor	Dressmaker	Mill overlooker	Builder
Compositor	n.s.	Compositor	Compositor
News manager	n.s.	Engineer	Mech. engineer
Printer	n.s.	Hat manufacturer	Hat manufacturer
Litho printer	Warehousew'n	Warehouseman	Tin plate worker
Printer	Weaver	Colour mixer	n.s.
Printer	Hat trimmer	Stoker	Joiner
Compositor	n.s.	Warehouseman	Mineralwater man
Printer	Dressmaker	Foreman engineer	n.s.
Engraver	n.s.	Draper	Timber merchant
Compositor	n.s.	Railway porter	Farm labourer
Printer	n.s.	Painter & decorator	Tripe dresser
Printer	n.s.	Traveller	Labourer
Litho printer	n.s.	Hatter	Weaver
Printer	n.s.	Saddler	Silk weaver
Printer	n.s.	Coal merchant	Labourer
Printer	n.s.	Fitter	Mason
Printer	n.s.	Machinist	Miner
Machine printer	n.s.	Spinner	Grinder
Compositor	n.s	Sgt Major	Coach painter
Labourer	Printer	Bleacher	Labourer
Printer	n.s	Packer	Gardener
Print finisher	n.s	Dyer's cleaner	Cotton operative
Compositor	n.s	Collier	Blacksmith
Printer	n.s	Dyer	Goods porter
Printer	n.s	Printer	School attendance officer
Printer	Reeler	Gardener	Gardener
Printer	n.s	Tobacconist	Hatter
Printer	n.s	Carder	Grocer
Compositor	Label sorter	Spinner	Accountant's assistant
Printer	Warper	Grocer	Grinder
Printer	n.s	Clerk in office	Coach builder

Sources: Compiled from: *Register of Marriages St Thomas's Stockport*, Vol. 1, 1875–87; Vol. 2, 1889–95; Vol. 3, 1895–1903; *Christ Church, Stockport*, Vol. 3, 1872–85; Vol. 4, 1885–97; *St Paul's Church, Stockport*, Vol. 6, 1909–15.

Out of the 42 printers identified on marriage certificates, not one married the daughter of a professional person, while in contrast nearly all daughters of solicitors, doctors and dentists married into families of similar standing. Only in two instances did printers marry into families that could be described as belonging to the lower managerial class (school attendance officer and accountant's assistant). Of the remainder, 18 married the daughters of skilled tradesmen and 19 married daughters of unskilled men, suggesting that in Stockport, printers married into families of similar or slightly lower economic and social status. Perhaps significantly, no printer married into a family where the father of the bride did work of a low status (scavenger, hawker, rag sorter). What the figures show is a tendency towards greater integration within the working class in line with the findings of Lummis.[133] As Crossick points out, the majority of labour aristocrats he studied were content with their positions and not necessarily interested in upward mobility.[134]

It is appropriate at this point to consider what occupations the sons of printers chose. Even before the period of this study it is claimed that occupational mobility within the working class, rather than upward social mobility, was the most common experience, and this appears to have been true of the sons of printers (see Table 3.8).[135]

Table 3.8   Sample of occupations of sons of printers, Stockport, 1875–1915

Father	Son
Printer	Grinder
Blockprinter	Labourer
Printer	Maker-up
Printer	Thread doubler
Stereotyper	Waterman
Gold printer	Warehouseman
Paper stainer	Cotton operative
Compositor	Doubler
Printer	Brushmaker
Printer	Compositor

Source: As for Table 3.7.

The information given in Table 3.8 is derived from marriage registers and therefore can only be taken as an indication of a general trend because it only represents 'married sons'. Nevertheless, no evidence is found to support the commonly held view that, in printing, sons followed their father in the same trade. This did happen in some parts of the country, where it is usually taken as a sign of a degree of paternalism on the part of employers. For example, throughout the nineteenth century *The Times* operated a patriarchal system whereby the tenants and labourers of the Bearwood estate of John Walter were employed as compositors and pressmen on *The Times*. As late as 1896 it was claimed that most people in the works were related.[136] Neither is there any marked pattern of the sons of printers entering other skilled trades (engineering, woodworking and building). Instead the dominant trend appears to be that of taking up semi-skilled and unskilled work (grinder, labourer, brushmaker).

The reasons for this are unclear, but might reflect some disillusionment with the trade on the part of printers, especially the long period of low pay during an apprenticeship and subsequent spasmodic unemployment. Those who had long experience of printing may not have been so anxious to put their sons into the trade. On the whole it was the mother who was influential in selecting the first job of sons and daughters, which might suggest that children were put into jobs providing immediate income benefits.[137] Conversely, there are numerous examples of the sons of other relatively well-paid workers (foreman engineer, mill overlooker, clerk) becoming printers, which tends to confirm the perceived view of printing as a well-paid, clean and respectable job. It is also worth remembering that a young person starting work in an apparently unskilled job might well have progressed and perhaps changed jobs, achieving a better social and economic position later in life.

What is abundantly clear, however, is that there is no sign to suggest exclusiveness of aristocratic labour among printers, the sons of printers in Stockport showing little in the way of upward class or occupational mobility. For instance, no sons of printers became clerks, which from 1861 became the fastest-growing occupational group, male clerks quadrupling in number between 1861 and 1891, from 91,000 to 370,000.[138] Clerical work, together with teaching, largely replaced small-scale ownership as the main route to upward social mobility.[139] As in printing, the qualifications for working as a clerk included literacy, accuracy and numeracy, but unlike printers, clerks distanced themselves from those they regarded as their social inferiors, not by income but by 'moral' superiority and the careful cultivation of status. From 1870 onwards, entry to the civil service was by competitive examination, effectively opening this up as a career for sons of families keen to promote upward mobility. But, once again, during the last quarter of the nineteenth century there is no evidence that the sons of printers in Stockport took advantage of this opportunity to gain occupational mobility.

Hobsbawm claims that members of the labour aristocracy were superior in social status to white-collar workers, and that it was the children of these skilled workers who became teachers. Using evidence from the Departmental Committee on Pupil Teachers (1898), which he claims gives the most comprehensive picture of this composite stratum, he then undermines this position by noting that, in Manchester, pupil teachers came from among 'labourers, mechanics and small shopkeepers'.[140]

The situation described may not have been the same in towns with a different occupational structure, but the results of this limited survey of Stockport between 1875 and 1915 make it hard to sustain the view that the majority of marriages took place within the subgroup of the labour aristocracy. If this group was clearly recognizable and had the distinctive characteristics identified by Hobsbawm, there would not have been so many marriages across the working class.[141] The data collected fail to support Hobsbawm's claim that, because a large number of sons of skilled workers followed their fathers into skilled work, this represented a relative advantage to the stratum in reproducing itself.[142] The trend identified among printers is of marriage within a broad cross-section of the working class rather than one of upward mobility. This does, however, contrast with the situation in Germany, where it is claimed that in 1900, 40 per cent of the sons of printers of working age were lawyers, technicians or teachers, suggesting that upward mobility had become newly important in that country.[143]

What is confirmed by the study of marriage registers in Stockport is the almost complete exclusiveness of the middle and lower middle class in respect of the occupations of fathers and sons, even though by 1871 this group had increased in size. Sons of fathers belonging to this stratum generally improved their status, gaining positions that would have demanded a

Table 3.9 Sample of fathers/sons following middle-class occupations, Stockport, (1875–1915

Father	Son
Railway inspector	Poor Law official
Mining engineer	Draughtsman
Chief constable	Insurance clerk
Inspector, NSPCC	Clerk
Broker	Solicitors clerk
Mercantile clerk	Civil service clerk
Schoolmaster	Schoolmaster
Station master	Bank clerk
Bookstall manager	Dentist
Merchant	Professor of history
Solicitor	Barrister at law
Civil engineer	Jeweller

Source: As for Table 3.7.

good standard of education, financial support and possible influence in securing the jobs (see Table 3.9).

General conditions of living

Hobsbawm's fifth indicator of membership of the labour aristocracy relates to general living conditions. Locality and quality of housing occupied by workers provide broad clues to their status in the community, where patterns of residence were seen as important social indicators.[144] Style, appearance and location of property were significant contributory factors to notions of respectability, distancing 'good' districts from multi-occupancy slum dwellings and tumble-down properties which were associated with overcrowding, unhealthy living conditions and moral decay.[145] Geoffrey Crossick, in his study of living conditions, looked at the number of rooms in homes occupied by workers in specific trades. His findings indicated that 74 per cent of printers lived in houses with three or more rooms, compared with 31.7 per cent of dock labourers and 59.6 per cent of smiths and tin workers. Both skilled engineers and shipwrights were close to printers, with 73.1 per cent and 77.7 per cent respectively. This can only be taken as a crude measure, of course, as it didn't take into account family size or indeed the size of the rooms; nevertheless it does suggest that printers avoided the worst kind of housing.

In the nineteenth century workers in many trades lived in close proximity to their place of work, forming relatively close-knit communities; this was especially true in the case of miners and textile operatives. In the case of printing, men were scattered throughout districts, mainly because they worked in small firms, which makes it difficult to draw general conclusions about the living standards of compositors as they inevitably experienced a similar lifestyle to their neighbours.

Table 3.10 represents the results of a limited survey of printers living in the Hazel Grove urban district of Stockport in 1907, the aim being to establish what kind of housing printers occupied and, importantly, who lived alongside them.

All printers listed in Table 3.10 were resident in a network of streets comprised mainly of modest two-up, two-down terraced houses typical of houses built after 1860, when municipal by-laws were introduced. Economy and convenience appear to have been all-important considerations as all the properties were located within a quarter of a mile of the English Sewing Cotton Printing and Box Making Company where most, if not all, the printers worked. The neighbourhood, while clearly 'respectable', was not 'mixed'. Middle-class housing in Hazel Grove was located on the opposite side of the main London Road, where houses were detached or semi-detached with gardens, providing homes for managers, solicitors and owners of small businesses.

Table 3.10   Addresses and near neighbours of skilled printers living in
Hazel Grove, 1907

Name and address of printers	Neighbours
Argyle Street	
Stephen Webb, printer	Card hand, mill hand
Walter Pidgeon, bookbinder	Collier, warehouseman
London Road	
William Kemp, printer	Collier, dairyman
Commercial Road	
Albert Garside, printer	Gentleman, box maker
Co-op Street	
A. Hacking, compositor	Mill hand, window cleaner
Newtown Street	
Thomas Booth, printer	Finisher, joiner
Peter Street	
John Bailey, printer	Traveller, hatter
Vine Street	
William Kemp, Printer	Cooper, painter

Source: *Stockport and Hazel Grove Street Directory* (1907).

In all cases printers lived next door to workers who would have earned similar wages (joiner, box maker, collier) or, in some cases, possibly less (window cleaner, dairyman, painter). The available evidence does not suggest any cluster of skilled labour aristocrats such as cabinetmakers or engineers in the neighbourhood, nor is there any hint that printers lived close to socially mobile groups such as clerks, foremen and shopkeepers. What emerges is a pattern of skilled and unskilled workers living in the same neighbourhood without apparent distinction on occupational lines.

This same mixed pattern is shown by the survey of the Ancoats district of Manchester, conducted in 1889 for the Manchester Statistical Society. Although it would be unwise to draw comparisons between inner-city Ancoats and the outer suburb of Hazel Grove, it is seen as significant that more than half the households surveyed in Ancoats were headed by skilled workers, and of these, almost one-quarter were classified as 'very poor', with only one-fifth listed as 'comfortable' (see Table 3.11).

Table 3.11   Occupations of heads of household, Ancoats district, 1889

Occupation	Numbers	% v. poor	% poor	% comfortable
Unskilled labourers	1,055	45	19.3	11.0
Unskilled superior workers	41	29	7.3	19.5
Artisans	610	24.4	16.2	19.0

Source: 'Report on the condition and occupations of the people of Manchester', paper presented to the Manchester Statistical Society by F. Scott (May 1889).

Scott's survey, based on Booth's work in London, did not specify individual trades but did indicate that a substantial number of skilled men were living in poverty in a neighbourhood inhabited by a mixture of occupations, the majority of whom were classed as 'very poor'. This finding tends to call into question those who claimed that skilled status almost guaranteed that the family would not fall below a certain level. Conversely, it confirms the view of McClymer, who maintains that the families of unskilled workers were only marginally less likely to fall within the standard poverty range than those headed by skilled workers.[146] The reason for this is that the father's occupation played only a limited role in determining whether a family remained out of poverty, occupational status of the head alone being insufficient to guarantee living standards. Although it is probable that most compositors earned sufficient to avoid the worst places to live, it mattered little if a printer earned a small amount more each week than another tradesman if better-quality housing was out of reach.

Only some aspects of living conditions are measurable by statistics. Quality of life depended on so many variables: sanitation and a clean water supply, educational provision, basic social services, as well as conditions in the workplace. Measures of poverty are somewhat arbitrary, but it is clear that factors such as the number of children and dependent relatives, and whether the mother of the family was in paid work, played a crucial part in determining the general living standards.

Scott, in preparing his study of Manchester, defined the 'very poor' as those 'who are always face to face with want', the 'poor' as those who live a hand-to-hand existence, and the 'comfortable' as those 'who are in a position to save, more or less'.[147] It was estimated that, in 1890, the very poor needed a minimum of 4s. per adult each week, the poor 6s. 3d. and the comfortable 8s. Scott assumed that two children would require the same expenditure as one adult. Using these figures puts a single compositor earning 30s. a week well into the bracket of comfortable; on the other hand a married man with a wife and four children, earning the same amount, would fall into the category of poor.

Prospects for advancement and those of his children

The sixth and final criterion used by Hobsbawm concerned a worker's ability to progress occupationally and socially. For two reasons, compared to many skilled workers the compositor had relatively good prospects for advancement. First, literacy and numeracy, central to the work undertaken, were qualities that often provided openings both within and outside printing. Second, relatively little capital was needed to start up in printing, allowing those who wished it the opportunity to start small printing firms.

If level of education, status in the community and importance of the work undertaken are part of a definition of a labour aristocrat, then it can be argued that from the fifteenth century to the present time the compositor has always been high in any hierarchy of workers. A reasonable standard of literacy, numeracy, manual dexterity and creative interpretation has at all times been crucial for a skilled compositor.'[148] As early as 1683 Moxon pointed out:

> It is necessary that a Compositor be a good English Schollar [sic] at least; and that he know the present traditional spelling of all English Words, and that he have so much sence [sic] and Reason, as to Point his Sentences properly ...
>
> (Moxon, *Mechanick Exercises,* p. 193)

Carey, in *The History of a Book*, written in 1873, claimed that in pre-industrial times:

> Printing was reckoned among the liberal arts; compositors were often men of gentle birth and Doctors of Learning were readers for the press but by the nineteenth century compositors did not belong to the aristocracy either of birth or letters, yet they are often clever and sensible men with a fair proportion of education.[149]

This is probably a reasonable assessment. A 'fair proportion of education' was obviously necessary, and there is evidence that the trade societies recognized this from an early stage. Throughout the period under consideration the trade societies expected compositors entering the trade to possess an appropriate standard of education and encouraged men to improve themselves. Most local societies provided reading rooms and in printing it was a traditional for men to take home copies of the work they had themselves worked on. Lectures covering artistic and scientific topics as well as trade subjects were provided for mutual improvement and trade betterment. As early as 1820, Newcastle upon Tyne Typographical Society ordered 306 copies of Hodgson's essay on stereotyping for their members, clearly an effort to keep members up to date with trade matters. Compositors benefited from a strong trade press, which not only encouraged high standards of craftsmanship but also catered for wider educational interests. As the *British Printer* acknowledged, 'our advice is often sought by employees who seek to improve themselves'. Competitions run by the *Printers' Specimen Exchange* fostered enthusiasm for artistic and creative interpretation of printed matter. Additionally, gold medal and prize essay competitions proved extremely popular, attracting large numbers of entries and indicating a general willingness on the part of workers to improve their education.

In firms producing work in foreign languages it was essential to employ some compositors with linguistic abilities. Even more skill and knowledge were necessary if the work involved non-roman fonts such as Greek, Arabic, Syriac or Hebrew. A minimum requirement for these men was to know the lay of the case and to understand the style of the country where the book was to be read. Again the setting of musical scores required not just an understanding of the complex notation but great skill in building up type forms in the correct fashion.

Although the conditions for the award of the William Bowyer's bequest could not be met by all compositors, at least some might have fulfilled its stringent requirements. The award was valued at £30 a year and the successful applicant had to meet the following conditions:

> A compositor who is a man of good life and conversation who shall usually frequent some place of public worship every Sunday, unless prevented by sickness ... he shall be able to read and construe Latin, and at least to read Greek fluently with accents; of which he shall bring a testimonial from the Rector of St Martin's, Ludgate. He should have been brought up piously and virtuously, if it be possible at Merchant Taylors', or some other public school, from seven years of age till he is full seventeen; and then to serve seven years faithfully, as a compositor, and seven more years as a journeyman.
>
> (*Notes and Queries*, No. 89, 12 September 1857)

It is little wonder, then, that the compositor enjoyed some prestige through the image that people had of his education and the literary associations of his work. It was claimed, too, that 'compositors had the pleasure of seeing and conversing with the men whose copy they put in type' (Anon., 1840). This is perhaps the reason why, in an earlier period, printing provided work for the downwardly mobile sons of the middle class.[150] In the obituary of E. Cave, who had worked as a printer before becoming the editor of *The Gentleman's Magazine*, the writer commented, 'this was a trade for which men were formerly qualified by a literary education and which was pleasing to Cave because it furnished some employment for his scholastic attainments'.[151]

It has been suggested that except for the intelligence of the compositors in interpreting copy, newspapers would never be produced, so it is not surprising that editorial work often provided openings for compositors because of the overlap of many of the tasks. This appears to have been especially true in instances where a compositor was interested in a particular cause, as in the case of Robert Hartwell, who had a long record of activity in radical politics. He had been a member of the National Union of the Working Classes, secretary of the Dorchester Labourers' Committee and attended the Chartist Convention. A compositor by trade, he took the job of sub-editor to George Troup on the *Bee Hive*.[152] Thomas Wooler, who established the political paper the *Black Dwarf* in 1819, was originally a compositor. Wooler succeeded Cobbett as editor of the *Statesman* and later practised as an attorney. Another compositor who prospered was Thomas Catling (b. 1838), an active Liberal and prominent freemason who worked on *Lloyds Weekly Newspaper* before becoming sub-editor and editor.[153] Other compositors progressed to become authors and journalists. Henry Beadnell served his time as a compositor and in 1875 wrote *Orthographical difficulties explained*, a guide for printers. Described as 'an example of a learned printer of the very highest type', Beadnell advised both Gladstone and Disraeli on taxation.[154]

Progressively in the period after 1850 there was an increasing demand in expanding printing firms for managers, overseers and foremen, providing opportunities for compositors to take on management responsibilities. Printing managers needed the kind of detailed knowledge and skill that was only available to time-served men, and throughout the period employers constantly expressed concerns that educational standards in the trade be maintained in order to provide sufficient managers for the future. Publishing and, from the late nineteenth century, advertising agencies provided opportunities for some occupational mobility for compositors, as did the increasing number of printers' supply houses. T. W. Smith, for example, the son of a Wesleyan minister, was apprenticed to an Isle of Wight jobbing office before working in a newspaper office. He became a commercial traveller for the Caslon Letter Foundry and eventually sole proprietor of this important firm.

For those compositors who were ambitious and prepared to speculate, by far the most attractive option was to start up in business, many such enterprises proving very successful. William Odhams served an apprenticeship as a compositor in Sherborne and in 1847 went into partnership with William Bigger. With an inventory of printing equipment valued at £423 2*s*. 4*d*., the firm made a fortune printing the *Railway Times* and the *Guardian*, and later, *John Bull*. Eventually Odhams bought the *Daily Herald* and opened a Manchester office.[155] Similarly, William Clowes, an apprentice compositor before setting up a press in London, left one of the largest firms in the country when he died in 1847.[156] John Tillotson, son of a notable nonconformist minister, was apprenticed in 1834 to R. M. Holden, a letterpress printer and stationer of Mealhouse Lane, Bolton. When Holden retired in 1850, Tillotson took over the firm which eventually became one of the leading printers in the country.[157]

No accurate figures are available on the number of compositors who set up in business on their own account. Almost certainly the figure would have been below the 5 per cent Hobsbawm suggested for the plumbing trade because the start-up costs would have been significantly higher.[158] It would be misleading to suggest that it was easy for the compositor to start a successful business because the short period many small firms lasted suggests that for every one that succeeded ten must have failed, but what is important is that the opportunity was there. The conclusion must be that throughout the period, the prospects for advancement were relatively good, and there is a real possibility that the apparent success of many compositors contributed to the notion that this was an 'aristocratic' trade.

Conclusions

Examining the experience of the skilled compositor in the light of Hobsbawm's criteria for identifying a member of the labour aristocracy presents a complex and often contradictory picture. Regional differences and local diversity of experience make it difficult to interpret living standards. Variations in earnings and working conditions, even within one trade, suggest that it is a mistake to identify any occupational group as belonging to an elite, as differences between men in the same trade could be as great as those between skilled and unskilled workers. Neither was the labour situation static: in printing the newer trades of photoengraving and lithography achieved status at least on a level with the compositor.

It is necessary to avoid taking for granted cultural diversity based solely on economic differences; family circumstances, too, were crucial in determining living standards.[159] The number of children and dependent relatives and the earnings, if any, of the spouse may well have made the difference between the compositor living in poverty or in comfort.

Gray, in discussing standard wages, points out that the greatest advances in wages were made by skilled engineers, builders and printers, but what is less clear is the regularity of earnings, level of unemployment and the significance of piecework.[160] The prevalence of seasonal and cyclical unemployment, confirmed by the large amounts of benefit paid out by the Typographical Association and the retention of tramp labour until 1914, must dispel the myth that compositors were always well paid.

Security, even more than level of income, was of crucial importance. As Lummis points out, domestic budgets were too tight to cope with irregularity of earnings, and high earnings followed by periods of unemployment could result in great hardship.[161] In May 1846 the *Typographical Gazette* complained that 'more than half the journeymen are unemployed during a portion of the year', a claim endorsed by Musson, who estimated that, in most years, between one-third and one-fifth of compositors were out of work or working as casual hands for at least part of the year.[162] Unemployment for part of the year could reduce the average wage of a compositor to between 10s. and 15s. per week. Frequent unemployment had consequences for the Typographical Association in that its resources were often stretched in meeting the immediate needs of its members. Rather than engaging in wider political debate and action, the Typographical Association devoted its efforts to internal trade matters, struggling to maintain a degree of craft cohesion.

No evidence is found of the exclusiveness of compositors in relation to marriage, calling into question Hobsbawm's assertion that this was how the labour aristocracy replicated itself. Neither is there any marked indication of upward mobility or family paternalism. On the other hand, the survey of the occupations of the families of printers represents the position in one town at one point in time, and there remains the possibility that some of these individuals may have later become successful both in terms of occupational progression and social mobility.

It is a mistake to consider material advancement alone. In spite of the number of indicators casting doubt on the position of the compositor as part of an aristocracy of labour, there still remain many features that set compositors apart from other workers. Lipset, in his study of American compositors, points out that their literary and cultural interests set them apart from the mass of workers while at the same time they were still manual workers who did not have the background or money to feel at ease with the middle class.[163] The work of the compositor involved a combination of intellectual and physical skills that many men were proud to possess. It is recorded that one composing-room overseer accused a designer who had prepared detailed instructions for the compositor: 'you are making hod carriers of us'. Many compositors liked their work because it was often interesting and challenging, providing scope for pride in craftsmanship and a sense of achievement. Some compositors were clearly interested in the aesthetic qualities of what they produced and the nineteenth-century examples of fine typography provide evidence of the dedication of many workers. Compositors needed manual dexterity, a good general education and acquired knowledge of the trade, qualities that allowed a degree of occupational mobility and opportunities to take positions of responsibility both within and outside the trade. Unlike some trades (engineering, textiles), where mechanization narrowed the gap between skilled and unskilled workers, developments in colour printing and mechanical typesetting meant that compositors needed more skill, not less, at the end of the period under consideration.

Comparatively, the working conditions of compositors were better, safer and cleaner than those in mining, engineering and building. Many printing firms supported and encouraged attitudes of respectability, providing social, welfare and sporting facilities for their employees. Membership in share purchase schemes and participation in rowing and golf suggest characteristics of the aspirant middle class rather than an impoverished working class.

By the last decade of the nineteenth century control by the chapel over working practices was reduced, partly as a result of the introduction of modern management techniques. However, loss of control was only partial. On issues relating to apprenticeship and the introduction of semi-skilled and female labour, compositors were able to maintain authority in the workplace. While the chapel appears to have been a close-knit, rather insular body, and in some senses the antithesis of trade unionism, it sometimes showed a great deal of strength in looking after the interests of its members.

It is a mistake to discuss any group as though it were a homogeneous social entity, but it is probable that compositors were part of the 40 per cent or so of workers who enjoyed reasonable living standards.[164] On balance, given a degree of stability of employment, compositors earned relatively high wages and were often engaged in interesting mentally challenging work, factors that indeed suggest that they belonged to an aristocracy of labour.

Notes

1. Howe, E., (ed.) *The London Compositor, 1785–1900* (London: Bibliographical Society, 1947) p. 1.
2. Fox, A., *History and heritage: the social origins of the British industrial relations system* (London: Allen & Unwin, 1986) p. 142.
3. Shepherd, M. A., 'The origins and incidence of the labour aristocracy', Society for the study of labour history, *Bulletin* no. 37 (Autumn 1978).
4. Ibid.
5. Fox, *History and Heritage*, p. 142.
6. Savage, M. and Miles, A., *The Remaking of the British Working-class 1840–1940* (London: Routledge, 1994), p. ix.
7. Hobsbawm, E. J., *Labouring Men: studies in the history of labour* (London: Weidenfeld & Nicolson, 1968), p. 274.
8. Gray, R., *The Aristocracy of Labour in Nineteenth Century Britain* (London: Macmillan, 1981), p. 46.
9. Hobsbawm, *Labouring Men*, p. 274.
10. Harrison, R. and Zeitlin, J. (eds), *Divisions of Labour* (Brighton: Harvester, 1985), p. 185.
11. Cole, G. D. H. and Postgate, R., *The Common People* (London: Methuen, 1961), p. 68.
12. Harrison and Zeitlin, *Divisions of Labour*, p. 3.
13. Ibid., p. 6.
14. Briggs, A. and Saville, J. (eds) *Essays in Labour History 1886–1923* (London: Macmillan, 1967), p. 116.
15. Penn, R., *Skilled Workers in the Class Structure* (Cambridge: Cambridge University Press, 1985), p. 9.
16. Gray, *Aristocracy of Labour*; Crossick, C. J., *An Artisan Elite in Victorian Society* (London: Croom Helm, 1978).
17. Harrison and Zeitlin, *Divisions of Labour*, p. 11.
18. Lummis, T., *The Labour Aristocracy 1851–1914* (Aldershot: Scolar, 1994), p. 46.

19. Meacham, S., *A Life Apart: the English working class 1890–1914* (London: Thames & Hudson, 1977), p. 135.
20. *Cyclical Unemployment,* Appendix 3rd report, PP Section 4577–4580.
21. Burnett, J., (ed.), *Useful Toil: autobiographies of working people from 1820s to 1920s* (London: Allen Lane, 1974), p. 108.
22. Ibid., p. 91.
23. Howe, E., *The London Society of Compositors* (London: Cassell, 1948), p. 206.
24. *British and Colonial Printer*, January 1894.
25. *British Printer*, March 1901.
26. *British Printer*, July 1900.
27. See for example Rule, J. in Joyce, P., (ed.) *The Historical Meanings of Work* (Cambridge: Cambridge University Press, 1987), p. 111.
28. Brown, E. H. P., *The Origins of Trade Union Power* (Oxford, Clarendon Press, 1983), p. 116.
29. Cole and Postgate, *Common People,* p. 206.
30. *Typographical Association: The first 50 years.* A Souvenir (1897).
31. Musson, A. E., *The Typographical Association* (Oxford: Oxford University Press, 1954).
32. McClellend, K. in Joyce, *The Historical Meanings of Work*, p. 201.
33. *Typographical Association: The first 50 years.* A Souvenir (1897).
34. See, for example, Hobsbawm, E. in Stearns, P. and Walkowitz, D., *Workers in the Industrial Revolution* (New Brunswick: Transaction, 1974).
35. Meacham, *A Life Apart*, p. 214.
36. Penn, *Skilled Workers*, p. 7.
37. Hobsbawm, in Stearns and Walkowitz, *Workers*, p. 145.
38. Hunt, E. A., *Regional Wage Variations in Britain 1850–1914* (Oxford: Clarendon Press, 1973), p. 49.
39. Lummis, *Labour Aristocracy*, p. 15.
40. Ibid., p. 342.
41. Manchester Typographical Society, Branch Minutes, 16 December 1914.
42. Musson, *Typographical Association*, p. 158.
43. For excellence of general printing in the last decade of the nineteenth century see *Printers' specimen exchange (1890–95).*
44. Riveirs, G. P., 'A Printer's Recollections', *The Monotype Recorder*, Vol. XXXII, No. 4 (Winter, 1933).
45. Musson, A. E., *Trade Union and Social History* (London: Cassell, 1974), p. 197.
46. Lummis, *Labour Aristocracy*, p. 8.
47. Manchester Typographical Society, Branch Minutes, 1827.
48. Child, J., *Industrial Relations in the British Printing Industry*, (London: Allen & Unwin, 1967) p. 43.
49. Harrison and Zeitlin, *Divisions of Labour*, p. 191.
50. *Craft Lectures of the Stationers' Company* (London, 1926), p. 15.
51. *Printing World*, centenary edition, p. 98.
52. Harrison and Zeitlin, *Divisions of Labour*.
53. Musson, *Typographical Association*, p. 105.
54. Manchester Typographical Society, Branch Minutes, February 1914.
55. *Report of the Royal Commission on the Poor Laws and Relief of Distress*, PP, Vol. VI, 1909, pp. 33–4.
56. Child, *Industrial Relations*, p. 124.
57. Musson, *Typographical Association*, p. 13.

58. Ibid., p. 26.
59. *Report of the Commission on Trade Societies and Strikes*, National Association for the Promotion of Social Science (London, 1860), p. 80.
60. Child, *Industrial Relations*, p. 127.
61. Hobsbawm, *Labouring Men*, p. 47.
62. Musson, *Typographical Association*, p. 50.
63. Child, *Industrial Relations*, p. 129.
64. Mussson, *Typographical Association*, p. 273.
65. Child, *Industrial Relations*, p. 127.
66. Ibid.
67. Smith, C. M., *The Working Man's Way in the World* (London, 1857; reprinted by The Printing Historical Society, 1967).
68. Child, *Industrial Relations*, p. 121.
69. *Printing History*, Journal of the American Printing History Association, Vol. VI, No. 2 (1984), p. 45.
70. *The Typographical Circular*, June 1891, p. 8.
71. Hobsbawm, *Labouring Men*, p. 48.
72. Burnett, *Useful Toil*, p. 96.
73. Adams, W. E., *Memoirs of a Social Atom* (1903) (New York: Kelly, 1968), p. 289.
74. Leeson, R. A., *Travelling Brothers: the six centuries road from craft fellowship to trade*, (London: Allen & Unwin, 1979) p. 175.
75. Adams, *Memoirs*, p. 289.
76. *British Printer*, May 1899.
77. Royal Commission on Labour, Fifth and final report, 1894 (PP).
78. Burnett, *Useful Toil*, p. 184.
79. Lummis, *Labour Aristocracy*, p. 30.
80. Musson, *Typographical Association*, p. 228.
81. Ibid., p. 282.
82. Royal Commission on Labour, Fifth and final report, 1894, p. 82.
83. Lause, M. A., *Some Degree of Power* (Arkansas: University of Arkansas Press, 1991), p. 42.
84. Clowes, W. B., *Family Business 1803–1953* (London: Clowes, 1953), p. 40.
85. *Typographical Association Circular*, No. 328, January 1880.
86. *Members' Circular*, Federation of Master Printers, June 1905.
87. Lefevre, T., *Guide pratique du compositeur d'imprimerie* (Paris, 1873).
88. *British Printer*, January 1893.
89. Woodword, E. L., *The Age of Reform 1815–1870* (Oxford: Clarendon Press, 1938), p. 587.
90. Hobsbawm, *Labouring Men*, p. 273.
91. Burnett, *Useful Toil*, p. 25.
92. Thompson, F. M. L., *The Rise of Respectable Society* (London: Fontana, 1988), p. 43.
93. Hobsbawm, *Labouring Men*, p. 278.
94. Johnson, J., *The Printer, his Customers and his Men* (London: Dent, 1933), p. 43.
95. Jones, G. W., 'The craft of the printer', The Worshipful Company of Stationers, Printing craft lecture, 1925.
96. Anon., *An old printer, personal recollections*, private circulation (London, 1896), p. 9.

97. Sessions, M., *The Federation of Master Printers: how it began* (York: Sessions, 1950), p. 348.
98. Ward, J. T. and Fraser, W. H., *Workers and Employers: documents on trades unions and industrial relations in Britain since the 18th century* (London: Macmillan, 1980), p. 67.
99. Manchester Typographical Association Notice of Special General meeting 28.9.1874 (ms., BPIF archive).
100. Ward and Fraser, *Workers and Employers*, p. 18.
101. Ibid.
102. St John, J., *Heinemann: a century of publishing* (London: Heinemann, 1990), p. 193.
103. Ibid., p. 194.
104. *Penny Magazine*, Vol. II, Issue 107, October/November 1833.
105. The Worshipful Company of Stationers, Printing craft lecture, 1925.
106. *Monotype Recorder*, Vol. XXXII, No. 4 (1933), p. 20.
107. Ibid.
108. Printing Historical Society, *Bulletin*, No. 4 (1995/6).
109. Bigmore, E. C. and Wyman, C. W. H., *A Bibliography of Printing* (London: Holland Press, 1978), p. 386.
110. Manchester Typographical Society, Branch Minutes, February 1914.
111. Stearns, P. N., *Lives of Labour: work in a maturing industrial society* (London: Croom Helm, 1975), p. 290.
112. Anon., *An old printer*.
113. Monotype Corporation Ltd, *Large size composition* (booklet, n.d.).
114. *Monotype Recorder*, Vol. XXXII, No. 4 (1933).
115. Factory and Workshops Acts Commission, Evidence of Lord Cavendish, PP 1875, p. 772.
116. Ward and Fraser, *Workers and Employers*, p. 150.
117. Musson, *Typographical* Association, p. 83.
118. Brown, E. P. H., *The Growth of British Industrial Relations* (London: Macmillan, 1959), p. 35.
119. Berg, M. (ed.), *Technology and Toil in Nineteenth Century Britain* (London: CSE, 1979), p. 148.
120. *Penrose Annual* (1951), p. 6.
121. Adams, *Memoirs*, p. 89.
122. Boyce, G., Curran, J. and Wingate, P. (eds), *Newspaper History from the Seventeenth Century to the Present Day* (London: Constable, 1978), p. 295.
123. *British and Colonial Printer*, July 1897.
124. Lummis, *Labour Aristocracy*, p. 147.
125. Howe, *London Compositor*, p. 142.
126. Gray, *Aristocracy of Labour*, p. 36.
127. Lummis, *Labour Aristocracy*, p. 149.
128. Ibid., p. 93.
129. Hobsbawm, *Labouring Men*, p. 273.
130. Thompson, *Rise of Respectable Society*, p. 97.
131. Lummis, *Labour Aristocracy*, p. 148.
132. Thompson, *The Rise of Respectable Society*.
133. Lummis, *The Labour Aristocracy*.
134. Crossick, *An Artisan Elite*, p. 145.
135. Thompson, *Rise of Respectable Society*, p. 83.
136. Bigmore and Wyman, *A Bibliography*, p. 280.

137. Ibid., p. 143.
138. Ibid., p. 68.
139. Harrison and Zeitlin, *Divisions of Labour* (Brighton: Harvester, 1985), p. 129.
140. Hobsbawm, *Worlds of Labour*, p. 274.
141. Thompson, *Rise of Respectable Society*, p. 96.
142. Hobsbawm, *Worlds of Labour*, p. 265.
143. Stearns, *Lives of Labour*, p. 52.
144. Thompson, *Rise of Respectable Society*, p. 152.
145. Ibid.
146. McClymer, J. F., 'Working-class living standards', a statistical approach based on 6th Annual Report Massachusetts Bureau of Statistics of Labor (1875), in *Journal of Interdisciplinary History*, Vol. XVII, No. 2, Autumn 1986.
147. Scott, F., 'Report on the condition and occupations of the people of Manchester', paper presented to the Manchester Statistical Society (1889).
148. Moxon, J., *Mechanick Exercises on the whole Art of Printing* (1683; reprinted London: OUP, 1962), p. 175.
149. Carey, A., *The History of a Book* (London: Cassell, 1873), p. 3.
150. Cannon, I. C., 'Social situation of skilled workers: London Compositors', unpublished Ph.D. thesis (London, 1961), p. 7.
151. *The Gentleman's Magazine* (1754), quoted in Cannon, 'Social situation', p. 20.
152. Coltham, S., 'The Bee Hive: its origins and early struggles', in Briggs, A. and Saville, J. (eds), *Essays in Labour History* (London: Macmillan, 1967), p. 187.
153. Ibid., p. 62.
154. Bigmore and Wyman, *Bibliography*, p. 42.
155. Odhams, W. J. B., *The Business and I* (London: Odhams, 1935), p. 4.
156. Clair, C., *A History of European Printing* (London: Academic Press, 1976).
157. Singleton, F., *Tillotsons 1850–1950* (Bolton: Tillotsons, 1950), p. 2.
158. Hobsbawm, *Labouring Men*, p. 296.
159. Gray, *Aristocracy of Labour*, p. 35.
160. Ibid., p. 17.
161. Lummis, *Labour Aristocracy*, p. 160.
162. Musson, *Typographical Association*, p. 21.
163. Lipset, M., Trow, M. and Coleman J., *Union Democracy: the internal politics of the International Typographic Union* (New York: Free Press, 1968), p. 108.
164. Lummis, *Labour Aristocracy*, p. 17.

CHAPTER FOUR

Workplace control and issues of gender

Overview

Throughout the period under consideration, the Typographical Association adopted an uncompromising policy of non-recognition towards, and exclusion of, female labour from the skilled printing trades. This policy was not, however, entirely successful. As the 1911 census abstracts show, in the provinces there were 699 skilled female workers in printing and a further 15,000 described as 'others in printing'.[1]

This chapter explores the experiences of women in the context of the wider debate about the aristocracy of labour. The case is made that the prevention of women playing a full role as skilled workers and trade unionists in printing was just one part of a wider struggle by craftsmen to exercise control in the workplace, maintain wages and consolidate their position as labour aristocrats, patriarchs and as 'natural' breadwinners. Exclusion of women from the chapel and its traditions, both symbolically and in reality, made women 'outsiders', unable to play any part in establishing working-class consciousness through the culture of work.

The aim here is not to attempt a comprehensive survey of the history of women in printing, but instead to examine some of the issues surrounding the introduction of women compositors. Following a brief consideration of the historiography of the subject, the main issues and problems associated with the topic are discussed. Account is taken of the transition of printing from craft to industry, as it is essential to have some understanding of the structure and functions of the trade in order to appreciate the differing views of craftsmen and their employers.[2] A summary of the different roles played by women in the past is provided and attention is given to the number of women employed and their status before going on to examine the arguments for and against the employment of women in the printing trades between 1850 and 1914.

Changing technology and growth in demand for printing in the mid-nineteenth century encouraged some employers to consider employing women in the composing room, coinciding with middle-class philanthropic efforts to provide suitable work for women. During the same period the Typographical Association, with increased membership and power, strengthened its opposition to any dilution of skilled, time-served labour. It is, however, important to stress that opposition to female compositors dates from the sixteenth century and was not a product of nineteenth-century industrialization.

With one or two notable exceptions, the subject of the employment of women as skilled compositors has received little attention from economic historians or from those interested in the printing trade. This gap is surprising because the employment of women in the composing room represents one of the earliest examples of women entering a long-established skilled trade. Possibly the reason for this neglect may be that women compositors were few in number, survived only a short time, and had little long-term impact on this male-dominated trade.

Three excellent works have, however, helped to redress the neglect of gender issues in printing, establishing a sound basis from which to test further work. Cynthia Cockburn's study of the skilled newspaper compositor explores how this work came to be 'men's work', providing an opportunity to consider the position of men in the industry from the nineteenth century to the present.[3] Ava Baron's work on the role played by women in the American printing industry is a good source of comparison with the experiences of women print-workers in England. Third, Sian Reynold's detailed examination of women compositors in Scotland illustrates the importance of gender in close-up.

In contrast to the rather sparse secondary sources, an abundance of primary source material from the nineteenth century clearly demonstrates how seriously the debate regarding women's role in the emerging industrial society was taken at the time. Parliamentary commission reports, trade journals and trade-society circulars all offer valuable information, and some company histories offer interesting insights into issues of gender in printing.[4] Minutes of Typographical Society meetings provide graphic accounts of the men's efforts to defend their position, whether the threat came from unskilled labour, excess apprentices or from women. *Women in the Printing Trades* (1904), a report by the Women's Industrial Council edited by J. Ramsay MacDonald (later to become the first Labour prime minister), contains a wealth of detailed information, and while by no means gender-neutral, provides valuable insights. A number of organizations contributed to this report, including the Royal Statistical Society, the Royal Economic Society and the Hutchinson Trustees. Individuals involved included Mrs Hammond and Clementina Black, a member of the Women's Industrial Council, a group that investigated over one hundred trades.

In dealing with the subject of women in the printing trades, methodological difficulties arise for a number of reasons. Women themselves are rarely heard in the literature of the time, and parliamentary reports and trade-union circulars mostly lack any contributions from women. What is available in abundance is evidence pertaining to men's views as to 'what was in women's best interests', confirming how deeply assumptions about gender were ingrained in nineteenth-century society. To a large extent, women can be seen as passive victims, as compositors struggled to maintain their status, identity and privileges.

To discuss the experience of women risks implying a universal claim that the position and experience of women was a common one, a strategy used by some feminist authors to fabricate a grand theory of oppression. This degree of generality is less than helpful in that it ignores important differences.[5] Generalizations, used on occasions by employers and trade unionists alike without regard for the roles open to women in the skilled trades, miss the deep-seated divisions among women and ignore the experiential diversity among groups of women. Only a detailed analysis of the precise roles played by women as employers and employees will throw some light on the important issues of gender in the workplace. Account must be taken of class, skill, age and education, together with acknowledgement of family roles and economic circumstances, before conclusions can be drawn about gender division; otherwise arguments are in danger of becoming reductionist. For instance, the question of age is particularly problematical in discussing women in the printing trade as it would appear that workers were often described as women when in fact they were really children of 12 or 13.

Difficulties also arise in interpreting the extant statistical information partly because of inaccurate observation and faulty measurement.[6] In many cases casual and part-time work was not recorded. Census information lists 'women printers', but the term is used to describe both compositors and those engaged in machine printing as layers-on, making it impossible to determine how many were engaged in each of these quite different jobs. Establishing the number of female trade-society members in those parts of the trade that did allow women membership is relatively easy, but, because of the large number of non-society firms, this is of little help in estimating the overall number of women employed in the industry. This is particularly so in the case of women working as compositors, as they were not members of any trade society.

Background

Before 1800 there is scant evidence of the involvement of women in the craft of printing, although there was some participation in the trade by the wives and daughters of master printers, usually those who inherited the business from a husband or father. In 1541, Jane Yetsweirt, widow of Charles Yetsweirt, held a patent for printing common-law books, the first woman to do so.[7] About the same time Louise Girand was a formal partner with her husband in a printing office and while he was imprisoned for heresy in 1542–4, she issued 13 editions under her own imprint, although it would be impossible to say whether she entrusted the work to a senior journeyman.[8] In sixteenth-century France women participated in a limited way in the trade, although it appears that this was an unwelcome intrusion disapproved of by the journeymen. In 1549, interference by the wife of a master printer in Lyon caused the journeymen to complain that their contract with the master was endangered because his wife was giving conflicting instructions, causing 'violation of natures orders', echoing the moral objections used by compositors in the nineteenth century.[9]

Davis, in her study of the women of Lyon in the sixteenth century, suggests that few women were actually engaged in the practice of printing. She maintains that pulling the press was regarded as men's work and that only a small number of artisanal women could read well enough to help with typesetting and proofreading.[10] In the seventeenth century, Mrs Agnes Campbell, who took over her husband's business on his death, dominated Scottish printing. As the King's printer, she held a monopoly and exercised what has been described as a 'reign of terror' in the trade.[11] In the USA as in Britain there were isolated examples of women taking responsible roles.

As in economic activity in general, the precise roles played by women are not easy to identify, but it has been suggested that between 1700 and 1840 the number of women heading printing businesses reveals a continuity of involvement, with no diminution in the female role over time.[12] In the north-west, Mary Tillotson (1844–1918), on the death of her husband, took over the running of the *Bolton Evening News*, where she managed a scheme of rebuilding, removal and expansion. Becoming well known for the interest she took in the welfare of the workers, it is recorded that she displayed remarkable business acumen in running this successful business.[13]

Having women in a position of authority did not of course guarantee that female employees would be well treated. From 1825, when the Society for Promoting Christian Knowledge and the British and Foreign Bible Society drove down the price paid for religious books and tracts, the result was a lowering of earnings of the many women who worked in bookbinding. One employer, Miss Watkins, having secured a monopoly of bible work, introduced piecework paying excessively low rates. Female employees earned an average of 6s. 2½d. per week for 64 hours' work, the women being subject to fines for spoiled work and learners being discharged as soon as they claimed an adult wage.[14] In 1849, when the women employed by Miss Watkins withdrew their labour in a strike led by Mary Zugg, they received support in their action from the London Union of Journeymen Bookbinders. This suggests that on some occasions of conflict questions of gender or membership of a trade society took second place to the interests of the trade as a whole. Nevertheless, female involvement in the trade as employers or the wives of employers represents only isolated examples having little direct impact on the working lives of journeymen printers.

While skilled compositors enjoyed some social prestige in society through the image that people had of their educational and literary associations, it was the combination of physical and mental attributes of the compositors that helped define the work as a masculine occupation, setting it apart from other manual trades.[15] Joseph Moxon in his *Mechanick Exercises* (1683–4), a detailed account of the craft of printing, makes no mention of any role being played by women. On the contrary, the language and descriptions of initiation ceremonies, rowdy banquets, drinking ale, physical violence and gambling suggest that women took no part in the trade.[16] As Sian Reynolds points out, it was hardly necessary to impose a formal ban on the employment of women in such a male-oriented environment.[17]

By the late eighteenth century the possibility of employing women as compositors was considered, but not by the emerging trade societies.[18] In 1792, Thomas Beddows, 'struck with the opening, which the printing trades seemed to offer women', gave his poem *Alexander's Expedition to the Indian Ocean* to be set by women in his village. He claimed that 'their nimble fingers seem well adapted to the office of compositor', described by his biographer as 'a benevolent hint'.[19] This appears to have been the first example of women working as compositors although it took a further 60 years for the notion to be tried on a large scale, by which time female labour became accepted without question in other sections of the trade.

Not until the early nineteenth century were women engaged in printing in significant numbers, when the division of labour caused by large-scale production and mechanization created many repetitive and simple tasks. Women were employed extensively in bookbinding to fold, gather and sew the printed sheets, and when mechanization came to the pressroom after 1820, women were employed to feed paper into the machines and to take off the printed sheets. In binding it was said 'the nimbleness of their fingers and willingness to undertake repetitive tasks made them most suitable for the work'. Women were brought in overnight to stitch and fold, as it was uneconomical to employ them full-time. Others collected work and distributed it round the neighbourhood; it was reported that women bringing barrow-loads of work back in the morning was a common sight in the alleys and courts of Drury Lane. Not only was some work described as women's work; certain types of work like folding and stitching were said to be 'the sort of work men cannot do; it is women's work'.

The nineteenth-century social and political movements dedicated to improving the status of women, combined with the growth in readership of women's literature, are two factors that had at least an indirect bearing on the position of women in the printing trade. Women were important buyers of printed matter, and printers themselves were open to influence from the feminist literature produced. Started in 1864 and printed by Hazells, the *Alexandra Magazine* bore the subtitle *Everywomen's Social and Industrial Advocate*. The aim of the magazine was to raise the social and economic status of women through the publication of articles suggesting suitable careers for women, including wood engraving and lithography.[20] Hazells themselves employed women, listing five women executives out of a total 59 senior managers.[21] The *British and Colonial Printer* took an optimistic view of the future for women in the trade, pointing out that, 'as printing is largely required by the class of persons who are chiefly interested in women's work and progress, there is a good chance for female enterprise'.[22] Emily Hill used the same argument but went further, arguing that it would be more convenient if women became employers in the printing trade.

The question is raised, then, as to why women were fully accepted in bookbinding and the pressroom but not in the composing room. Two explanations are possible. Mechanization of printing presented a new situation, one in which the male operative took responsibility for the skilled work of setting up the machine while the employment of women to feed the machine relieved the skilled printer of that tedious task. In short, women did separate work, which was supervised by men and posed no immediate threat to the status of the skilled printer. Women's work in the pressroom was low-paid, monotonous and on occasions dangerous. The second reason for the acceptance of women into machine printing was related to the fact that in the early decades of the century, the printers were less well organized than the compositors. In contrast, by the time the threat of female labour in the composing room materialized, the trade society was well established and in a strong position to control entry to the trade.

The frequent mention of class in nineteenth-century discussions relating to the employment of women in printing indicates clearly that machine printing and bookbinding provided employment for working-class women. The Salvation Army, for example, set up a bookbinding factory 'for rescued women who were unfit for domestic service', an indication of the perceived status of this work as below that of domestic servant.[23]

In contrast, the work of the compositor was seen by some to provide opportunities for middle-class women. One reason given was 'the widespread distress occasioned by increasing competition in the more beaten paths of feminine enterprise'.[24] The drive towards the employment of women compositors came in part from the Social Science Association. By 1860 new classes of women were seeking work. A female correspondent wrote to the Scottish *Circular* pointing out 'that with ample servants, women spend most of their time idling, reading periodicals or gazing listlessly at their lily white hands', and therefore any opposition to the employment of female compositors was just encouraging idleness.[25]

Others argued against the employment of women, citing women's natural instincts for caring as reasons for the objections. In August 1862 *Blackwood's Edinburgh Magazine* published a virulent article denouncing the idea of women compositors and claiming that 'the nobility, clergy, political leaders who had expressed themselves in favour of the scheme are very foolish – being wholly ignorant of the details of the printers' work'. It was argued that the notion of equality of the sexes was false, as 'society has devised its own regulation where certain vocations have been assigned to each sex'. This 'separate spheres' ideology of work plainly put women in the domestic sphere, and those women who dared encroach on men's work risked losing their femininity. The same article claimed that 'effeminacy can go no further as women only establishments were wholly impolitic, interfering with the distribution of work'. Notions of gender-specific work were not addressed solely to women. Men too were attacked for not sticking to manlier labour, particularly tailors and haberdashers, who took what was perceived as women's work. The adage 'nine tailors make a man' was quoted to illustrate the ill effects of men taking women's work.

Emily Hill, writing in the *Women's Signal* (1897), expressed the opinion that 'composing, the setting up of type for printing, is often regarded as a sort of half way house between industrial and higher grade occupations'.[26] In part this notion is related to ideas of what kind of work was seen to be appropriate for women of different classes. The journal *Practical Engineering* defined women's work as 'simple tasks that could be performed by any girl', a definition that appears to have fitted women employed in machine printing where little education was needed to feed sheets of paper into a machine.[27]

In contrast, with respect to the compositor's work, it was necessary to be able to read well and have knowledge of grammar and spelling, qualities more associated with middle-class values. As the *Printers' Register* pointed out, 'the girls employed in composing have been drawn from a higher social stratum than the general run of men doing similar work but at a profit'.[28] MacDonald appeared to confirm this in his report of 1904, mentioning one Leeds firm which 'employed 120 girls of a very superior class'. Issues of class were of significance for employers in other ways. The kind of women they needed to attract were 'the more educated refined kind', the very group who do not appear to have been especially attracted to the unpleasant environment of many printing offices. As Alexander Fraser of Neil and Company, the Scottish printers, pointed out, 'the class of girls we would wish to have, we could not possibly ask to come in at six in the morning'.[29]

Table 4.1 shows the number of women employed in printing, lithography and type-founding in England, Wales and Scotland between 1841 and 1901. The data, extracted from census returns, must be treated with caution because of suspected under-numeration of women workers and the inclusion of subsidiary helpers.[30] A further limitation occurs because the figures provide insufficient detail of the breakdown within the various trade groups, making it impossible to determine just how many women compositors were employed. The category 'printers' would include 'layers-on', who were employed on the machines to feed the sheets. The figures for 1851 are further complicated because they include women employed in bookbinding. Allowing for the weaknesses in the statistical evidence, the figures do demonstrate that

Table 4.1   Women employed in the skilled printing trades, England, Wales and Scotland, 1841–1901

	1841	*1851*	*1861*	*1871*	*1881*	*1891*	*1901*
England and Wales							
Printers	161	3,926*	419	741	2,202	4,527	9,693
Lithographers	12	6	–	–	147	349	1,043
Type-founders	–	–	11	–	32	55	183
Scotland							
Printers	21	710*	70	113	839	1,430	2,860
Lithographers	–	–	2	36	153	400	731
Type-founders	–	–	–	–	71	75	53
Total women	195	4,642*	502	890	3,444	6,836	14,563
Total males (inc. Scotland)	19,558	29,078	40,557	51,170	74,910	96,811	119,289
Percentage of women	0.9	16	1.2	1.7	4.5	7.0	12.2

*   The numbers for 1851 include all trades.

Source: MacDonald, *Women in the Printing Trades* (1904).

women were greatly outnumbered by men. Notwithstanding this fact, however, the number of women employed doubled each decade and the ratio of women to men grew from 1:100 in 1841 to 12:100 in 1901.

Introduction of female labour into the composing room

As Ramsay MacDonald noted, the general emancipating influences of the time and the great demand for compositors were two major reasons why the employment of women in the composing room became an issue in the mid-nineteenth century. The so-called great demand for compositors was of course only temporary, and the majority of men suffered seasonal unemployment.

Although the introduction of women into the composing room coincided with the introduction of machine composition, it cannot be claimed that women were brought into the trade for that express purpose. The advent of mechanical typesetting threatened the status of the hand compositor in that, for the first time, there was the real possibility of using cheap unskilled labour to displace time-served compositors. Early composing machines required at least two workers to operate them, clearly not an economic proposition if skilled men were employed. Employers took the opportunity to engage poorly paid female labour, much to the disgust of the *Compositors'*

Source: St Bride Printing Library, Negative 31.

Figure 4.1   The Young–Delcambre Composing Machine
The Young–Delcambre Composing Machine was patented in 1840. Used by women typesetters on the *Phalanx* and the *Family Herald*, the machine was only in use for about three years. It was still a further 40 years before an efficient composing machine came into use.
The image shown is rather romanticized, demonstrating the machine as ideal for women to operate.

Source: *Illustrated London News*.

Figure 4.2   The Victoria Press
The Victoria Press, London, was started in 1860 by 25-year-old Emily Faithful,
a women's rights campaigner, together with Bessie Parkes, founder member
of the Society for the Promotion of Women's Work. A number of the females
in the illustration appear to be quite young children. The figure in the
background is Wilfred Head who managed, and later took over the running
of, the ill-fated venture.

Chronicle, which claimed that the proprietors had to pay £16 for what might
have been done for £7 10*s*. It would appear that women were used during this
interim development stage of the composing machine for economic reasons,
employers becoming less interested in employing women as the machines
were perfected, requiring only one person to operate them. Both the *London
Phalanx* and the *Family Herald* (1842) were set by female labour on these
early typesetting machines.

   One of the earliest experiments in the employment of women compositors
in mainstream commercial printing was at McCorquodales of Newton-le-
Willows in 1848, where it is reported that women received 'systematic training'.
This represented an isolated example that was not taken up more widely for a
further 12 years.[31] In 1860 Emily Faithfull, supported by the Society for the
Employment of Women, started the Victoria Press in London amidst great
publicity.[32] Established with the intention of providing skilled work for women,

this press, perhaps more than any other, is credited with spreading the idea of employing women compositors. The Caledonian Press in Edinburgh, another enterprise set up to employ women on similar lines to the Victoria Press, inspired the master printers in the city to try female labour on a large scale in book houses.

Emma Paterson, who had served an apprenticeship in bookbinding, was a keen supporter of Emily Faithfull's attempts to promote women's printing societies, a move seen by the Typographical Association as a campaign dedicated to lowering trade-union rates. Paterson had visited America and, inspired by the success of the Women's Typographical Society, founded the Women's Trade Union League (WTUL), the purpose of which was to assist groups of women to found their own unions. Between 1874 and 1886 the League established between 30 and 40 women's societies, including the successful Society of Women Employed in Bookbinding.[33]

Seen by some as the 'wild schemes of social reformers and cranks', these early philanthropic ventures alerted the Typographical Association to what was seen as a dangerous trend, and throughout the English provinces disputes arose whenever women were engaged. In Manchester the intention to engage women compositors was announced in quite a dramatic way. A large public gathering was held at the Memorial Hall, where an American man named Felt set out to demonstrate that it was possible to teach girls to set type in seven hours rather than the seven years taken up by the traditional apprenticeship. For this purpose he assembled 30 young women in the orchestra gallery where, before the assembled audience, he proceeded to teach them the rudiments of typesetting. This rather eccentric event was further complicated because the promoter introduced a system of typesetting where letters that occurred frequently were combined in order to save time, a totally unworkable idea because it increased the size of typecase by more than 40 boxes. Felt's meeting was attended by many supporters of the right of women to work as compositors, including Dr Pankhurst, Lydia E. Becker and Dr Mackie, proprietor of the *Warrington Guardian*. However, the supporters of Felt's proposals were heavily outnumbered by members of the trade society who made their objections clear with shouts of 'humbug, gammon, nonsense', the meeting becoming quite rough and disorderly.[34]

Within three days of the meeting at the Memorial Hall, the Manchester Typographical society received a deputation from the compositors of the *Guardian* chapel objecting to any ideas of involving women in the composing room. A month later the Society passed a resolution stating 'under no circumstances are women to be entertained in any society office in the city'.

While not especially successful, the early attempts to employ women as compositors still represented a threat to the dominance of the male compositor. In 1872, when the Scottish Typographical Association made a claim for a reduction in hours, this was refused by the employers, and 880 printing workers came out on strike for three months. In retaliation the employers brought in non-union labour from England and trained women, and while it is not claimed that the women broke the strike, the men were defeated and the way opened for the employment of women compositors. Within a period of eight years the movement had begun which resulted in the large-scale recruitment of women compositors in Scotland.[35] Eventually, in 1899, the Edinburgh Typographical Society supported a women's section, but this ceased after a year. Although opposed to cheap labour, the Scottish Typographical Association had to face up to the fact that substantial numbers of women were employed, and in 1911 Edinburgh's Female Compositors Society was approved. Eventually an agreement was made by the union that women should be paid 70 per cent of the men's rate.[36]

Table 4.2 provides evidence that all the firms employing women were relatively large book houses, and in each case, a reasonable number of male compositors were retained, presumably to provide training and supervision of the newly recruited females. Women compositors employed in the Edinburgh book trade were paid on average 12s. a week, against the men's 32s., explaining the employers' keenness to reduce the number of men employed.[37]

Table 4.2   Firms employing more women compositors than men, Edinburgh

	Women	*Men*
Morrison and Gibb	136	112
Neill and Co.	109	37
Green	42	23
Riverside	35	8
Oliver and Boyd	29	14
Colston	28	13
Murray	31	8
Skinner	19	6
J. and J. Gray	9	8

Source: Reynolds, *Britannica's Typesetters*, p. 13

In France there was similar opposition to the employment of women in printing, and in 1862 the Paris compositors initiated a major strike over the introduction of women into the composing room. The French printers were supported by a loan from the London Society of Compositors, indicating a degree of international co-operation in the struggle to keep the composing room a male preserve. The French compositors appear, however, to have been less successful than their British counterparts.[38] At the Didot company at Mesnil, near Dreaux, one of the most important offices in France, it was reported in 1873 that 'nearly everything is done by women, peasant girls have been taught to read and compose in French, Latin and Greek, even copperplate engraving is executed by women'.[39]

The experience of women who sought employment as compositors in the USA was only marginally better than in Britain. When an employer-member of the Philadelphia Typographical Society announced his intention to engage women as compositors, there was so much resentment that he was forced to abandon the idea.[40] As in Britain, typesetting was considered a male trade but during the Civil War, when the workforce was depleted, women were employed. It was claimed that on the new land of the west coast 'self sufficiency and skill of women was valued just as much as that of men'.[41] About the same time as Emily Faithfull's ventures in England, a number of women-owned or -staffed presses were started in America, one of the most successful and prolific being the Women's Co-operative Printing Union (WCPU), established in 1868 by Mrs Agnes Peterson. Early letter headings of the WCPU proclaimed 'women set type! women run presses!' Producing a variety of general commercial work, the advertising for the WCPU stated 'we invite criticism'.[42]

In the American context, it is interesting to make a brief comparison between the experience of female telegraphers in the 1850s. Like compositors, telegraphers needed to be literate and numerate, able to work at speed and maintain accuracy. It was work undertaken by men until Western Union, the main company involved, saw the opportunity to lower costs by employing women operators – a chance the women themselves seized upon to gain equality and recognition. The response of the men in the industry was similar to that of the compositors in Britain. The case was made that women were taking away men's jobs and that they were inferior workers: 'the indisputable fact, that much the larger proportions of errors, in transmitting and receiving messages are made by female operators'.[43] However, the situation differed from that in the printing trade in that the women were admitted to the union where they were able to argue their case and take a full part in its affairs.

Apprenticeship as a means of control

What gave the Typographical Association a great deal of power and set it apart from many other unions was its absolute resolve in ensuring that only time-served men entered the trade. This meant regulating the supply of labour through restricting the number of apprentices, a powerful mechanism of control serving to restrict the entry of women into the skilled sections of the printing industry. The knowledge and skill of the compositor needed to be acquired over time through an apprenticeship, an instrument used both to control entry to the trade and as a vehicle for transferring and maintaining the customs and secrets of the craft from one generation of male workers to the next. Craftsmen were unrelenting in their insistence that only time-served men should work in the composing room.

Until 1800, entry to the craft of printing was through an 'indoor' apprenticeship of seven years, a system which had its origins in the control exercised by the medieval craft gilds through what Cynthia Cockburn calls a 'patriarchal ascendancy'.[44] The very fact that the apprentice would have lived as part of the master's household for a long period was hardly conducive to the employment of women, given the social and moral conditions of the time. The seven-year-long apprenticeship of the compositor also discouraged women. Those promoting entry of women into the trade attempted to overcome the problem of formal apprenticeship by providing training, a service for which they charged. Wilfred Head, manager of the Victoria Press, offered women apprenticeships on 'very moderate terms and thus qualify them to earn a respectable livelihood in other offices'. At the Victoria Press 18 women were employed, supervised by eight journeymen compositors. At another firm, Mr & Mrs Lavender 'received women on payment of a £5 premium', although they allowed women who could not afford the fee to forgo wages until the premium was paid.[45]

For reasons discussed in Chapter Two, a consequence of the increased demand for printed matter was the need to specialize: newspaper production, jobbing printing and book production effectively became separate trades. Variations in the level of skill demanded for differing classes of work resulted in a hierarchy within the trade. Notwithstanding seasonal and cyclical changes in demand for different kinds of work, time-served compositors were flexible and able to take these on, an argument that was used against the employment of women. London newspaper compositors, the subject of Cockburn's study, required a minimum of skill but great speed at typesetting as the newspapers needed to be on sale quickly – a situation that afforded the London compositors great bargaining power and the opportunity to earn high wages on piecework.[46] Alleged lack of speed of women compositors was the subject of constant complaints by the unions and some employers.[47]

In contrast, jobbing work, where the greatest number of compositors were employed, required varying degrees of skill, but afforded little in the way of bargaining power. Little expertise was needed for the simple setting of notices and posters in crude styles, in contrast to complex foreign-language and mathematical setting or for the nineteenth-century American style of artistic printing where a great deal of creative skill and effort was needed.[48]

The book trade became the main section of the industry to employ women compositors because of the quantities of straight text-setting involved, leading to the disparaging description of women as mere 'type lifters'. Book production, especially the setting of novels and encyclopaedias, involved tedious, repetitive setting of straightforward text and, unlike newspaper work, gave few opportunities for strong bargaining in the workplace. Evidence suggests that where women were employed, the work was broken down to allow them to specialize in carrying out minor tasks, for example leading and brassing out.[49]

Arguments for and against the employment of women in the composing room

Ramsay MacDonald, in his report *Women in the Printing Trades* (1904), summarized the advantages and disadvantages of employing women in the trade as follows:

Advantages:
A woman accepted half a man's wage.

She was not a member of a trade union and was therefore more amenable to the will of the employer.

Women workers were more steady workers than men and were less ambitious.

She will do odd jobs that lead to nothing.

Disadvantages:

Women have less skill than men and are not good all rounders. Very likely to leave when they are getting useful.

Employers do not like mixed departments.

They take more time off through illness, have less strength than a man, and are preoccupied with domestic duties.

The advantages and disadvantages listed by Ramsay MacDonald will be considered in turn as they provide a useful framework for discussion, although in some cases the rationale for deciding precisely what was an advantage and what was not is unclear. It must be obvious from the outset that the MacDonald report was not a neutral one, but written primarily from the employer's standpoint, largely ignoring the disadvantages to women and to members of the printing trade unions.

Advantages of employing women

1.   A woman accepted half a man's wage.
Both supporters and opponents of the movement to employ women compositors acknowledged that the main reason for employing them was that they

were prepared to work for lower pay, a situation that MacDonald identified as the 'paradox of entrepreneurs paying at very different rates for factors of production which are not so different'. Typographical Association records show that women employed in the composing room were paid between one-third and one-half of men's wages.[50] Women averaged 12s. to 15s. a week against the men's 32s. and those on piecework were paid 2½d. per 1,000 ens compared with the rate of 6½d. for men.[51]

Some firms took the view that employing women was an alternative to installing machines to save money. In 1880, the *Warrington Guardian* paid women only one-third of the men's rate, the proprietors claiming that the cheapness of women's labour made it unnecessary to introduce mechanical composing machines. In Manchester, one employer estimated that women were two-thirds as valuable as men but earned only half a man's wage.[52] On the other hand, some employers were against the employment of women because of the danger of starting a dangerous trend of undercutting of prices.

Economic arguments from tradesmen usually followed the line that married-women compositors would depress wages as they only needed a little to supplement their husband's wages, claiming that they usually married skilled artisans and had their husband's wages to fall back on.[53] It can be stated that at least some of the arguments expressed in support of women entering the trade were of an irrational kind. As Reynolds points out, Emily Faithfull, subscribing to the view that printers were paid too much anyway, showed little awareness of the consequences that the employment of women would have had in lowering wages in the trade.[54]

Keeping women out of the trade helped ensure a family wage for the male breadwinner and, importantly, helped maintain the position of the compositor in the hierarchy of labour. Respectable families were those who could survive on one income; less respectable were those families where it was necessary for the wife and children to go out to work. At the 1875 Trades Union Congress the view was expressed that:

> it was the duty of trades unions to bring about a condition … where wives and daughters would be in their proper sphere at home, instead of being dragged into competition for livelihood against the great and strong men of the world.[55]

Initially a firm advocate of female compositors, by 1898 the *British and Colonial Printer* had taken the opposite view. It pointed out that 'the injudicious avowal of Emily Faithful that one of the good results of the success of women would be the lowering of wages in the trade' was 'a notion that was imprudent as well impudent'.[56] The following year, the *British Printer* denounced the employment of female compositors as 'not being in the interests of the trade or the women themselves', pointing out that the three-year apprenticeship meant the women were only type-lifters.[57] The trade societies feared that women would reduce wages, increase unemployment and lower working standards, arguments countered by Emily Hill, who dismissed compositors as 'nothing more than artisans', adding 'there are several trades that demand more intelligence'.

It is worth noting that it was not just in the context of women's employment that attacks were made on the wages of compositors. Although printers were at the forefront of the fight to remove the taxes on knowledge and the author himself was highly paid, Professor Jevons, Cobden Chair of Political Economy at Owens College, Manchester, wrote:

> If the printers' and compositors' unions keep their wages at a higher level the excess is paid in every newspaper and book, hindering the diffusion of knowledge. We have removed the advertisement, newspaper stamp and paper duties, because they hindered the diffusion of knowledge and yet you continue to pay a small TAX to a body not exceeding 30,000 men.
> (W. H. Wood, Sec. M&S Trades Council leaflet, p. 16 MCRL, n.d.)

2.   Women were not members of trade unions and therefore more amenable to the will of the employer.

Conflict between the typographical unions and those who saw printing as an ideal occupation for women is amply documented. Initially the impetus for employing women as compositors came not from employers but from pioneers of women's emancipation. Emily Faithfull's efforts to make the trade of compositor a woman-only one stemmed from a middle-class philanthropy, which showed concern for women but not for working-class solidarity.[58] Women who did gain employment as compositors were not allowed to join the Typographical Association. The trade societies were astute in demanding equal wages for women, as this removed the benefits which employers sought. When a proposal that an effort be made to organize the women was put to the Typographical Association members in 1896, the motion was lost by a large majority, the union remaining fundamentally opposed to the idea of accepting into membership anyone who had not served a seven-year apprenticeship.[59]

The question therefore arises as to why employers acquiesced to demands for artificially high wages for men, particularly when women were less likely to have protection from trade societies. Claims that lack of trade-union membership left women more amenable to the 'will of the employer' were clearly demonstrated by the persistence of employers in resisting all attempts to control the hours worked. Women were permitted by law to work 14 hours per day, that is, from 6.00 a.m. to 8.00 p.m. or, with permission, from 7.00 a.m. to 9.00 p.m. (Clause 14, Factory Act 1867), but this did not suit employers, who argued for the right to employ women for three hours per day extra for five consecutive days per month. Master printers claimed that the volume of work was outside their control, citing the case of law papers which had to be completed the same day. At the *Warrington Guardian*, where the proprietor found a way of employing women profitably, it is reported women worked as late as midnight.[60] Evidence does suggest that employers insisted on the freedom to determine the hours worked. From 1874, when the employment law changed to provide for a compulsory break after 4½ hours' work, the master printers argued 'that this was not practical in printing and in any case the women can have tea while working'. Women were required to work long hours, often to the detriment of their health, although they themselves often wanted the freedom to work overtime.

Unlike those in the bookbinding and machine-printing sectors of the trade, the women who gained employment in the composing room did not benefit from the protection that membership of the union afforded; neither did they receive support from the men they worked with. Acceptance of female labour in machine printing and bookbinding did not, of course, mean equal pay. As late as 1911 women were employed as 'feeders' on presses at between 5*s*. and 14*s*. for a 50-hour week as compared with the male rate for such work of £1.10*s*.[61] A few firms did eventually pay women the same rate as men. In 1894, Hazell, Watson & Viney, which employed women in the composing room, gained recognition from the Typographical Association on granting all women compositors the branch rate. However, while tacitly recognizing women, the trade society did not allow the women to join.

3. Women are steadier than men are and less ambitious.
The claim in the MacDonald report that women were more 'steady' than men appears to contradict one of the disadvantages he lists: 'that women took more time off and were more preoccupied with domestic duties'. One possible explanation for the description 'steady' is that women were mainly employed to set continuous text, work that gave them little opportunity to move away from the frame to associate with other workers. Employers even took precautions to ensure that women did not talk to each other while working by arranging the frames in single lines so that they did not face each other. In contrast, men who undertook complex work had to move around the workroom, which gave them opportunities for contact with others. One suspects that 'more steady' may have been associated with the fact that the women were not organized and therefore less likely to become involved in disputes.

Even if the claim that women were steadier than men was partially true, not all experiments in employing women compositors were successful. In 1868, the *World* publication explained that it had tried nearly 100 female compositors but found them 'incapable of performing so much setting as men, incapable of setting correctly and even of learning to decipher bad manuscript'.[62]

4.   Women will do odd jobs that lead to nothing.

The final advantage listed by MacDonald, that women would do jobs that lead to nothing, is an example of how women, unprotected by trade-union membership, were exploited for the short-term gains of employers. For example, when the Hattersley type-composing machine was introduced, the Typographical Association was forced to allow girls to distribute the type after use. But this was agreed by the union in the full knowledge that this work did not impinge on the status of the skilled compositor, distribution of type being repetitive, boring and despised by the men. For skilled male compositors who had served a seven-year apprenticeship and were ambitious, there were many openings within management, editorial work and with supply houses, positions in the trade that would not have been generally available to less experienced women.

The *Printers' Register* defended the position of women compositors on the grounds that women who were untrained or otherwise unfit had been placed in positions where their performance was made to contrast with men – men who 'had years of training and discipline, inherited qualification and the influence of associations and surroundings which made them apt for the job'.[63] What made the men 'apt for the job' were the qualities associated with the labour aristocrat: full apprenticeship, membership of an exclusive craft group and the support of a well organized trade union. In contrast, it has been demonstrated that most women working as compositors spent only a few years in the trade and received no support from the trade societies.

Disadvantages of employing women compositors

1.   Women have less skill than men and are not good all rounders. They are very likely to leave when they are getting useful.

One danger was that the repeated reports of the failures of women in the workplace increased in the popular mind the belief that women were unfit for responsible work when in fact the real problem was that women were only partly trained. Placing women in jobs where their performance was compared to that of men was unfair. Men had inherited qualifications and tradition, a different educational experience and had formed a close-knit group in the workplace.

The problem of comparing the experience of women and men in the workplace, highlighted by the *Printers' Register*, partly explains MacDonald's claim that women had less skill and were not good all-rounders. If women were only trained to do text-setting, possession of limited skills would suffice. According to MacDonald this situation appears to have been both an advantage and a disadvantage, less skill allowing employers greater control over the women but less freedom to employ them as 'all-rounders', that is, on a wide range of work.

In constructing arguments about gender division in the workplace, it is important to note that, in the context of the nineteenth century, female labour often meant child labour. In printing, claims that women were paid the full rate really meant that they were paid apprentice wages, possibly paying premiums and certainly working for a period without wages.

Table 4.3 shows that the majority of girls employed were aged between 14 and 20, none of whom would have completed the full period of training or qualified for the full rate of pay, a fact that may bear out the common claim by employers that 'it is not worth training women as they rarely stay in the trade long enough'. One employer estimated that the average period women remained in the trade was 12 years, although the figures suggest that the period was considerably shorter than this.[64] Few women were employed after the age of 20. Sidney Webb acknowledged this view, pointing out that women left after training; 'therefore men offered an employer greater net advantageousness'.[65]

Table 4.3   Number of females employed as printers at various ages, England and Wales, 1901

Age	Unmarried	Married or widowed
10	394	–
14	988	–
15	4,898	7
20	1,999	76
25	730	120
35	146	112
45	42	65
55	21	56
65	4	23
75+	1	11

Note: This table does not include Scotland, where more women compositors were employed.

Source: MacDonald, Census of 1901, Appendix VII.

Opponents of female labour in the composing room were quick to use the age of the girls as a reason not to consider their views on conditions in the trade. When asked by the Parliamentary Inquiry of 1876 if the women had been consulted regarding hours worked, Mr Wilson of the Operative Printers Union indignantly replied: 'No, certainly not, the girls employed are so young and not able to think for themselves on such matters.'[66]

From the employers' point of view, child labour of this kind was conveniently out of the control of the trade unions and could be exploited. It is reported that many young girls were unaware of the Acts, working every night of the week, raising the possibility that middle-class philanthropic efforts to involve women in the trade may have resulted in the exploitation of children. Many printing offices employed children illegally, many of them girls. In Manchester, a number of the well-known firms, both large and small, were fined for employing unregistered children. Between 1875 and 1877 John Heywood, Henry Blackwell and John Roberts were all fined amounts between 10s. and £2. Harris and Co. were fined £2 for employing ten females at 10.30 p.m. on 30 June 1876, clearly very little deterrent given the low wages of the children.[67] In Glasgow, Murray & Gibbs, for example, employed 60 children at 3s. per week.[68]

Other employers were unenthusiastic about improving working conditions. Robert Leader, proprietor of the *Sheffield Independent*, was quite proud to point out that he 'fully supported the desirableness of making the age at which children should begin work ten instead of nine'.[69] The same employer admitted that the children worked on Christmas day. Mr A. K. Murray, a master printer who employed 60 children at 3s. a week, complained that restricting the hours worked had been disastrous:

> Restricted hours have increased wages but have not bettered the conditions of the working class as the cost of living is greater and the demand for luxuries more ... the lost hours being filled with questionable amusement, producing a serious deterioration of the moral health.[70]

Neill & Company, the Edinburgh printers, employed between 30 and 40 female compositors, starting the girls at 13 in order to 'educate them'.[71] Even suppliers were aware that equipment would have been used by children, with one manufacturer boasting in their advertising for a new self-inking press: 'it can be worked by a child of ten'.[72]

2.   *Employers do not like mixed departments.*

One explanation of the low number of women over the age of 20 employed in printing relates to the general custom in the trade for women to cease work on marriage. Printing was a deeply conservative trade that for moral and economic reasons expressed widespread condemnation at the prospect of married women working, to the point of arguing for the complete abolition of married women's work. The few married women who did work were only employed as casual job hands, evidence suggesting that many married women did not wish to continue working. This was one of the reasons why the Scottish experiment failed, one employer venturing to suggest that the success at their skilled job was the quality that gave them success in the marriage market. Presumably the social and educational standing of women employed as compositors was thought to have enhanced their marriage prospects.[73]

There was a clear perception at the time of what constituted appropriate work for 'respectable women'. Ideally the work had to be clean, light and demand a reasonable degree of education. If possible it had to be carried out in the presence of other women and present no possibility of moral danger. Where women were employed as compositors, they were usually segregated in their own composing rooms, with perhaps one or two men to lift heavy formes of type and generally supervise the work. Even this arrangement caused some employers to complain about the expense of providing separate facilities. It was believed that the indiscriminate mixing of the sexes 'soon rubs out natural modesty'. Similar arguments were made in respect of women who worked in the telegraphy industry, which was described as: 'not a proper occupation for women as it brings them into conflict with too many of the rough corners of the world and requires an understanding of such matters as womanly women cannot be expected to possess'.

Underpinning the moral objections to married women in the workplace was the view that those who chose to marry should be at home, and that there was something morally suspect about women who wanted to work – views not unconnected with the status of the printer in the hierarchy of trades. These sentiments came from employers and employees alike, forewomen especially complaining that the talk of married women had a corrupting influence on unmarried women.[74] Moral damage caused by extravagance was another frequently quoted reason why married women should not work, reasoning that 'the husband will only spend the surplus in beer'.[75]

Employers were divided about the moral arguments, the stance taken depending on whether they were of a coercive or paternalistic nature. When hours of work were discussed, one employer claimed that when women worked late at night, 'they were beset on all sides when they were going home and great moral mischief arose'. This argument was quickly countered by another employer, who suggested that if women worked late in the evening they had less time to get into mischief.[76]

Arguments against the employment of women as compositors were not confined to the unions. Employers themselves were divided on the issue and in furthering their case used a whole range of economic, social and practical reasons to explain their dislike of women in the composing room. Charles Wyman, Chairman of the Master Printers' Association, told the Parliamentary Inquiry in 1876 that:

> as a fact women will never make good compositors, except as tending machines, it is not a business well suited to them. Physically they have got all the aptitude for manipulating the type but they cannot lift weights, they never see their work right through so they never realise how imperfectly they have done it. When composing machines are perfected – they are something like a pianoforte – women will be able to deal with them better than men.

The reference to imperfect work, through not seeing their work right through, results from women not being fully trained in all the aspects of the compositor's work and employed to do a limited range of tasks.[77] It would appear that, rather than being an objection to the employment of women, this was an explanation of why women were paid low rates. A number of firms, which were 'fair' in the city, opened branches in the country employing female and boy labour. For example, Wymans, following the lead of many large London book houses, opened a large branch in the provinces, employing women and non-union labour at low rates.[78] In Manchester, when the Co-operative Printing Society considered the employment of women compositors, the committee were evenly divided on the issue, but, following an amendment, it was agreed that the subject be closed, as it was feared 'that in the infancy of the society this new feature might weaken it'.[79]

3.   A woman takes more time off through illness, has less strength than a man, and is preoccupied with domestic duties.
It is difficult to present an objective assessment of women's health issues relating to the printing industry because of the prevalence of prejudice, misinformation and the absence of detailed case studies. Ramsay Macdonald claimed that women took more time off work and had less strength than men, although his report is rather dismissive regarding health problems.

There is ample evidence to suggest that printing was not a healthy industry. Exposure to lead, especially in typesetting, and the extensive use of gas jets for lighting produced an unhealthy working environment. Even with the emergence of larger firms, few printers operated in custom-built workshops, the majority being located in unsuitable mill or factory premises vacated by other industries.

Issues of health were used selectively to oppose the employment of women as compositors. As Klein points out, the persistence of exclusionary policies directed solely at women ignored health hazards to men.[80] In physical terms, women entering the printing trade were introduced to an unpleasant, alien working environment, a fact that the trade unions were quick to point out, suggesting that any parents who allowed their daughters to work in printing were 'irresponsible'. This was the environment that helped define the masculinity of the work, working in the heat and fumes for long hours being appropriate to men but not to women.

Employers, too, were faced with the dilemma that the very women they wanted to attract as compositors, the 'better educated daughters of middle-class tradesmen', were possibly the least likely to be attracted to such a poor working environment.[81] As Ramsay MacDonald put it, 'the printing trades do not attract the most genteel girls'.[82] Opposition to women workers came mostly from the self-interest of those concerned. Women themselves were blamed for having little stamina and strength and being inferior to male workers – reasons that were also used to justify low pay. Master printers frequently maintained that women were 'irregular attenders, due to ill health', one manager suggesting they 'imagined themselves to be ill when not really ill at all'.[83] Trade-union objections took on a more protectionist tone, with the Operative Printers' Society authoritatively telling the Parliamentary Inquiry, 'we say the employment of women in the composing room is decisively unhealthy'.[84]

Dangers from lead poisoning and its effects on the reproductive systems of both women and men appear to have been largely ignored, although the Operative Printers defended their attempts to exclude women from working the Linotype on the grounds that the fumes and gases from lead were injurious to health. A fact that appears to be supported through the many references to women fainting when the room was hot. As one factory inspector reported in 1877, 'when working long hours it was common for some of the women to have fits, and of a bad kind'.[85] Klein, in her detailed study of the way health issues have been used to exclude women from the composing room, also confirms that the hazards of lead poisoning were particularly damaging to women, perhaps more so than standing for long periods.[86]

Medical evidence from the USA, most of which centred on the problems women encountered through standing for long periods at the case, was used by the Scottish Typographical Society to support their objections to the employment of women.

> Mr M_____, brought up in the business from a boy, now engaged in it for 18 years, having worked in offices with female 'compositors' ranging from 1 to 20 in number, and including from 200 to 300 in his observation, states 'Few girls can continuously set more than 5,000 ems per day.' (I may explain that is types in Scotland that would be 10,000, as we reckon in a different way from those in America.) 'While men will set from 7,000 to 8,000; not because the girl is not quicker in movement and perception, for she is, but because she cannot 'stand it; she is not strong enough. It seems to be the back that gives out. Girls cannot work more than eight hours, and keep it up; they know it, and they rarely will, and even this seems to pull them down; so that it is extremely rare that a girl continues more than a few years at the business'. Then further on we have the evidence of a female compositor, who says: 'we cannot stand at the case. It increases back and headache, and weakness of limbs as well as a dragging weight about the hips. I have been at this work for five years, but have been frequently obliged to give up for vacations from peculiar troubles and general debility.' Then the medical evidence is this: 'Dr B_____, a physician to dispensary patients, says, 'I have seen quite a number of female typesetters who were suffering from uterine troubles, and disturbed menstrual conditions. I think that these, with obstinate constipation and occasional cystitis (inflammation of bladder), are their chief troubles, besides the ever-present "headache." Mind and body are compelled to act so quickly in that work, that I am not surprised at nervous effects, particularly in young women not fully developed.'
>
> (Sixth annual report of the Bureau of the Statistics of Labour by Messrs. Wright and Long, the commissioners appointed by the Legislature of Massachusetts, 1875)

Another argument used frequently was that it was necessary for women to lift heavy weights, although this is not strictly valid. Only a small number of compositors, those employed as stone hands, were required to lift the assembled pages on to the press and in any case the same objection could have been made about men of poor physique or the many women who worked in domestic service and were required to carry heavy coal buckets and trays of crockery.[87] It is reported that at Hazells, a large book printers, with few exceptions men would not go out of their way to help the women, and, if a forme needed lifting, a woman usually called the foreman 'to do the amiable'.[88]

Unlike the employers, who were by no means united in their opposition to the employment of women, the trade unions representing the skilled printworkers mounted a vociferous campaign against the employment of women in the composing room. Fearing that women would increase unemployment and lead to reductions in wages, the men displayed deep-rooted social and moral prejudices in arguing their case. As the *Scottish Typographical Circular* reported, 'people are beginning to see that making women printers ... will only unfit them for the active and paramount duties of female society'.[89]

At the Conference of Typographic Societies held in 1886, it was agreed that 'women were not physically capable of performing the duties of a compositor'. However, with some reluctance, the main societies did agree to accept women into the trade, but with the proviso that 'women must have served the full apprenticeship and be paid in accordance with the scale'. These were unrealistic conditions given that the main reason employers were keen to introduce women compositors was to reduce the wage bill, and, for reasons of status, it was unthinkable for skilled men that women should be paid the same rate. The dilemma faced by the union meant that admitting women members amounted to recognition of low rates of pay.

The stance of the Typographical Association contrasted with that of the bookbinding trades, where there was complete assimilation of women into the union, the executive recognizing that 'we are between two alternatives – that we get the girls in our power, or leave them disregarded for employers to use against us'.[90] With the exception of one brief period, women were effectively barred from participation in the Typographical Association, leaving them the option of joining the segregated Women's Printing Society, which provided some short-term advantages alongside the disadvantage of isolation from fellow workers in the trade. Outside London the Typographical Association refused to recognize women who competed with men in unorganized districts. Where the union was well organized, for example in Manchester and Liverpool, the Typographical Association took swift action whenever attempts were made to introduce women.

Throughout the period under discussion, their poor standard of education was frequently given as the reason why women would not make good compositors. In 1865 the Typographical Association closed the local news-paper at Bacup on account of the employment of women compositors; the explanation given was 'the lack of intelligence in the women'.[91] In 1898 the *British and Colonial Printer* reported that large numbers of girls leaving board schools, having completed their fifth or sixth year, were rejected for work in printing on account of 'defective reading'.[92] Ramsay MacDonald apparently accepted this view when he commented: 'no doubt a girl who has only an elementary education is not the best material to make a compositor'.[93]

Other objectors questioned the ability of women to work at speed, claim-ing 'few girls will set more than 10,000 ens per day, while men will set between 14,000 and 16,000'.[94] Given that many compositors were engaged on piecework, speed of setting was essential to earn a living wage, the incentive to work fast being very great. Men also expressed fear that if women were employed they would work overtime and apprentices might also be brought in to work without the supervision of journeymen. This concern was part of a strategy to prevent dilution of labour in the composing room where, unlike many other printing trades, there was no place for semi- or unskilled workers. Compositors were adamant that the liberty they had to work overtime should not be granted to women.[95]

Conclusions

Many of the nineteenth-century gender arguments relating to printing fail to take account of continuity and change within the trade or changing social patterns. This was a craft that, by 1850, had remained largely unchanged for 350 years, retaining many pre-industrial traditions during a period of rapid economic and technical change. As the technology developed, becoming more accommodating to the employment of women, compositors used argu-ments based on craft traditions of an earlier period to restrict women's entry to the trade. For example, objections raised by the trade unions and some employers that the education women received in 1850 did not fit them for the craft, even if they did have substance originally, were no longer valid in 1914, but these arguments persisted.

Underpinning many discussions about the role of women is the idea that women themselves wanted to go out to work, although in many cases this was not so. Women's wages were reduced in having to pay for domestic help, and emancipation for many women amounted to escape from paid work into their own world of home and family. On the other hand, by 1881 there were a million more women than men in Britain, consequently many women re-mained single or were widowed and needed to earn a living wage.

Changes took place in the conditions of the trade and in the strength of the unions during the period under discussion, making it hard to consider printing as a homogeneous industry and causing much confusion in the historiography of the subject. Some idea of the complexity of the printing trade is indicated by the fact that in 1900, more than 50 trade unions represented the printing workers. Many firms were small, old-fashioned 'one-man' jobbing shops, outside the control of the unions and leaving little in the way of documentary evidence of their existence.

It is important to incorporate gender into labour history without denying differences between men and women or segregating men and women completely. The real issue is not whether men and women were different, but who had the power to define those differences, an idea central to this study, where numerous examples illustrate how issues of gender have been used selectively to gain power and advantage by trade unions and employers alike.[96] While the printing-trade societies deplored the exploitation of women, they still refused them membership and made no effort to help them receive the union rate of pay. As Thompson points out, the logic of capitalist development was not simply to seek the cheapest forms of labour, but to connect to an existing and recognizable form of stratification. In the case of printing, the skilled compositor belonged to a long-established stratum far removed from young, partially trained females who were destined to work in the trade for only a short time.[97] Acknowledgement of the similarities of men and women must be made, as the study shows that many women possessed the right attributes to work as compositors and yet their working life in printing was severely curtailed. Women were not a separate species of workers, both men and women being subjected to the same changes in the organization of work.

It was an iniquitous system which allowed women to be paid so little. Men's wages and prices for different classes of work were fixed by arrangement between trade unions and associations of master printers but women, outside the unions, were unrepresented and paid low wages.[98]

Opposition to the employment of women only applied to the composing room, where the threat was seen as the start of a process of deskilling, coinciding with the introduction of machinery. In reality, when composing machines were introduced, more skill was required of the operator, not less. In the case of machine printing, women were fully accepted as 'layers-on' and in bookbinding women were trained in many skilled parts of the work without problems.[99]

The introduction of female labour in the composing room was just one of many fronts to be guarded against. Excess apprentices, turnovers and foreigners all needed to be controlled if the skilled men were to retain their position according to long-established custom and practice. As the MacDonald report of 1904 demonstrated, the climate of sexual discrimination in printing was very slow to change. Arguments against the employment of women in the composing room shifted as situations changed. When one set of circumstances changed, the justification for not employing women also changed, leading to the conclusion that, at best, the reasons offered were misplaced or invalid, with the single exception of wages. As the Typographical Association gained strength, it was able to put pressure on the employers to pay women full trade-union rates for the job, at which point the employers lost interest in employing women in the composing room. It is clear that on many occasions trade unionists and employers were united in their opposition to taking on women as compositors, even when the initial objections no longer had any validity.

Concern over the implications for women's health of standing for long periods had to be abandoned with the introduction of the Linotype and Monotype machines, where the operator was seated, prompting the *British and Colonial Printer* to suggest that a 'Linotypist' was an ideal occupation for a woman. In fact a substantial number of women were employed as Monotype keyboard operators in the Edinburgh book trade.

Instead, arguments shifted from physical fatigue to concern about women's ability to stand the mental stress of working a keyboard, a particularly difficult claim to substantiate given the widespread feminization of clerical work after the introduction of the typewriter.[100] By the turn of the century general education for all had improved and trade schools were commonplace, so lack of education and skill were not valid excuses. The gradual development of larger firms offering welfare and recreational facilities in custom-built factories displaced earlier fears about the suitability of the working environment for women. Concern about the moral well-being of women compositors was also misplaced, given the very large numbers of women engaged in other sections of the trade. Although outside the scope of this book, it is worthwhile noting the role women played in running or exercising creative skills as typographers and illustrators in private presses. Presses of this kind were outside the control of trade unions and the commercial considerations of general printing.

Nineteenth-century objections to the employment of women in the skilled printing trades are especially interesting because similar reasons have been used to exclude women until recent times.[101] Gladstone attacked the printers for excluding women, and even at the outbreak of the First World War, requests by the government and employers to allow women to train as compositors were rejected. In 1916 the Typographical Association refused urgent requests by the government to allow the introduction of female labour. The policy of exclusion by the Typographical Association was on the whole successful: there was no large-scale incursion of women into the composing room.

Notes

1. Musson, A. E., *The Typographical Association* (Oxford: Oxford University Press, 1954), p. 102.
2. The language used in the printing trade frequently makes gender assumptions; for example, craftsman, master, father of the chapel.
3. See Baron, A., *Work Engendered: towards a new history of American labor* (London: Cornell University Press, 1991); Cockburn, C., *Brothers: male dominance and technical change* (London: Pluto, 1983); Reynolds, S., *Britannica's Typesetters: women compositors in Edwardian Edinburgh* (Edinburgh: Edinburgh University Press, 1989).
4. Company histories provide a good source of information about family roles. See, for example, Keefe, H. J., *A Century in Print: the story of Hazell's 1839–1939* (London: Hazell, Watson & Viney, 1939) and Singleton, F., *Tillotsons 1850–1950* (Bolton: Tillotsons, 1950).
5. Baron, *Work Engendered*, p. 32.
6. Sharpe, P., 'Continuity and change: women's history and economic history in Britain', *Economic History Review*, Vol. XLVIII, No. 2 (1995), p. 355.
7. Bell, M., *A Dictionary of Women in the London Book Trades, 1540–1730* (Unpublished MA thesis, Loughborough, University of Technology, 1983).
8. Ibid.
9. Wright, B. D., *Women, Work and Technology: transformations* (Michigan: University of Michigan Press, 1987), p. 174.
10. Ibid.
11. McDougal, H. (ed.), *Reputation for Excellence: a history of printing in Edinburgh* (Edinburgh: Napier, 1990).
12. Barker, H., 'Female involvement in the English printing trades c1700–1840', unpublished ms. (1996).
13. Singleton, *Tillotsons*, p. 32.
14. Drake, B., *Women in Trade Unions* (London: Virago, 1984), p. 7.
15. Thompson, P., *The Nature of Work: an introduction to debates on the labour process* (Basingstoke: Macmillan, 1983), p. 215.
16. Moxon, J., *Mechanick Exercises on the Whole Art of Printing* (1683–4; reprinted 1962), p. 323.
17. Reynolds, *Britannica's Typesetters*, p. 19.
18. Drake, *Women in Trade Unions*, p. 8.
19. MacDonald, R. J., *Women in the Printing Trades: a sociological study* (London: WIC, 1904), pp. 24–5.
20. Keefe, *Century in Print*, p. 65.
21. Ibid.
22. *British and Colonial Printer*, 14 October 1897.
23. Ibid., August 1888.
24. *Printers' Register*, 6 January 1868.
25. Gillespie, S. C., *A Hundred Years of Progress: a record of the Scottish Typographical Association 1853–1953* (Glasgow: Maclehose, 1953), p. 104.
26. *British and Colonial Printer*, October 1897.
27. *Practical Engineering*, 14 August 1941.
28. *British and Colonial Printer*, August 1897.
29. Factory and Workshops Acts Commission, Minutes of evidence, PP, Vol. II (1876).
30. MacDonald, *Women in the Printing Trades*.

31. Reynolds, *Britannica's Typesetters*, p. 29.
32. Cockburn, *Brothers*, p. 25.
33. Ibid., p. 12.
34. Manchester Typographical Society Minutes of branch meeting, Dec. 1869.
35. Reynolds, *Britannica's Typesetters*, p. 37.
36. Gillespie, *A Hundred Years of Progress*.
37. *British and Colonial Printer*, 14 November 1897.
38. Howe, E., *The London Society of Compositors* (London: Cassell, 1948), p. 169.
39. Lefevre, T., *Guide pratique du compositeur d'imprimerie* (Paris, 1873).
40. Baker, E. F., *Printers and Technology* (Columbia: Columbia University Press, 1957), p. 8.
41. Keats, P. L., North Baker Research Library, California Historical Society (Internet).
42. Ibid.
43. *Telegrapher*, 28 November 1864, quoted in Jepson, C., *My sisters telegraphic* (Internet).
44. For details of indoor apprenticeships see Moxon, *Mechanick Exercises*.
45. *Printers' Register*, 6 February 1868.
46. Cockburn, *Brothers*.
47. *Printing History,* Journal of the American Printing Historical Society, Vol. XIV, No. 2 (1992).
48. See, for example, the *Printers' Specimen Exchange*, which was a showcase for high-quality work.
49. Leading: inserting strips of metal between lines. Brassing out: inserting running heads.
50. Musson, *The Typographical Association*, pp. 102–3.
51. *British and Colonial Printer*, 14 October 1897, p. 11.
52. MacDonald, *Women in the Printing Trades*; p. 46.
53. This was not true for many women, for example spinsters and widows.
54. The view that printers were paid too much was common amongst supporters of the movement to introduce women into printing. See, for example, the extract from the *Women's Signal* in the *British and Colonial Printer and Stationer*, 14 October 1897.
55. Turner, H. A., *Trade Union Growth, Structure and Policy: a comparative study of the cotton unions* (London: Allen and Unwin, 1962) p. 185.
56. *British and Colonial Printer*, 22 September 1898.
57. *British Printer*, May 1899.
58. Emily Faithfull led a move to make the trade of compositor a women-only job. See Ratcliffe, E., *The Caxton of her Age* (Upton-upon-Severn: Images, 1993).
59. *Typographical Association Circular*, No. 525, June 1896.
60. Reports of Inspectors of Factories for the half-year ending 31 October 1874. PP, 1875, p. 109.
61. *British and Colonial Printer*, June 1911.
62. *Printers' Register*, 6 November 1868.
63. Ibid.
64. Ibid.
65. *Economic Journal*, Vol. I (1898), p. 635.
66. Factory and Workshops Acts Commission, *Minutes of Evidence*, Vol. II, PP, 1876, p. 779.
67. Ibid.
68. Ibid.

69. Ibid.
70. Ibid.
71. Ibid.
72. *British and Colonial Printer*, 15 November 1878.
73. MacDonald, *Women in the Printing Trades*; p. 174.
74. Ibid.
75. Ibid.
76. Factory and Workshops Acts Commission, *Minutes of Evidence*, Vol. V, PP 1876, p. 44.
77. MacDonald, *Women in the Printing Trades*; p. viii.
78. Musson, *The Typographical Association*, p. 237.
79. Hall, F., *History of the Co-operative Printing Society 1869–1919* (Manchester: CPS, 1919), p. 53.
80. Wright, *Women, Work and Technology*, p. 101.
81. Reynolds, *Britannica's Typesetters*.
82. MacDonald, *Women in the Printing Trades*; p. 67.
83. Factory and Workshops Acts Commission, *Minutes of Evidence*, Vol. V, PP, 1876, p. 777.
84. Ibid.
85. Reports of Inspectors of Factories for the half-year ending 30 April 1877, PP, 1877, p. 30.
86. Wright, *Women, Work and Technology*.
87. The stone hand assembled pages on a flat table (stone), locking these into a metal frame for transportation to the press.
88. Keefe, *Century in Print*, p. 77.
89. Reynolds, *Britannica's Typesetters*, p. 36.
90. Bundock, C. J., *The National Union of Bookbinding and Paper Workers* (Oxford: Oxford University Press, 1959), p. 69.
91. *Typographical Association Circular*, June 1865.
92. *British and Colonial Printer*, October 1898.
93. MacDonald, *Women in the Printing Trades*.
94. Factory and Workshops Acts Commission, *Minutes of Evidence*, Vol. V, PP, 1876, p. 777.
95. Ibid.
96. Baron, *Work Engendered*, p. 25.
97. Thompson, *Nature of Work*, p. 208.
98. *British and Colonial Printer*, 27 October 1898.
99. 'Layers-on' were employed to feed sheets of paper into the press.
100. Cockburn, *Brothers*, p. 3.
101. Until equal opportunity legislation was introduced in the 1970s, by which time printing had undergone major changes, in particular the demise of letterpress printing.

CHAPTER FIVE

Skilled compositors, their trade union leaders and employers

Overview

The earlier chapters in this work have demonstrated the complexity of the printing trade in that, while remaining traditional and conservative both in outlook and practice, it accommodated and adapted to change. Attention so far has mainly focused on the experiences in the workplace; therefore it is now appropriate to consider the trade in the wider context of local and national politics and the emergence of a formalized system of industrial relations. Where appropriate, this chapter focuses on Manchester, acknowledging the importance of the city as a centre for commerce, industry and printing trade unionism.

The first section of the chapter considers stages in the development of formal associations of employers: first as *ad hoc* groups coming together to negotiate scales of wages; second the emergence of local associations responding to trade problems in particular districts; and finally the establishment of a national federation. It will be shown that employers' organizations developed in parallel with the growth and consolidation of trade union activity, especially during the last 20 years of the nineteenth century.

The non-representative character of the employers' associations is emphasized and attention is drawn to differences among district associations, some of which reacted in a very confrontational manner to the trade unions. Significantly for the printing trade unions, the conflict of interests between the employers in the general trade and the newspaper owners is shown to have caused divisions which proved advantageous to the unions. The positive attitude of the Typographical Association towards the employers' federation, particularly in respect of collective bargaining and the later Joint Industrial Council, raises the interesting question as to whether the Typographical Association would have achieved the success it did without the existence of the employers' federation. Given the complex nature of wage scales and the preponderance of small firms, the union may well have exhausted its resources in dealing with countless minor disputes.

The development of the Typographical Association from a collection of small insecure branches at mid-century into a relatively well-organized trade union at the end of the century is considered next. Reliance on past customs, perseverance and slow but steady progress of the typographical unions illustrates how a strong occupational consciousness developed, eventually leading to the formation of the industry-wide body, the Printing and Kindred Trades Federation (PKTF). Aspects of the changing nature of the union are then examined, demonstrating how the narrow sectionalism of the traditional craft societies was questioned in the light of the success of some 'new model' unions. Importantly for the theme of this book, the role of the leadership of the union, both nationally and locally, is considered in order to look for any divergence of opinions between the leadership and the rank-and-file members.

A short account is given of the part played by printers in politics during the Chartist and immediate post-Chartist era in order to draw contrasts with the apolitical stance of the Typographical Association leaders at mid-century. This position in turn gave way to the support offered by many leaders of the union to the Conservative Party and finally the swing towards the Independent Labour Party (ILP) at the end of the century.

Three events of significance to the printing trade in Manchester are then singled out for consideration. First, attention is given to the Ship Canal Movement, as this exercise in popular capitalism was supported by leaders of the printing unions, who were very active in making a success of this venture. Second, the formation of the Co-operative Printing Society, largely through the efforts of the leadership of the Typographical Association, is reviewed, demonstrating how the leader of the Typographical Association confirmed their reputations as responsible and respectable citizens. Finally the provision of technical education in printing is considered. This development illustrates the dilemma faced by the union in that for the first time forces outside the trade were able to influence, and possibly undermine, the control the union had over traditional apprenticeships.

In different ways, all three events serve to illustrate how compositors, albeit in part through the leadership of their trade society, came to live up to the reputation they had gained as a 'better class of workmen', well able to engage in the commercial and civic life of the city.

Employers' organizations

At the risk of oversimplification, it can be said that employers' organizations in printing developed in three stages. From the late eighteenth until the middle of the nineteenth century employers had no formal associations but simply came together in *ad hoc* groups when the need arose. During the second half of the century local associations were formed in many districts and, finally, from 1900 the printing employers formed a national association to co-ordinate policies throughout the country.

According to Child, the strategic difference in the printing industry between workers and employers was that workers needed a formal, well-organized body built up over a long period if they were to have sufficient resources to defend their interests.[1] In the case of the employers, it was only necessary to act collectively in times of crisis in order to deal with a particular problem. The overstocked labour market was sufficiently in their favour to prevent serious disputes and financial resources could be quickly made available should the need arise, making a permanent organization unnecessary.

In Manchester the crisis that brought the employers together for the first time appears to have been the demand by the Typographical Association for a revised scale of 'remuneration for news and jobbing labour and an end to the practice of balancing time'. George Faulkner, one of the best-known Manchester printers of his day, called the meeting of employers at his offices on 27 January 1874, and 33 firms were represented. At this meeting it was unanimously agreed by the employers to reject the claim made by the Typographical Association and to establish the Manchester and Salford Association of Master Printers (MSMP). The new association met on 6 February 1874, when George Faulkner was elected chairman (later president), Harry Rawson secretary and James Collins hon. treasurer.[2] At this meeting a letter was read from W. H. Wood of the Manchester Typographical Society informing the employers that members of the union were tendering a fortnight's notice of a strike. In response, the employers proposed that the wage claim should be settled by arbitration, on condition that the men withdrew their notice. When the issue was put to the membership of the union, the employers' proposal was rejected after the men voted:

> For the employers' proposals 249
> For arbitration 30
> For the original demands 393

It would appear from these voting figures that there was substantial minority support from the men for the employers' case, illustrating how difficult it was for the union at this time to gain a consensus and confirming the moderate stance of many printing craftsmen. After a number of meetings between the two sides, a compromise was reached, although the employers expressed regret that the men had turned down the offer of arbitration and issued the following statement in the Manchester newspapers:

> The public are respectfully informed that the following firms of letter-press printers have, in compliance with the requisitions of their work people, consented to make an advance in the wages paid to them [followed by a list of Association members].[3]

The claim for a wage increase was conceded by September 1874, when the Typographical Society held a dinner to celebrate 'the advance of wages'.[4]

Of the two issues which prompted the formation of the MSMP – a claim for new wage rates and the dispute over 'balancing time' – it was the latter that was seen as the more serious. It had been the custom in the trade to make

overtime payments after 55 hours had been worked, but the employers insisted that, in the case of men who had been absent from work for any part of
the week, they should complete 55 hours before overtime rates became
payable. It would appear that a small number of employers were prepared to
take a lead in challenging the authority of the union. Documents show that
the practice of 'balancing time' occurred frequently in the office of George
Faulkner, the President of the newly formed Master Printers' Association,
while other employers in the city admitted they were not interested in the
issue of balancing time, as they 'cheerfully paid the extra rate'.[5]

The bitter dispute centred on the question of who should take responsibility for inefficient workmen – the union or the employers? The question of
responsibility is a recurring one throughout the history of industrial relations
in the trade. The Typographical Association argued that it was unfair for
conscientious workers to be punished for the actions of a few, and that it was
the responsibility of the employer to discharge men who were absent from
work without reason. For their part the employers felt it was incumbent on
the union to enforce discipline and order in the trade.

The formation of the Master Printers' Association in Manchester was in
part a response to the increased strength of the Typographical Association
and probably marks the beginnings of a formal system of industrial relations
in the trade. A reduction in state intervention in specific trade matters and
moves towards a liberal democratic state resulted in a shift in responsibility
from government to individual employers and trade unions.[6] Master printers
constantly campaigned for less government interference, arguing that legisla-
tive aid was not called for and amounted to unnecessary interference with
trade. For example, the employers complained that they had been forced to
provide light, airy workrooms and now factory reform legislation meant that
these had to be repainted regularly, causing unnecessary additional cost.
Employers also pleaded that the government should leave the men alone as
'they are quite capable of minding their own interests'.

It is not suggested that all employers welcomed conciliation with the
unions; nor is it implied that individual members of the Association were not
anti-union. However, individualism and sectionalism appeared to be as strong
among printing employers in the city as they were among tradesmen, not
least because the parties were competitors in a very competitive industry.

Representing approximately 20 per cent of the printing employers in Manchester, the 33 firms involved with the formation of the MSMP tended to be
the larger, more influential ones. As late as 1974, eight of these original firms
were still members of the Association:

> McCorquodale & Co. Ltd (The George Faulkner Press)
> James Collins & Co. Ltd
> John Barnes (Printers) Ltd
> Jesse Broad & Co. Ltd

John Roberts & Sons
A. Megson & Son Ltd
Palmer & Howe
H. Rawson & Co.

Growth in membership of the Master Printers' Association appears to have been slow, with only 26 firms paying the annual membership fee of £1 in 1875. However, the membership did represent the largest employers in the city, including:

Bradshaw and Blacklock
Jesse Broad and Co.
George Faulkner and Son
John Heywood
Thomas Sowler and Son
Taylor Garnet Evans

By 1876 the membership was widened to include lithographic printing houses, bookbinders and rulers, in part because limiting the association to letterpress printers resulted in little support and few issues to deal with. For instance, the *Annual Report*, dated 3 March 1876, stated that 'during the past year no issues had risen that called for the direct action of the Association, although the question of apprentice ratios was still unresolved'.[7]

Lack of enthusiasm for combination by the employers, especially before the 1890s, was partly because they had little to fear from the unions in the prevailing conditions of surplus labour.[8] Bringing together a cohesive group of employers presented considerable difficulties. Many printers were small 'one-man' firms that had little in common with large employers of capital but a great deal in common with the craftsmen printers. For their part, newspapers, together with the larger specialist printers, who were coming to terms with rapid mechanization involving large-scale investment, had little in common with the numerous small 'jobbing offices'.

National newspapers, important channels for the expression of political ideas, were competing for an expanding readership. Already committed to particular social and political objectives, newspaper owners like the Harmsworth brothers – later Lords Northcliffe and Rothermere – and Lord Beaverbrook were becoming influential in moulding public opinion and were formidable employers for the unions to deal with. On the other hand, newspaper proprietors were anxious not to gain reputations as unjust employers, as this might adversely affect circulation. It was well within the power of the Typographical Association to publicize details of bad employment practices, which could be taken up by other newspapers and used to damage their competitors.

Problems arose because of the complex nature of a trade in which agreements as to wages, output and hours worked not only varied from locality to locality but also from firm to firm in the same district. It is also worth noting, especially in the period before 1900, that associations of employers were not fully representative of the trade. Often members represented 'open houses' or non-society firms and in these circumstances felt under no obligation to honour agreements made with the trade unions. *The Times*, for example, was closed to union members and in other cases firms were not only non-union, but also actively anti-union. D. C. Thomson, the Scottish printer/publisher, for one, would not employ union members, requiring its employees to sign an agreement promising not to join a union.[9]

As John Saville pointed out, the industrial events of the 1890s must be seen in the context of a 'developing counter attack by the propertied classes against the developing industrial organisation of the working people'.[10] *The Times* newspaper in particular took the view that the restrictive practices of the trades unions were a threat to the well-being of the economy. Strong unions ran counter to mid-Victorian ideas of liberalism in that the closed shop was said to take away a worker's freedom of choice.

It is clear that some printing employers were prepared, when necessary, to respond in a determined and aggressive way. In evidence to the Royal Commission of 1892, the Dublin printers reported very low morale in the trade through the perpetual aggression of the employers 'by encroaching our rights and increasing the number of apprentices in order to decrease the number of journeymen'. In the same year, when there was a combined approach by the unions requesting a reduction in the working week by $2\frac{1}{2}$ hours, the Yorkshire FMP refused the request. A strike followed and immediately the master printers formulated rules for their members which stated:

> No strike hands from any part of the country to be employed. A list of names of those on strike be printed and circulated. The Association to inaugurate and control a workmen's employment bureau.

To ensure cohesion, employers who did not adhere to this policy were liable to a fine of £50 by their association, indicating just how determined the employers were to break the unions on this issue. Employers were required to assist any firm in dispute with a trade union through undertaking work in hand at minimum profit levels so that the firm did not suffer financially. Additionally, the employers formed a Mutual Benefit and Aid Association to provide benefits for those employees who agreed to relinquish union membership, the intention being to rival the benefits provided by the unions.[11] The Yorkshire FMP included two of the largest employers in the country, McCorquodale & Co. and Petty & Sons. In the face of such determined employers, the Typographical Association and the Bookbinders withdrew from the dispute, leaving the Amalgamated Society of Lithographic printers (ASLP) to continue alone. The dispute lasted a year and in the end the ASLP were defeated and forced to return to work. In spite of a 2*s.* a week levy on the ASLP members, the dispute cost the union more than

£1000 and in the end many older members of the society were not taken back to work.

The Typographical Association was basically conservative in its ambitions, striving to preserve privileges from the past rather than pressing for improved conditions in the light of the changing industry, and in this respect, the unions had the sympathy of some employers. For its part, the association welcomed the formation of the employers' organization. It believed that where changes in the established order came about, for example the introduction of mechanical composition and formal technical instruction, stable relations between workers and employers could only be maintained through a process of negotiation.[12] Agreements that would command nation-wide acceptance were preferable to countless small disputes and, in return for a degree of compromise on the part of the workers, the Typographical Association acquired a greater role in collective negotiations.[13] What gave the union a certain degree of security was that, while there were often unemployed men seeking work, there was, in comparison with some trades, no large pool of labour for employers to draw on in the case of a lockout. Unlike the building trade and the docks, where in the event of a dispute workers could be replaced with 'free labour', only skilled labour could be used in the composing room, somewhat restricting the employers' opportunities to recruit replacement men.

Although at local level competition between firms was so keen that master printers could rarely present a united front to the unions, changes in technology, competition from abroad and the growth and consolidation of the printing unions made the formation of a national federation of employers inevitable. In June 1901 the Federation of Master Printers (FMP) was formed with Walter Hazell as its first president setting the tone of the organization. Hazell was a paternalistic employer and philanthropist who was not in any sense anti-union.[14] The priorities of the FMP included the representation of the industry in legal matters, for example on copyright laws and in regard to Parliamentary Bills; the avoidance of 'unhealthy' competition through the introduction of a standard costing system; the support of technical education through a system of examinations, and the conduct of negotiations with trade societies.[15]

The FMP was not entirely passive. Within a year of its formation the Abstract of the Factory and Newspaper Act 1901 was circulated by the FMP as a model for printers to follow. In accordance with the Truck Act, 1896 members were reminded of their rights to make deductions from the wages of their employees in respect of bad or negligent work and to fine workers for acts or omissions.[16]

A Brief Abstract of the Factory and Newspaper Act 1901 so far as applicable to Printers, Federation of Master Printers, London 1902

Department	Specified act or omission
Composing	For not returning Type Cases or materials to their proper places when done with
Printing	For careless Laying-on at Machine
Binding	For failing to return to the proper person, or to carefully preserve surplus sheets of any uncompleted job
Warehouse	For passing badly printed work, work wrongly set, or broken, torn, or soiled sheets
Paper	For giving out Paper without a proper order, or giving out wrong Paper or quantities, or in such a way as to make unnecessary remnants
Engineers	For not keeping Lubricators on all engines filled and working
Generally	For losing 'Copy' or 'Orders' For wilful destruction of the Company's property For throwing materials or any missiles For using lighted paper for any purpose For using as waste any Sheets of an uncompleted job For throwing orange peel or other refuse on the floors of the rooms, balconies, staircases, yard, or into the lavatories, w.c.'s or urinals, or improperly using the lavatories, w.c.'s or urinals For using foul or abusive language For gambling on the Company's premises For playing about or quarrelling on the Company's premises For being too long on an errand For careless breakage of windows For allowing lights to remain burning unnecessarily, or water to run to waste For absence from work without leave; coming late to work; or leaving work before the proper time

(BPIF Archive)

This was not simply an idle threat: printers frequently stopped wages for carelessness or mistakes at work. An examination of the wages book belonging to Megson and Son, the Manchester printers, shows that stoppages from wages were a regular occurrence. During the week ending 2 November 1878, out of 35 employees listed, 15 workers had deductions made from their wages of between 1*d*. and 1*s*. 8*d*. Stoppages were made for spoilt work, lost time and 'money owing'.[17]

It was the issue of conducting negotiations with the trade unions that caused continued divisions among employers. The problem arose because of the power of the newspaper proprietors, who were not prepared to adhere to conditions laid down for the general printing industry and thereby risk loss of production on newspapers through strikes generated in general printing. Newspapers could not afford to suffer disruption of production; neither did they want to risk loss of readership through gaining a reputation as unfair employers, particularly at a time when they were competing to build up a large working-class readership. For these reasons, requests for increases in wages by Typographical Association members working on newspaper production were frequently met, leaving general printers no alternative but to agree increases.[18]

The answer to this problem was to set up a separate organization to cater for the interests of the newspaper proprietors. The first grouping of newspaper proprietors was the Linotype Users' Association (LUA), formed in 1895 to negotiate with the Typographical Association on national rates and conditions for Linotype operators. The LUA, representing the owners of virtually all regional newspapers, was later reconstituted, and changed its name to the Newspaper Society. In 1906 the Newspaper Proprietors' Association (NPA) came into being in order to represent the interests of proprietors of national newspapers. The NPA was founded as a direct result of a dispute between the London Society of Compositors and the Master Printers' Association, a dispute in which the newspaper proprietors were anxious not to become involved. The newspaper owners decided to leave the MPA in order to negotiate directly with the association on the understanding that the Typographical Association would not involve newspapers in disputes concerned with general printing.[19]

The existence of three distinct groups of employers (representing national newspapers, regional newspapers and general printing) is of significance because it allowed the Typographical Association greater bargaining power when conducting negotiations on wages and conditions. A degree of competition existed for experienced labour, enabling newspaper compositors to maintain differentials while compositors in the general trade were quick to take up vacancies in news work. This situation was especially prevalent in Manchester, where both regional and national newspapers were produced alongside an extensive general printing trade.

Until the national body of the FMP reorganized its structure and constitution in the post-1918 era, it remained unrepresentative and had little authority. Nevertheless, the printing unions were up against the forces of mass capital in the form of local master printers, a national federation of newspaper proprietors and a federation of employers' associations.

The nature and development of compositors' trade societies

A constantly recurring theme in any study of the printing trade is the value placed on past custom, and it was this concern for tradition that played an important part in setting printers apart from the 'new trades' of the nineteenth century. Constant reference to past ways of working informed the behaviour of skilled compositors even in the machine age of the late nineteenth century. It is therefore appropriate at this juncture briefly to consider the development of the compositors' trade societies, as this represents one of the main vehicles through which a strong occupational consciousness was sustained and developed throughout the period.

Although it cannot be claimed that the early trade clubs were directly descended from the old guilds, it is clear that from the early sixteenth century printers came together to safeguard their interests. It is recorded that the first regular society of compositors was formed in 1785 in order to agree a scale of prices and to limit the number of those entering the trade. By 1801 this society organized meetings, elected a committee and collected subscriptions. Before the repeal of the Combination Acts, in 1825, 12 typographical societies were established and by the 1830s this number had increased to more than 40. In turn, these local societies formed three regional federations: the Northern Typographical Union (NTU), the Irish Typographical Union and the General Typographical Association of Scotland.[20]

The NTU, forerunner of the Typographical Association, was founded in Manchester in 1830, providing an early indication of the importance of the city as a centre of trade unionism in the trade. By 1840 the NTU consisted of 44 member societies with 1000 members, but it suffered from friction between local societies and shortage of funds, prompting it to canvass for a national association of all printing unions. At a special delegate meeting held in Manchester in 1844, the National Typographical Association was formed, taking in all the old regional unions, many independent societies and the London Union of Compositors (LUC). The principal objectives of the new national union were:

1. The centralization of authority in respect of strikes and disputes.
2. Equality of remuneration for the unemployed.
3. Abolition of tramp relief and the introduction of out-of-work allowances.

Despite a promising start with 4000 members, within four years the national union collapsed and the influential London compositors withdrew. Within a short time the unions reformed and the Provincial Typographical Association was established in June 1849. ('Provincial' was dropped from the title in 1877.) The main objectives of the Provincial Typographical Association at its formation were the improvement in terms of employment 'through the limitation of the number of apprentices, restriction of the hours of labour, regulation of the standard of wages, and the general supervision of all matters affecting the interests of the printing profession'.[21]

During the first five years of the union's existence no major trade difficulties had arisen, but four branches, including Macclesfield, had been struck off for non-payment of subscriptions, illustrating the kind of difficulties encountered nationally in attempting to enforce rules on small branches, many with fewer than 20 members.

In 1852 the Manchester Society joined the Provincial Typographical Association, accounting for a substantial rise in membership figures, and at a delegate meting held in March 1852, Thomas Gregory was elected chairman and Christopher Burgess secretary, both men belonging to the Manchester Society which continued to dominate the national union.[22] At this first meeting the main item discussed was the 'taxes on knowledge', and a memorial on the question was sent to the House of Commons.[23]

Progress of the Provincial Typographical Association can be seen to have taken place in two stages. Between 1850 and 1875 priority was given to ensuring that established wage scales were adhered to, administering tramp relief and controlling the influx of labour, especially apprentices and female labour, in order to give the union greater bargaining power in wage negotiations. In the period after 1875 changes in employment practices made many of the old rules out of date or difficult to enforce, so the union consolidated its power by increasing its membership in non-society offices and the provision of greater benefits.

Changes in the newspaper stamp and advertising tax in 1853 did not result in the expected improvement in trade, and the Typographical Association was concerned about levels of unemployment. The number of casual workers increased, and although the Crimean War caused an increased demand for newspapers, it was said to have had a bad effect on the book trade.[24]

Problems arose in removing men from an office declared unfair because the society had to provide a loan to the men for removal, but few men paid this back. Typical of the problems facing the union was the case of two Chester compositors who drew full strike allowance and then used their cards to draw double travel payments, before returning to their original firm.[25] Conditions like this meant that, in the early years, the finances of the Provincial Typographical Association were in a poor state. In 1856, the cost of one dispute in Birmingham was £291, reducing the balance of the association's funds to £149.[26] In 1858, a dispute in Liverpool over the treatment of casual labour cost the union £1304 1s. 9d., and smaller disputes in Manchester forced the Typographical Association to appeal to other trades for support. The Amalgamated Society of Engineers donated £50 and a levy was imposed on members.[27] Eventually the Provincial Typographical Association followed the lead of the larger unions, becoming imbued with a spirit of thrift and caution, tending to show reluctance to risk resources on strikes sometimes clamoured for by its members.[28]

In April 1865 the headquarters of the Typographical Association moved from Sheffield to Manchester, where meetings were held at the Seven Stars tavern on Withy Grove, although within a year the union had moved to its own offices, reflecting the growing desire for respectability, and distancing printers from the use of the 'common tavern'. The headquarters of both the Lithographic Printers and the Society of Lithographic Artists were located in Manchester and it is clear there was close of co-operation between officers of the three unions.

The Typographical Association: continuity and change

Many labour historians use the Typographical Association as an example to illustrate the traditionalism and conservatism of the 'old' type of craft union and in some respects this is valid although the reality is more complex.

From 1860 it is possible to identify changes taking place within the Typographical Association which suggest a weakening of the old order and a developing interest in the characteristics of the 'new model' unions. Before considering these changes, however, it is worth exploring some of the qualities which firmly indicate the traditional craft characteristics of the Typographical Association.

Irrespective of the national policies of the Typographical Association, the real basis of power lay with the chapel and its immediate concerns. Clearly aware of this, the executive avoided taking a confrontational line with employers, arguing instead that acceptance of union regulation was in the best interest of the trade as a whole. 'Smooting' (working for more than one firm) was banned because the extra work reduced the energy and attention of compositors; limitation of overtime encouraged efficiency by improving health; and control of the number of apprentices was necessary in order to ensure proper instruction. Employers were to be persuaded that union regulation in the workplace was in their best interests, the union arguing that even if union rules restricted an employer's freedom, they provided a code of conduct for journeymen. Otherwise there was the possibility that unscrupulous individuals would take advantage of every opportunity to gain for themselves.

Second, if rules were necessary because of the technical nature of the work, it was better that they should be framed by qualified men, that is society men. Additionally, it was argued, common conditions allowed employers to compete with each other on equal terms The three objectives in forming such rules were to establish a rate of exchange for labour, to maintain a degree of craft control and to ensure that work was shared out equitably between firms. Concentrating on work-related issues diminished the relevance of wider ideological issues, which the union saw as having little to do with immediate concerns at chapel level. A reasonable degree of security and well-established benefits meant that the majority of members were not prepared to sacrifice what they had built up over a long period in the interests of wider political and social objectives.

Throughout the period the Typographical Association took the view that both employers and employees had responsibilities. The mid-Victorian liberal ethos, which emphasized independence, self-help and pride in workmanship, suited the highly skilled workers in printing. As T. J. Dunning, secretary of the Bookbinders' Union, pointed out in 1860:

> We have said before that the true state of employer and employed is that of amity, and that they are the truest friends, each of the other – for each derives his revenue from the other ... it should be the duty of both to prevent this harmony from being interrupted. Each should consider its interruption the greatest of calamities.[29]

The Typographical Association never advocated revolutionary doctrines but totally accepted prevailing social and economic structures, its leaders content to work within the existing political framework.[30] In 1841 the Secretary of the Manchester Typographical Society welcomed:

> the feeling of respect and goodwill shown towards us by our employers; due to the fact that in every dispute it has been our study to adopt a quiet, respectful, but determined conduct. Reason and justice have prevailed, where threatening and intimidation would have failed.[31]

The executive committee of the Typographical Association sent an observer to Sheffield at the establishment of the Alliance of Organized Trades, but decided it was outside their authority to take part.[32] Although the union leadership was aware of the defects of a system which resulted in failure to provide continuous employment at adequate rates of pay, *laissez-faire* capitalism was accepted with a complacency that verged on servility. In evidence to the Royal Commission on Trade Unions in 1869, the leadership of the Manchester Typographical Society stated:

> we never sanction acts of intimidation or annoyance ... our members decidedly belong to the more industrious intelligent and skilful portion of the men, employers acknowledge that the most able workmen are unionists.[33]

This view of the typographical unions contrasted sharply with sections of the building and cutlery trades which had been involved with the 'Manchester and Sheffield outrages', the main reason why the commission was set up. It was clearly implied that the compositors were not in the same class as workmen who were prepared to indulge in physical violence.

As Able Heywood, the Manchester printer, pointed out to the 1892 Commission:

> The practical absence of strikes in the trade serves to show the relations between employers and employees to be very good. There is a high degree of intelligence among printers which is a guarantee against strikes being needlessly entered into.[34]

In England and Wales, between 1881 and 1890, no serious strikes took place in printing. Approximately 70 small disputes occurred, far fewer than in the earlier period. Disputes arose mostly in relation to the employment of non-society men, excessive numbers of apprentices, and piecework rates. In Manchester the Typographical Association paid out £4500 in strike benefit during two lockouts but there were no disputes in Liverpool or Oldham.[35] In 1898 there were only nine disputes in printing in the whole country, affecting 163 workers, who lost 11,789 hours, an average of less than six days for each worker involved.[36] Statistics show that in the last decade of the nineteenth century printing experienced far fewer disputes than other trades.

Table 5.1   Percentage of union members involved in trade disputes in England and Wales, 1894–1900

	1894	1895	1896	1897	1898	1899	1900	Average
Printing	0.1	0.1	0.1	0.3	0.1	0.1	0.2	0.1
All trades (excluding agriculture & fishing)	3.9	3.2	2.4	2.8	3.0	2.2	2.2	2.8

Source: Board of Trade, *Report on strikes and lockouts* (1901).

Compared to England, labour relations in Scotland were often poor, the employers in both Glasgow and Edinburgh issuing quarterly 'black lists' of men who had taken part in strikes. Possibly because of the concentration of large book printers and publishers, strikes were rather more frequent, with employers prepared to use women compositors and non-union labour and insisting that men who trained on the Linotype sign two-year contracts.

The caution in relation to strikes shown by the Typographical Association in England applied in other countries too. Between 1878 and 1882 in the Department of the Seine there were only three strikes involving printers compared to 24 in the furniture trades, 17 in construction and 20 in metalworking.[37] G. D. Kelley, secretary of the Amalgamated Society of Lithographic Printers, visited America in 1900 to study the printing trade and reported that the hours worked, pay and the number of apprentices were similar to Britain, but he noted that American printers were more ready to take on new methods and improved machinery.[38]

Trade disputes were not, of course, the prerogative of the trade societies; problems arose in non-society firms too, although these are not so well documented. A number of disputes arose at *The Times*, an office which remained closed to society labour until 1914. In France, the Dupont Company successfully excluded trade union labour, renounced collective wage agreements and introduced women compositors. However, in 1903, 500 printers went on strike in protest at a foreman who was 'too severe'.[39] In part this was a protest against new-style management

There was a tendency on the part of the leadership of the Typographical Association to identify with the aspirations of the employers rather than other trade unionists. Blaming workers for lack of ambition and sheer selfishness, they accepted the view that wages must inevitably depend on supply and demand, a position that did no go unnoticed by the employers. As Edward Hulton, proprietor of the *Sporting Chronicle*, told his employees in 1878 on the occasion of the firm's annual social event, 'the interests of employers and employed were doubtless identical'.[40] Richard Hackett, secretary of the Manchester Typographical Society in 1899, the year of its diamond jubilee, boasted that 'printers were at the front of a movement for moderate and unaggressive policies'.[41] Writing in a booklet published to commemorate the jubilee, Hackett attacked the 'baneful spirit of selfishness of some trade societies, where the mutuality of interests, as a principle was neither understood nor appreciated'. Clearly distancing the union leadership of the Typographical Association from any idea of radical action, Hackett boasted that 'members of the Typographical Association have a bequeathed heritage of sympathy with industrial aspirations'. The identification of union members with the interests of the employers may have been understandable 50 years earlier, when there were many small printing firms, but by the year of Hackett's address there were a number of large firms established in Manchester, including major national newspapers. Adopting a high moral tone, the leadership of the Typographical Association overstated the emphasis on moderation, describing the proceedings of the union as having 'stateliness and an elaborate parliamentary formality'.[42]

The moderate ethos of the union was reflected in the *Typographical Circular*, the monthly journal of the union. Until about 1900 the *Circular* contained little or no political comment but was mainly devoted to the interpretation of trade rules and to encouraging self-help. Moral improvement was clearly high on the agenda of the Typographical Association. During the 1890s the *Circular* was showing marked religious influences, with reprints of articles from the *Church Times*, and taking a lead in attacking the Sunday press for causing work to be carried out on the Sabbath. There appears to have been an underlying assumption that all members of the trade were Christians of the evangelical persuasion. In the April 1899 issue a long article appeared entitled 'What would Jesus do?', urging members to consider all kinds of trade matters in the light of the gospels. This theme was taken up again in the January 1900 *Circular*, where a description was given of two kinds of 'free labourers': one was the man who considered trade union problems in the light of scriptural teaching; the other was the evil man who underbid the rate for the work.[43] The religious influence evident in the *Circular* appears to have been powerful in other ways. The membership certificate of the Typographical Association, for example, contained numerous references to God and the Bible, suggesting that the greatest achievement of printing was to bring the word of God to the masses, in contrast to darkness and superstition before the advent of printing (see Figure 5.1).

By the turn of the nineteenth century the *Circular* began carrying more political comment. Reports appeared celebrating the success of labour candidates in the local elections, and G. H. Roberts, the Typographical Association-backed Member of Parliament, provided regular expositions. Even so, the *Circular* attacked socialism and supported Labour because it believed the party would benefit the trade. Even the distribution of the *Circular* mirrored the cautious philosophy of the union and its obsession with thrift, as the journal was not given to every member, but one copy was provided to be shared between three members.

Caution must be exercised in drawing conclusions solely from the content and tone of the *Circular*, as it was very much the organ of the executive rather than the membership. Indeed, some members complained that the *Circular* dealt with trivia. Nevertheless, in the period before 1900 little encouragement appears to have been given to questioning the *status quo*.

By the last decade of the nineteenth century, the policy of moderation meant that organized printers were becoming recognized, respectable and sometimes influential in local society. Clearly relations between the leadership of the Typographical Association and the Employers' Federation were mostly amicable. When Colonel Sowter, proprietor of the *Manchester Courier* and *Evening Mail*, was awarded a knighthood, the event was greeted with great enthusiasm by the chapel and by the Manchester Society, who held a presentation to mark the occasion.[44] Again, when the Manchester Typographical Society built its new headquarters, Caxton Hall, in 1903, the official opening was performed by the President of the Master Printers supported by the Secretary, and the President of the Manchester and Salford Trades Council.[45] In 1900, the Annual Soirée and Ball of the Liverpool Typographical Society was attended by the Lord Mayor, most of the city council, and many titled guests, including Sir Archibald Willock.[46] Willock, who was the editor and proprietor of the *Liverpool Courier* and Chairman of the Press Association, sat as a Conservative MP. During the speeches it was stated that the society was not in any way aggressive, a claim demonstrated by drawing attention to the accounts of the society which showed the following expenditure:

Source: The National Museum of Labour History, Manchester.

Figure 5.1   Typographical Association membership certificate *c*.1910
Essentially the content is of a religious nature, the Bible featuring very
strongly in the centre of the picture. In style, the design belongs to the age of
Gutenberg and Caxton. Frequent use is made of the the the gothic letter, a
letterform that went out of use in England in 1500.
The deliberate antiquarianism represents homage to the past traditions and
makes no concessions to wider working-class consciousness.

Unemployment pay	£722
Benevolent payments	£2000
Superannuation	£559
Funeral payments	£433
Strike pay	£22
(not connected with Liverpool)	

Importance of the Manchester branch

Throughout the period under consideration, the Manchester branch of the Typographical Association was the largest and most influential branch in the country, although it came into dispute with the trade in many localities due to its insistence on a policy of local independence. The Manchester Typographical Society covered Manchester, Ashton, Bury and Oldham, but the surrounding towns were in disarray because, although they belonged to the Manchester branch, they were not paid Manchester rates. In 1865 the Manchester branch negotiated a reduction in hours from 59 to 55, but this caused problems in Ashton-under-Lyne, Bury and Oldham, where employers argued that they could not compete with the Manchester firms, because of the 'superior machinery used'.[47]

It would appear that the Manchester branch was well thought of, particularly by compositors from other parts of the country. J. W. Rounsfell, in his account of life as a tramping printer published in 1887, eulogized the trade in Manchester:

> Manchester! The branch of the typographical luxuries; the ideal branch for wages, hours, and general conditions of labour; the model branch carved out of the perseverance of its members collectively; the branch in the enjoyment of the full fruits of a life of industrial combination; the pioneers of the annihilation of piecework; the home of the annual weeks holiday; the privileged branch whose members have earned their privileges; the branch 'from whose bourne no traveller returns'; the metropolis of typography; the seat of government – I was on my way thither! I arrived![48]

In many respects Rounsfell's enthusiasm was overstated. The Manchester branch, run as it was by officials, could hardly be described as the ideal branch, and piecework was by no means annihilated, but instead was the preferred method of payment by many newspaper compositors in the city. What Rounsfell's comments do suggest is the variation in conditions experienced by members working in different parts of the country, many small societies having little power to dictate local conditions. The Nottingham branch, for example, allowed one firm to increase the number of apprentices from four to nine, although three of the eight men employed were non-society men. In this instance the proprietors of the firm had themselves recently been branch officials of the Typographical Society.[49]

While both the union and the employers agreed that each had obligations, there was a good deal of argument as to who should take responsibility for particular shortcomings. At the annual social gathering held for all the Lanca-shire branches of the Typographical Association in 1887, a Manchester employer told the assembled members:

> the weak point in your association is that you are troubled with lot of inefficient men, some not up to their work, others given up to that greatest curse, drink. If you had better men, employers would be pre-pared to pay more in sickness benefit.[50]

This view was at variance with the Manchester Society's belief in a minimum rate for all:

> if one man is inferior to another, the employer has the advantage of the average. If men unsuited to the business are admitted, the fault lies with the masters who indenture them, for apprentices are always taken on trial before being bound.[51]

Partial decline of the 'old order'

Up to this point stress has been placed on the moderate and conciliatory nature of the Typographical Association, but it is desirable at this stage to look at aspects of trade unionism in printing which indicate some disillusion-ment with the polices of traditional craft unions. Members were intelligent enough to realize that living standards depended on more than the parochial affairs of the chapel and the intransigence of a few master printers.[52] War and political instability in Europe, together with serious economic depression in the mid-1870s led at least some printers to question the limited scope for change offered by the old-style craft union.

For the first time printers were confronted by the realities of capitalist modes of production, where labour was treated as a commodity to be bought for the lowest price. The price lists for piecework composition remained in force after the break-up of the National Typographical Association and the dissolution of many of the employers' organizations, it being left to the unions to maintain these prices. Employers took the view that wages were on a level with a commodity whose price had to be determined by the market, and that they alone should fix prices. On the other hand, if the price of labour was fixed by the market, it was difficult to argue on principle that other trade conditions could be seen as part of a contract of service. Undue competition among employers acted continuously to reduce wages during depressions but without comparable pressure to raise wages in busy times.[53]

The Typographical Association existed as an unregistered society because the executive felt that intervention by the registrar was unnecessary and would impinge on their authority, although this seems to have been against the wishes of the membership. Often there was little grass-roots support, leaving the Association to be run by officials who spent much of their time visiting firms to settle minor disputes concerned with the interpretation of complex rules. Two aspects to the stance taken by officials can be identified: on the one hand there is evidence of co-operation in working with employers, and on the other of taking a belligerent attitude in public and constantly seeking to amend the rules.[54]

A major difficulty with the Typographical Association was that it was made up of small branches, making it difficult for the executive to enforce discipline; rules were interpreted according to local conditions rather than according to national policy. Few sanctions were available to the union against members until the last quarter of the century, and the loose federal structure of the union, especially in the period before 1890, meant that men travelling to another district had to obey local rules. Offices declared fair by one district were judged unfair by another, leading to poor inter-branch relations. Taking up resources and energy in minor disputes between branches left little time for officials to address longer-term political and economic issues affecting the trade.

It would appear that while the executive of the Typographical Association often took a conciliatory stance towards employers, the rank-and-file membership were less prepared to do so, and there is some evidence that the executive were not carrying out the wishes of members. As early as 1865, the Liverpool branch maintained that only members of the union should feed machines (it was in their rules), but the Liverpool branch did not get the support of the executive, who thought it sufficient to have skilled men in charge of the machines.[55]

Evidence suggests a certain amount of disillusionment by rank-and-file members with what the unions had achieved. In the 1891 report, *The Present Position and Future Prospects of the LSC*, it was claimed that 'in fair offices, abuses of all kinds [took place], abuses that are as a rule all in favour of the employers and antagonistic to the interests of the workmen employed therein'.[57] In part this kind of observation implied some dissatisfaction with the leadership of the union particularly in the context of the substantial success of the mass trade unionism of the dockers, miners and gas workers. Dissatisfaction with the leadership and the continued existence of 'gifts' was so great in 1891 that the London Society of Compositors Reform League was formed with the express aim of opposing the leadership of the union. Particularly singled out was C. J. Drummond, the conservative and unapproachable secretary of the LSC. The Reform League declared its specific aim to 'fight the bastard trade unionism of Drummond and his colleagues and to get new men elected to the executive'.[57] The league achieved some success in that Drummond resigned and the radical grouping won three seats on the executive. One of those elected was W. H. Hobart, a socialist who had worked with

Ben Tillett during the Tilbury dispute of 1885. Drummond's successor as secretary of the LSC was the Fabian C. W. Bowerman.

In the provinces, too, the radical faction within the Typographical Association made moves to replace the Conservatives Wood and Nicholson from the executive and to break the influence of the powerful Manchester branch which held all the seats on the committee. According to Musson, the centralized absolutism practised by the Typographical Association executive left it reluctant to trust the independent initiatives of its members.[58] Exercising control through the *Typographical Circular*, the executive avoided having a delegate meeting for 14 years from 1877.[59] Evidence suggests that many chapels were unhappy about this situation, nevertheless in the provinces all the progressives achieved was the concession to hold delegate meetings every five years. Similarly the bookbinding trades experienced discontent through the existence of jobbing chapels. While not on the scale of the London 'gifts', it was claimed that these groups 'encouraged cliqueism, organising disorder at our meetings'.

Printers, like many other trades, were experiencing the effects of counterattacks by the employers, drawing attention to the need for greater working-class co-operation. According to John Child, the union leadership had difficulty in persuading branch officials and members to distinguish between humanitarian aid and strategic objectives. Preece, in his study of the Bradford Typographical Society, found from 1870 onwards numerous examples of support for other unions 'to aid them in their struggle against the employers'.[60] In 1875 sums were donated to the miners and in 1894 money was given to the striking shuttle-makers, the same branch voting to become affiliated with the newly formed Workers' Municipal Election Committee. Examples of rank-and-file support for other workers can be found in different areas. In 1877, when printers in Limerick struck for an increase in wages, the employers attempted to starve the men out and, during the strike, which lasted six months, the men were supported by a donation of £27 10s. 0d, £25 coming from the Manchester branch.[61] In 1894 the Manchester society donated £3 each to the Sheffield Wool Shear Makers and the Belfast Shirt, Collar and Apron Cutters.[62] It is important to note that support often came from individual chapels, rather than the Association or the branch. The compositor's chapel at the Co-operative Printing Society received a delegation of striking workers from the chain-makers of Cradley Heath, agreeing to support the strike with weekly subscriptions. Blacklock's chapel gave a contribution of £2 to the same dispute and also collected weekly for the men on strike.[63]

From 1900 there were signs of change in the policy of the Typographical Association at national level away from the sectionalism of the earlier years towards greater concern for other groups of workers. The Typographical Association gave assistance to other unions. For example, in 1900 the Association made a loan to the AEU of £5000. The set-back rendered to trade unionism by the Taff Vale judgment of 1901 not only slowed trade union activity, but also served to bring into focus the importance of mutual support. Two large printing employers attempted to exploit the Taff Vale case. Ward Lock & Co. brought an action for damages against the Operative Printers' Assistants; and at Straker & Sons, where a strike was called because the firm engaged women Monotype operators, the LSC was brought before the court. The LSC had the backing of the Printing and Kindred Trades Federation (P&KTF), which called out all union members in the firm. The Straker case is of particular interest because the claim for damages included '£10,000 because the plaintiffs suffered losses in having to employ inferior workmen' – that is, non-society men.[64] Both cases went to appeal, the courts finding in favour of the unions; nevertheless these incidents did underline how even moderate unions were vulnerable.

Relatively minor local disputes were common to the trade in the late nineteenth century, but when an employer did fight back the union leadership at national level were left with the problem of negotiating a settlement. It became imperative that union leaders and employers have a mechanism to resolve disputes, but this was not always seen as a good thing at branch level because it threatened the autonomy of the chapel.

By the 1890s some socialist members of the Typographical Association had started to demand more democracy in the constitution of the union and greater solidarity with other workers, leading to the union taking a greater interest in widening the craft base of the society.[65] Although unable to bring unskilled men into the union in the fashion of the 'new' unions, they did manage to make the case for other skilled men to join the Typographical Association.[66] Pressmen, readers and monotype caster attendants were not recruited into the Typographical Association until after 1900, and the neglect of the machine section of the industry stemmed, at least in part, from the compositors' attitudes of exclusiveness and superiority.[67]

In 1897 there were 54 printing unions with 350 branches and a total membership of 52,527.[68] The Typographical Association alone had almost 10,000 members in 99 branches and a general fund of £17,000.[69] Although lending numerical strength, the inclusion of other trades opened the way for more inter-trade conflict over demarcation issues, particularly in machine printing where some machinery had dual functions, for example paper bag making and printing. The persistence of small printing firms also militated against forceful trade union activity, as it was virtually impossible to stamp out every breach of rules relating to job demarcation. Union membership in larger offices was more militant and displayed greater propensity to take collective action, although it would be wrong to dismiss the effectiveness of the union in smaller offices. One keen supporter of union ideals working in a small firm might have very direct contact with all those working in the office, perhaps wielding a disproportionate amount of influence.

More damaging than inter-trade arguments was the disharmony between and the Typographical Association and the London Society of Compositors. Relations between the two unions were frequently strained, and especially so in 1902 when the LSC proposed to extend their radius from 15 miles from central London to 30 miles. A serious dispute arose between the two unions as this change would have taken in 12 Typographical Association branches. The situation worsened between 1906 and 1910 when the Typographical Association set up a branch in London and the LSC formed a branch in Reading. The cause of this problem was the London differential, which the LSC did not wish to see eroded. From the Typographical Association's point of view, men who moved to London were treated unfairly, experiencing obstruction in gaining employment in the city.[70] Disunity between the two unions arose in part because both were long-established societies with deeply embedded customs and practices.

Although the printing unions had taken a step in the direction of industrial unionism, the influences of 'new unionism' were short-lived. The Typographical Association in its established form had grown numerically and its policy of restricted entry to the trade appeared to have paid off, increasing further the authority of paid officials. Local typographical societies were for many years run by committees, and while this suited small branches, with the growth in membership it became increasingly difficult to organize large branches in this way. In 1871 the Manchester Typographical Society decided that the business of the union should be conducted by delegates elected from various chapels in the city. In turn it became the responsibility of the delegates to elect the branch committee and a full-time secretary, changes which removed the society from the direct control of the members. This form of indirect government tended to lessen the direct participation of individual members in trade matters and in many cases induced apathy, reducing union membership to mere payment of weekly subscriptions.

Manchester, though a relative stronghold of trade unionism in printing, suffered from low participation at branch level and between 1860 and 1890 the executive exploited the apathy of the membership to fend off outside influences. Records show that the Manchester branch, with a membership of over 1200, had an attendance at meetings of only 30 or so members, and on many occasions was not able to get a quorum. Interestingly, given the compositor's reputation as a respectable artisan, there were many complaints in the *Circular* that those attending were 'a rough element who indulged in language unfit for any meeting'. This seems to be borne out by the number of members who were fined for disorderly conduct during meetings and had to pay sums between 2s. 6d. and 7s. 6d.

Co-operation with other trades

By the last decade of the century the proliferation of small unions within the printing industry made some sort of alliance necessary, and in 1891 the Printing and Kindred Trades Federation (P&KTF) was formed to bring together the disparate unions in the trade. One of the aims of the P&KTF was the avoidance of costly inter-trade strikes by taking a collective and conciliatory approach to disputes. The federation did not, however, inter- fere with the internal policies or finances of its member unions, and no strike could be sanctioned without the consent of the executive of indi- vidual unions, each union retaining absolute autonomy. Most printing unions were federated within the P&KTF for national negotiations on issues such as hours and holiday entitlement, but on the question of wages each union acted independently. In the time-scale of its development the P&KTF paral- leled the employers' federation and in 1908 the two organizations formed a joint board of conciliation.

The Typographical Association carried on an extensive debate over the federation of trade unions, concluding that while it was good in principle it would not work in practice: each union should become strong in its own right.[71] Initially the Typographical Association was unenthusiastic about such a federation, partly because it did not want to lose its independence or become embroiled in polices that might lead to strikes. There was also concern that there could be a 'levelling down' of pay and conditions as the Typographical Association was the largest union involved and its members were among the highest-paid workers in the trade. For similar reasons the London-based unions formed their own federation, fearing that a provincial organization would not fight to keep the London differentials. Eventually, however, the Typographical Association came to play a full part in the P&KTF. By 1901, 13 unions were affiliated to the P&KTF, representing 42,000 mem- bers, and by 1914 this number had grown to 23 societies with 82,000 members.[72]

The P&KTF was unable to avoid completely inter-union disputes, al- though it did gain recognition in respect of collective bargaining.[73] In 1909 the federation moved to secure a 48-hour week, but the employers refused this request. The P&KTF asked for support for a 50-hour week from January 1911 and a 48-hour week from 1912, putting a further question to the mem- bers asking them to accept a 3d. per week levy to build up a fund to press for the issue of the shorter week if necessary. The members failed to give this proposal the necessary support of a two-thirds majority, and the P&KTF suffered some humiliation when the rank-and-file membership failed to give their backing to the fight for a reduced working week.[74]

Fair trade

The idea that the compositor belonged to an elite body did not extend to men who were not members of the society. Throughout its history the Typographical Association put great emphasis on exclusiveness of its members at the expense of the 'inadequate men' who did not belong to the society. From 1850 the society regularly published lists of both 'fair' and 'unfair' offices with the aim of drawing attention to those employers who did not employ society men and pay a fair day's wage for a fair day's work. Warning the general public to avoid such firms was only a short step away from extending the strategy to campaigning more generally by issuing warnings to political parties, other trade unions and public bodies not to support 'unfair' firms.

In October 1894, when the Manchester Corporation sought tenders for the printing of the Codification of the Local Acts, a number of Manchester printers tendered for the work but the contract was awarded to a firm outside the city. The Manchester Typographical Society mounted a campaign against this decision by distributing 10,000 'fair contract' handbills to trade unionists in the city. All councillors who supported the contract going outside the city were named and a plea was made to trade unionists not to vote for these councillors in the forthcoming election. Similarly in Blackpool, when the contract to place an order for 100,000 Blackpool Guides came before the council in 1899, the fair wages issue developed into a major political debate. While the trade union had one supporter on the council, there were eight other aldermen or councillors who were owners of newspapers or printing and publishing companies, all of course opposed to fair trade ideals. On the grounds of interference with free trade, the Liberal group on the council overwhelmingly rejected the plea that the work should be placed with a fair office paying union rates.[75]

Undeterred by opposition to the fair wages campaign, the Typographical Association extended its activities to take in the printing of parish magazines and other parochial work. However, this provoked a bitter response from a number of Church of England clerics who strongly objected in principle to interference from trade unions. The union was accused of trying to gain a monopoly, a situation judged to be grossly unfair to employers. Objections were made to the element of compulsion in the union's policy and to paying men the union rate rather than according to the ability of the individual.[76]

While the Typographical Association led the way on the fair wages issue, encouraging other unions to act in a similar way, it cannot be claimed that the actions of the association in respect of fair contracts were political. There was no party bias, but the episode did demonstrate how influential the union could be. Individual councillors, and indeed printing firms, did not welcome the publicity the campaign brought, and it would appear that many such firms did in fact become 'fair'. In particular, local newspapers which were owned or had an allegiance to political parties were concerned about the affect on circulation such adverse publicity might have. After a dispute over wages at Emmott and Co., the firm engaged non-society men – an action which prompted the Manchester Society to publish a poster which announced: 'The attention of all trade unionists is drawn to the fact that the daily sporting paper the *Sporting Telegraph* is produced by non-union labour.' Emmotts then took the society to court for libel; however, the judge found in favour of the union and eventually the firm reverted to employing society men.[77]

Radical politics and printers

It has been suggested that the artisans of the radical political movements of the first half of the nineteenth century were not the product of the new industrial order, but were printers and other tradesmen who, out of independence and respect for past traditions, were reacting to the injustices of industrialization.[78] Even though Hobsbawm suggests that the revolutionary crowds of 1848 probably contained more printers, joiners and locksmiths than any other trades, the printing trade societies generally distanced themselves from the potentially violent behaviour associated with Chartism and the agitation of 1830–32 before the passing of the Great Reform Bill.[79] There were few references to Chartism in the literature of the typographical societies, but it is clear that some societies supported the political aims of the Charter and certainly the more 'respectable' Anti-Corn Law League.[80]

Although the printing-trade societies may have overtly remained aloof from Chartism, many individual printers were active in various strands of radicalism and the signs are that printers often took a lead in early radical politics. Dorothy Thompson, for example, argues that compositors played an important part in early radical working-class movements throughout Europe. Three of the signatories to the Charter were printers – Hetherington, Vincent and Watson – and Chartist autobiographers included Thomas Frost and John Bedford Leno.[81] Undoubtedly, one reason for this degree of participation was the extent of literacy among printers and the importance of printed broadsheets, pamphlets and newspapers to the dissemination of ideas. The skills of the compositor in interpreting manuscript copy and editing text meant that the progression from compositor to sub-editor and then editor was quite common; such skills were essential to further the cause of any radical political movement. Robert Hartwell provides such an example, having a long record of activity in radical politics. He attended the Chartist convention, was a member of the National Union of the Working Classes and secretary of the Dorchester Labourers' Committee. A compositor by trade, he became the sub-editor to George Troup on the *Bee Hive*.[82]

W. E. Adams is fairly typical of many nineteenth-century printers who belonged to the radical tradition. Born in 1832 into a Chartist family, Adams was apprenticed on the *Cheltenham Journal*, becoming a member of the National Charter Association and working on Linton's *English Republic*, which was printed at 'Brantwood' in the Lake District. W. J. Linton, acknowledged as one the best nineteenth-century wood engravers, was a radical politician who produced the *National*, Bronterre O'Brien's journal of advanced radical theory, and, between 1851 and 1855, his periodical, *English Republic*. Adams then worked in Manchester as a reader/compositor in the office that printed the *Alliance News*, and at the same time studied English grammar, Latin and French at the Working Men's College under the Revd William Gaskell. His experience in Manchester clearly contrasted with that in Cheltenham, where he served his apprenticeship, providing valuable insights into aspects of the trade. He found that compositors in Manchester were of 'a higher order and of a more refined taste' and that Manchester printers took an intelligent interest in literature and politics, attributing this to the free library, the Working Men's College and the radical tradition of the city.[83]

It is important to note that early enthusiasm for radical causes did not necessarily translate into support for wider working-class interests. The early radical background of Adams and his admiration for the Manchester compositors was not consistent with his fierce opposition to the emerging socialist movement. He opposed the closed shop, advocated personal independence and self-help, and believed that men should feel affection for their work because 'work is worship'. Adams was especially critical of the 'policy of skulk', by which he claimed workers demanded a good day's pay for a bad day's work.[84] On social questions Adams was equally vehement, claiming that 'a grievous charge against some of our charitable institutions is that they contribute to the maintenance and multiplication of persons who are mentally and morally diseased'.[85] Adams clearly showed many of the characteristics attributed to members of the 'labour aristocracy' – independence and enthusiasm for self-help. Eventually he became editor of the *Newcastle Daily Chronicle*, one of the most important radical provincial papers of the day. Support for radical causes did not always extend to endorsement of trade-society principles. For example, Feargus O'Connor, the Chartist leader, was a printer and owner of the *Northern Star*, although he was denounced by the trade society for being 'an unfair employer' on account of his unreliability in paying wages and the excessive number of apprentices he employed.[86]

For others, opposition to the stamped press provided a common cause for printers to take a lead in radical politics. Henry Hetherington, who served an apprenticeship to the Parliamentary printer Luke Hansard, became attracted to Owenism, joining the Co-operative Printers' Association in 1821, before starting his own press in 1831. Co-founder of the National Association of the Working Classes and the London Working Men's Association, Hetherington

184   THE SKILLED COMPOSITOR, 1850–1914

was an active Chartist, leading the struggle for the unstamped press.[87] In 1835 his presses were seized and he spent numerous spells in prison for offences relating to the publication of the unstamped *Poor Man's Guardian*.[88]

A number of men who contributed to the radical cause were owners of printing offices. Abel Heywood (1810–93) opened a bookshop and penny newsroom on Oldham Street, Manchester in 1831 and, like Hetherington, was an active Chartist, spending time in prison for selling unstamped newspapers. His business was very successful, by mid-century handling 10 per cent of the newspaper trade in Britain. Heywood became a respected politician, helping to form Manchester City Council and serving as Mayor on two occasions.[89]

Another compositor who became a printer, bookseller and publisher was James Watson. Watson was a radical politician who helped draw up the People's Charter and was twice imprisoned for his activities relating to the unstamped press and the publication of liberal and free-thought literature.[90] Other printers came to the radical political tradition from within the Church. Andrew Aird, for example, started work in a Glasgow printers at the age of nine, eventually becoming a journeyman compositor. Aird was active in the Church and was ordained an elder, founding the Christian Institute for Young Men.[91]

The changing political stance within the Typographical Association

It has been suggested that, in printing, the search for new strategies to control the uses of machinery resulted in a shift from the non-political stance of the mid-Victorian period to a more political one towards the end of the century. While there is some truth in this, a difficulty arises in defining just what constituted political behaviour in the nineteenth century. Provided that issues to be dealt with were concerned with the 'trade', they were considered non-political, although of course in today's terms many of these issues would be distinctly political. For example, the question of the legal status of trade unions was very much a political matter, but the agitation for improved working conditions or improved factory legislation was not seen in the same light. Recognition of this dichotomy helps explain the somewhat contradictory behaviour of leaders of the Typographical Association who stood by principles of justice and fairness for the working man on issues such as fair wage agreements for public contracts, while giving active support to the party of free enterprise.

In the USA socialism never took hold in the pressmen's union as it did in the garment workers' and carpenters' unions, as the American printers took the view that the most potent defensive and offensive weapon was good craftsmanship. The National Typographical Union of America admitted employers in the hope of avoiding cut-throat competition.[92]

To a large extent the degree of politicization within different Typographical Association branches depended on its officers. It is worthwhile, therefore, examining briefly the political interests of some of the trade union leaders who took a leading part in determining policy, not only in Manchester, but nationally. Claims by the leadership of the Typographical Association that it was important to keep the society free of politics really amounted to keeping 'party socialism' at bay. In 1867, both Nicholson and Wood (Treasurer and Secretary, respectively, of the Manchester Typographical Society) campaigned for Conservative candidates, boasting that 7000 working men had voted Conservative as a result of their efforts.[93] W. H. Wood, together with Henry Slatter, were the organizers in Manchester of the Social Alliance. Founded in London, the 'New Social Alliance' was an initiative between an influential group of Conservative peers and trade union leaders to influence domestic legislation.[94] Alan Kidd, in discussing working-class Toryism in Manchester, draws attention to the part played by Nicholson in organizing the mass demonstration of support for Disraeli on his visit to the city in 1872. It was during this time that Disraeli was in opposition, where he successfully attacked Gladstone's Irish policies.[95] Samuel Nicholson was also a prominent member of the Orange Order and general secretary of the Order of Druids.[96]

Henry Slatter was general secretary of the Typographical Association from 1869 until 1897. Born in Birmingham in 1830, the son of a baker, Slatter had very little schooling, except for what he gained from the Mutual Improvement Society of the Unitarian Church. Moving to Manchester in 1865 to work as a compositor on the *Manchester Daily Examiner*, he became a member of the Manchester branch committee, representing the Typographical Association several times at the TUC.[97] Slatter was one of the founding members, and a director of, the Manchester-based Co-operative Printing Society, and took an active part in the civic life of the city, becoming, on 21 May 1885, the first working man to be appointed a magistrate in Manchester. Slatter took a leading role in the Ship Canal Movement, was a member of the School Board, the Manchester Sanitary Association and chairman of a charity providing cheap meals to city children. In his spare time he acted as a scorer at county cricket matches.

In considering the life of Slatter, it becomes clear that he was not in any sense a radical prepared to risk conflict with employers. Instead, he advocated that questions in a dispute should be 'talked over fairly by masters and men', gaining a reputation for his persuasiveness. There are clear signs of what Gore describes as 'embourgeoisement' of union leaders as they became incorporated into civic life.[98] The long period he spent as general secretary of the Typographical Association (nearly 30 years) and his very active civic life, together with his reputation as a 'self-made man', confirmed his qualities of reliability and respectability. In 1877 Slatter spoke at the TUC proposing support for the co-operative movement, and while he was given support, questions were asked about wage rates paid by the Co-operative Printing Society. Described by the *Manchester Evening News* as a 'trade unionist of the old school', Henry Slatter was a member of the TUC Parliamentary Committee from 1877 until 1890, when he resigned following the success of the socialist 'new unionists' at the Trades Union Congress held in Liverpool in 1890.[99] During this period of increasing politicization within the trade union movement, it is recorded that Slatter wanted the Typographical Association to carry on in the same steady way as in the past.[100]

In May 1867 the Manchester branch refused to take part in the 'Great Reform Demonstration of Working Men', claiming: 'that sort of thing was foreign to the objects for which the Manchester Typographical Society was formed'.[101] However, the moderate stance of the Manchester Society appeared to be changing, as it supported the Agricultural Labourers in their dispute of 1874, taking part in a 20,000-strong march through Manchester. On this occasion the Manchester branch members had set up a printing press on a dray, printing and selling copies of a letter of support for the agricultural workers from the Bishop of Manchester.[102]

From the mid-1890s there were increasing signs that the Typographical Association was moving towards support for the newly formed Independent Labour Party (ILP). This contrasted with the earlier situation in Manchester where there was strong active support for the Conservatives from within the Typographical Association executive, the branch and the Trades Council. Caution must be exercised here, as examples of support for Labour were not general and cannot be taken as evidence that the majority of union members were of a radical disposition. It is also important to differentiate between the rhetoric of public statements made at meetings of the executive of the union and the actions actually taken by rank-and-file members.

Local branches of the Typographical Association varied a great deal in their degree of politicization. Bradford, for example, was one of the principal centres of support for the ILP, and in this town a number of committee members of the Typographical Society were actively involved in labour politics. In Sheffield, William Dronfield, secretary of the Sheffield branch of the Typographical Association, was very active in working-class politics during the 1860s and 1870s. Dronfield assisted the Yorkshire and North Derbyshire miners to organize and acted as secretary of the Sheffield Trades' Defence Committee in the wake of the 'Sheffield outrages'.[103] Dronfield was a member of the Reform League, taking an active part in the Reform Bill agitation of 1866–67, and the Sheffield branch secretary, Tom Shaw, was also a member of the ILP executive.

Like their counterparts in Sheffield, the Nottingham Typographical Society branch officers were involved in Labour politics. In 1900, A. Jones from the Nottingham branch was elected general secretary of the Typographical Association. Jones was very active in Labour politics and a member of the ILP.

His election was seen as a 'triumph for the new school'. His successor, Herbert Skinner, held similar views.[104]

Even though there is ample evidence that the moderate and conciliatory approach of the typographical unions was changing, there was still a front that suggested otherwise. The Manchester branch of the Typographical Association was less than fully committed to the Labour movement. In 1896, when a vote was taken whether to support the May Day Labour demonstration, members voted against the motion by a majority of 424.[105] In 1898 the London Society of Compositors showed great pride, not in its militancy, but boasting instead that 'no party [political] decisions have ever stained the records ... it is the quality of the management of the society and its auditing arrangements that matter'.[106]

Only one year later, the same society displayed a degree of militancy when it withdrew its delegates to the London Trades Council because of the reactionary character of the council. There was some criticism at the time that the trades councils were more interested in 'deputations in connection with various semi-political and pseudo philanthropic movements' than the real issues affecting the working classes.[107]

Less than 20 years later, during their attempts to get a reduced working week, the LSC started the *Daily Herald*, initially as a strike sheet. Formed with capital of £300, the venture had the backing of C. W. Bowerman, MP (who had previously worked as news secretary of the LSC) and W. Matkin, secretary of the General Union of Carpenters and Joiners, representing the parliamentary committee on the *Herald*'s board of directors.[108] The *Daily Herald* became devoted to the radical policies of the Left, attacking Ramsay MacDonald for his support for the Liberal government.[109]

In the last decade of the nineteenth century a number of Typographical Association members were actively seeking election to Parliament. T. R. Threfall, from Liverpool, was one of the first Typographical Association members to stand for Parliament. Nominated by the Trades Council, he was defeated in the 1892 Election when only three independent socialists were returned. At the same election another compositor, Fred Maddison, failed to get elected but eventually gained the seat in the Brightside division of Sheffield as a 'Lib–Lab' in 1897, becoming the first member of the Typographical Association to gain a seat in Parliament.[110] Maddison took a radical political stance, favouring the introduction of land taxation and the reform of the House of Lords.

Fifty Labour Representation Committee candidates stood at the General Election of 1906 and 29 were returned to form a compact parliamentary group. In addition to the LRC members, there was a trade union group of 22, mainly miners, but including Fred Maddison of the Typographical Association. G. H. Roberts, a compositor by trade, stood successfully for Parliament in the 1906 election. Roberts, who was President and later secretary of the

Norwich branch of the Typographical Association, was a member of the ILP. Described as an ardent socialist, he became the first Typographical Association Parliamentary representative, the association providing full financial backing. Roberts became chief Labour Party whip from 1908 to 1914, eventually joining the National Democratic Party. At the General Election of 1926, however, Roberts contested his seat as a Conservative.

In Manchester, the Labour Representation Committee had its first parliamentary success at the General Election of 1906, when G. D. Kelley, a former Liberal, overturned a large Conservative majority to gain the seat for south-west Manchester.[111] This was seen as a great victory for the trade unions because Kelley took the seat from Charles Galloway, a large engineering employer whose activities in relation to the Trades Disputes Bill and his insistence on employing 'black' labour gave him some notoriety among trade unionists. Kelley was general secretary of the Lithographic Printers and a founder member of the P&KTF. A Justice of the Peace and Manchester councillor, he served as Labour member for south-west Manchester from 1906 until he retired in 1910. Both Slatter and Kelley were members of the TUC's parliamentary committee, Kelley for five years and Slatter for 13.[112]

Another printer, Charles W. Bowerman of the LSC, was one of the most influential Labour politicians of the day, gaining a seat in the election of 1906. Bowerman was employed as a compositor before becoming general secretary, and later parliamentary secretary, of the LSC. He was a strong supporter of labour representation and a Fabian socialist. Elected Labour member for Deptford from 1906 until 1931, and junior whip, he became president of the P&KTF and secretary of the TUC from 1911 until 1923.[113] The conclusion must be that by 1900 printers did play a full part in labour politics but it is equally important to stress that printers who embraced radical politics were not all successful. For some, involvement in socialism barred them from a career in printing. Thomas Alfred Jackson (1879–1955), the son of a compositor, started work as a reading boy at the age of 12 before becoming an apprentice, but after serving his time as a compositor he was unable to find work as he had been branded by employers as a socialist agitator. Eventually Jackson was employed by the Communist Party as a sub-editor/editor on party journals, subsequently becoming a journalist on the *Sunday Worker.*[114] Other printers left the trade out of choice, working to assist other trade unions. For example, W. H. Hobart, a compositor by trade, worked with Ben Tillett during the Tilbury dispute of 1888, and Edward McHugh, an Irish-born compositor, described by Taplin as a left-wing radical, became the first general secretary of the National Union of Dock Labourers.[115]

Trades councils and the TUC

From the late 1850s trades councils were set up in many towns, usually at the initiative of the skilled trades, to provide a forum for the organized trades to meet to discuss national policies and matters of mutual concern. In Manchester, the Trades Council was formed in September 1866, rather later than similar groups in other main towns and cities, by which time the building trades were suffering a great deal of unrest. The reasons for the formation of the proposed Trades Council were outlined by Wood and Nicholson, the two members of the Typographical Association who were instrumental in setting up the council:

> Manchester, although a great stronghold of union principles, is comparatively weak, consequent upon the the different trade societies being isolated in their operations, and not united for mutual protection against the encroachments of capital, – a want of sympathy being thus engendered.[116]

The reference to 'encroachments of capital' did not imply any desire for radical action because the main aim of the council was the prevention of strikes and lockouts and the encouragement of principles of co-operation, conciliation and arbitration. Nicholson and Wood, both Conservatives, became chairman and secretary, respectively, of the Manchester and Salford Trades Council. By the 1890s this council had changed from the conservative body of the 1860s to a campaigning group working closely with the Labour Representation Committee and the Social Democratic Federation.[117]

In 1868, two years after the formation of the Manchester and Salford Trades Council, the first TUC was convened in Manchester. Earlier attempts to organize unions nationally had failed, but two factors now gave greater urgency to the need for the trade unions to be represented by a national body: the Royal Commission on Trades Unions and the implicit promise of the Reform Act of 1867 that working men could now use their vote to return working men to Parliament.[118] It was Nicholson and Wood, in their capacity as president and secretary of the Manchester and Salford Trades Council, who signed the proposal to hold the first congress in Manchester. Based on the pattern of the British Association for the Advancement of Science and the Social Science Association, the intention was to provide a respectable and restrained forum for the discussion of 'previously prepared papers'.

Although the future importance of the TUC as a powerful political force was not anticipated, it is likely that the formation of the TUC brought the Typographical Association more closely in touch with political matters affecting the working class. There were still some inconsistencies and contradictions in the union's attitude to political matters, but the distinctions as to what could be called political were becoming less blurred. However, the

Typographical Association was not always fully committed to the TUC and on occasions declined to send delegates to the annual conference.

The Ship Canal Movement

The lead taken by officials of the Typographical Association in the formation of the Trades Council and the TUC was equalled by their enthusiasm for the great civil engineering project, the Manchester Ship Canal. The idea of linking Manchester to the sea had been discussed from 1820, but firm proposals to open up the city directly to the world sea trading routes by means of a canal were not put forward until 1882. Bypassing the port of Liverpool, the objective was to increase the importance of Manchester, especially in relation to its exporting activities in textiles and engineering. The canal was constructed between 1887 and 1894 at a cost in excess of £15m., more than three times its estimated cost, the scale of the project alone demanding extensive support across all sections of society. Typographical Association leaders played an important role in gaining working-class support for the Ship Canal venture, and in doing so helped to confirm the idea of responsible and respectable trade unionism.

Trade union support for the canal scheme was not spontaneous, but was carefully orchestrated, the Ship Canal Movement being described as the most effective local propaganda campaign conducted in Victorian Britain.[119] It is therefore worthwhile at this point to examine the role played by the leaders of two of the major Manchester printing unions, Slatter of the Typographical Association and Kelley of the Lithographers' Union. Through both the trade unions and the co-operative movement these two men played an important part in mobilizing working-class support for the Ship Canal scheme. To this end in November 1882 a mass meeting of the working classes of Manchester and Salford was held at the Free Trade Hall. Chaired by H. Slatter, general secretary of the Typographical Association, the meeting was supported by six other union officials, representing the engineers, spinners, lithographic printers, carpenters and tailors.[120]

The Ship Canal campaign served as a convenient vehicle for developing a cross-class ideology of co-operation and mutuality of interest, and it was imperative for this employer-led scheme to have wide working-class support through links with the trade union movement.[121] Slatter in particular was able to deliver this support; Ian Harford describes his role as most significant.[122]

Kelley and Slatter argued that the Ship Canal would bring new industries and create jobs, and for these reasons gave strong backing to the idea of popular capitalism through working-class share-holding.[123] The leaders of the printing unions were well experienced in taking a moderate and cautious approach to industrial relations rather than a confrontational one, and this is probably why they were called upon to show a lead to the cotton, engineering and building unions. Professional leadership, experience of public speaking and dealing with finances, and reputations as responsible public figures were the precise qualities that made Slatter and Kelley indispensable to the Ship Canal campaign.

Slatter's involvement in the Ship Canal Movement probably came as a result of his association with J. T. W. Mitchell, chairman of the Co-operative Wholesale Society, one of those present at the inaugural meeting of the Ship Canal Company. Slatter played a pivotal role in the Ship Canal Movement, chairing most of the large meetings and acting as a fundraiser. In three inner-city wards he was largely responsible for raising subscriptions of £12,000, mostly in small amounts.[124] Second only to Slatter was G. D. Kelley, general secretary of the Lithographic Printers and secretary of the Trades Council (later Liberal councillor on Manchester City Council). Kelley used his influence on trade councils in Hyde, Oldham and Stalybridge to rally mass support for the meeting at the Free Trade Hall on 13 November 1882.[125]

The evidence provided by the Manchester scheme suggests the growing power of 'respectable' trade unions and a fair degree of co-operation with employers. When the Linotype school was opened in Manchester in 1894, it planned to offer free training on the machines to unemployed men, irrespective of whether they had worked in the trade or not. Instead of conflict, the Typographical Association responded in a conciliatory way, avoiding any strike action. It is suggested that Slatter's role as general secretary of the Typographical Association was likely to have stood him in good stead, as the chairman of Linotype was Joseph Lawrence, campaign manager of the Ship Canal Provisional Committee and, from 1901 to 1906, Conservative MP for Monmouth.[126]

Although the Ship Canal Movement involved considerable co-operation between employers and trade unions, it would be wrong not to acknowledge elements of dissent. Manchester did not display the simple class power structure of a small industrial town, but a more complex mix with factions from manufacturing and mercantile capital; between the established Church and nonconformists; between Liberal and Tory, and between new unions and the old craft unions. Evidence suggests that some rank-and-file members of the Typographical Association were less ready to co-operate with employers than their leadership, with strong feelings at this time that employers were encroaching on trade customs. There was also some hint of scandal in that it was alleged that the costs of many of the demonstrations in support of the movement were met by commercial interests, Harford suggesting that it represented a compact between manufacturing capital and trade unions.[127] Reservations about funding the Ship Canal proved well founded, as in 1902 the Ship Canal Company still owed the City Council £6m.

The energetic fundraising of the elite trade unions for the Ship Canal Movement coincided with a period of great instability in the labour market.

While it could be argued that this gave the movement added urgency, it must also have highlighted the contrasts between the relatively secure section of the skilled labour force and the mass of unskilled and unemployed labour. During 1886 there was a great deal of unrest by the unemployed in both London and Manchester, posing a serious threat to public order. Protest demonstrations were held daily outside the Town Hall and in Stevenson Square, where 'socialist speakers' addressed the demonstrators. The mayor handed out work tickets on a daily basis for men to work on the Queens Road refuse tip and to shovel snow in outlying districts. This emergency measure, usually restricted to the first 700, enabled men to earn 2s. per day. Many of the unemployed were Irish, and the situation was further aggravated by the Irish question, 1886 being the year of the first Home Rule Bill.[128]

It is clear that the whole history of the Ship Canal enterprise has been marked by controversy; nevertheless it does illustrate a unique partnership between capital and labour, a partnership that the leaders of the printing unions played an important role in securing.

The Co-operative Printing Society

Founded in 1869 as 'an association of craftsmen, as a means of ameliorating the conditions of labour', the North of England Co-operative Printing Society (CPS) was started in Manchester by leading members of the Typographical Association. Its first committee consisted of well-known figures in the co-operative movement together with representatives of the trade unions, including John Bradley, Robert Stapleton and Henry Slatter.

The CPS was relatively easy to set up, as only a small amount of capital was needed and there was a considerable amount of trade available from sympathetic consumer co-operatives, trade unions and friendly societies. In the early stages, printing was carried out at the *Manchester Guardian* offices, but after a short period of time plant and premises were acquired.

The CPS was not intended to be a workers' co-operative, but a labour co-partnership. No special provision was made for workers to sit on the managing committee or to have any say in the running of the company. Employees did participate in profit sharing, after a 7½ per cent return had been paid to investors – an arrangement that greatly favoured capital and generated a good deal of criticism. As Holyoake pointed out:

> The Manchester Printing Society gives 7½ per cent to capital, where capital has small risk, seeing that the co-operative societies are at once shareholders and customers; and these well secured, overpaid shareholders come in for a second share of profit with labour's one share, so that the workpeople have a shabby award insufficient to create pride,

interest, or exertion on their part. This is imposture profit sharing, but very good capital sharing.[129]

The Manchester venture proved to be commercially successful, remaining in business to the present day and serving as a model for other co-operative printing ventures. However, as Musson notes, the CPS was more like 'an enlightened, profit sharing joint-stock company than a producers' co-operative association'.[130]

Although the Typographical Association was instrumental in forming the co-operative printing venture, and retained shares in the organization, there is no indication that the co-operative movement had any special interest or appeal to the rank-and-file membership of the Typographical Association. A number of writers testify that the CPS was a good employer, but there are numerous records of minor problems, which cast doubt on this assertion. John Hardman, the first manager, rather optimistically believed that if the trade unions supported the co-operative movement, ultimately the co-operative movement would take the place of trade unionism.[131] Certainly in the later period, when a number of firms started 'house unions', which specifically barred trade societies, the Typographical Association came into conflict over the CPS's insistence on dealing with such firms.

In addition to the CPS, a number of smaller co-operative printing societies were formed, usually with the express aim of providing work for the unemployed. In part the impetus for these co-operatives resulted from the very large sums trade societies spent on printing: it was estimated that in 1901, the combined trade union expenditure on printing was £200,000, the profit on this being in the region of £30,000.[132] One such venture was the Manchester Labour Press, set up to undertake election work for Labour candidates. The executive of the Typographical Association invested £200 in this venture but lost all the money when the press collapsed in 1901.

In the context of this study, the development of the CPS bears little relevance to the conditions of labour, but it is significant because it demonstrates how the co-operative movement assisted trade societies and the Labour movement in general. It also illustrates how the co-operative movement provided another vehicle to be used by trade union officials in gaining acceptance as respectable and responsible individuals, able to contribute to the civic and business life of the city.

Technical education

By the last quarter of the nineteenth century it was acknowledged by employers and trade unions alike that the training given to many apprentices was inadequate. The advent of new processes of reproduction and the introduction of mechanical composition, together with increased specialization, meant that few apprentices were sufficiently trained to meet the increasing demands placed on them. In printing, the large number of small offices meant that on completion of their apprenticeship many relatively inexperienced men were forced to seek employment in larger firms.

State provision of technical education developed during the last quarter of the nineteenth century partly as a response to the mounting concern by industrialists and politicians about Britain's prominence in world trade.[133] Generally speaking, the government was not keen to disturb the existing system of boys receiving instruction in the workplace; neither were they in favour of the system operating in many European countries whereby students studied in college until they were 22 or 23. The Royal Commission on Technical Instruction (1882) urged that all children should be taught the rudiments of science and given instruction in drawing, but as far as further education was concerned a selective system was envisaged whereby higher-level studies would be provided at a limited number of colleges.

The engineering industry, concerned about the level of theoretical knowledge of trainees, led the way with extensive training schools for apprentices. For example, Mather and Platt, the Salford engineers, provided a private technical evening school for over 80 apprentices, taking the view that it was better to bring school to the workplace. There were only a few isolated instances of printing firms organizing systematic training for their workers. From 1860 onwards both Eyre and Spottiswoode and Bembrose of Derby, two of the country's largest printers, had schools for their own employees, and some 20 years later Hazells began a school for apprentices. There were of course other providers of more general education. From the mid-nineteenth century the mechanics' institutes were providing lectures and library facilities, as did the co-operative movement. More formal classes were organized through the university extension movement and later the provision was further extended by the Workers' Educational Association (formed 1903).

Employers in particular were anxious to raise the standard of those seeking apprenticeships. With the introduction of mechanical typesetting, corrections of any kind were difficult to make, mistakes resulting in the loss of any benefit gained by the new composing machines. In 1891, the editor of the *British Printer* made a plea that 'the mechanical calling of compositors must command a higher standard of qualification than at present ... spelling, punctuation and well advanced in general intelligence'.[134] What was needed in the late nineteenth century was training based on an appreciation of art, design and science rather than simply on past traditions. The sectionalism of the traditional system of apprenticeship meant that many compositors had little knowledge of the new trends and processes that were needed by future managers, overseers and estimators, a concern frequently expressed by employers.

Collectively, employers were favourably inclined to technical education but individually many were distinctly hostile to the idea. As the *British*

Printer pointed out in 1900, 'many employers, although publicly supporting technical education, privately treated it with contempt'. Master printers were often reluctant to pay the technical school fees of apprentices, and some large employers failed to support day-release classes when these became available.[135] In practice, the success of technical classes depended on the interest and support of the few employers who took an interest in education, individual firms often providing machines and equipment.

On the question of technical training outside the workplace, the Typographical Association faced a dilemma. The provision of craft training in technical schools represented a break with the 400-year-old tradition whereby the mysteries of the craft had been imparted within the confines of the chapel. Allowing training to take place outside the workplace represented some loss of authority and control over apprentices by the chapel. There was real fear in some quarters that the system of apprenticeship was under threat. The view at the time was that printing had to be learned by imitation over a long period and could not be taught. Many older craftsmen put forward the view that school training had not been necessary in the past, but this opposition might have reflected deeper concerns that they might be displaced by 'new men' who were more scientifically trained.

In spite of reservations, it was in the union's interests that men were trained to a high standard of craftsmanship as a pool of incompetent workmen could easily cause costly disputes which the union were forced to defend, becoming a drain on the society's benefits provision. As a matter of principle, the union had always argued that it was the employers' sole responsibility to teach apprentices the trade, and there was a good deal of reluctance to allow this duty to be passed to a third party. Underpinning this principle was the belief that if incompetent workers emerged, it was the fault and responsibility of the employers alone, and had nothing to do with the trade society. For example, in 1891 the printing employers proposed that the union should supply men with a certificate of competence, but this was refused by the union, who argued 'it was the employer's responsibility alone to train apprentices properly'.[136]

From the 1880s, as the trade became increasingly specialized, the union acknowledged with some reluctance that is was no longer possible for an apprentice to receive the 'all-round training' that had been given in the past. In part this response reflected the conservative nature of the ancient craft of printing, together with insecurity brought about by rapidly changing conditions. Technical-school learning was seen by many as pedantic and of little relevance to the 'real' work of the compositor that could only be learned in the confines of the chapel. Grudgingly, the general secretary of the ASLP described technical education as 'a useful auxiliary to workshop instruction'.[137]

Concern was expressed by the Typographical Association that the provision of trade classes might allow outsiders to take advantage of the opportunity to learn the trade without the benefit of a seven-year apprenticeship and for unscrupulous employers to undermine the system of apprenticeships, flooding the trade with 'school-trained boys'. In 1890 the union stated: 'we would place no obstacle in the way of technical education … but to throw open classes for individuals in one trade … will defeat the object and make workmen far less skilled than those today'.[138] In the event, attempts by the Typographical Association to control further education provision were unrealistic, as technical education was supported by public funds and could not be made available solely on the basis of union membership. Many apprentices attending classes were employed in small non-society offices, often simply because the Typographical Association was not organized in that district. Neither could the trade union insist that its own members provide all the instruction.

In many ways the Typographical Association's constant, and often reactionary, appeal to tradition allowed the union to be overtaken by events. General enthusiasm for printing was boosted by the private presses and the Arts and Crafts Movement. The popularity of sophisticated typographic fashions and a great proliferation of new typefaces meant that advertising agencies and publishers were beginning to take an interest in work that in the past had been the sole responsibility of the compositor. Suppliers of equipment, too, were beginning to offer training as part of their sales strategy. Both Linotype and Monotype were quick to set up schools providing keyboard training on their machines.

At another level there was some opposition by supporters of the liberal–radical tradition to increased government involvement, any centralized intervention by the municipal authorities being seen as state socialism. The independent-spirited working class with its own culture was committed to resisting the individualism of a hierarchy of men with college qualifications.[139] Additionally, acceptance of 'outsiders' becoming involved in the training of apprentices amounted to an acknowledgement that the trade was no longer exclusive; there could no longer be 'secrets of the trade', given that apprentices were taught alongside non-society apprentices and possibly by non-society instructors.

Rather than outright opposition to technical-school trade classes, the Typographical Association opted for a policy of restriction. At the 1886 Conference of Typographical Societies a resolution was passed 'that the imparting of technical knowledge in Technical or Board schools should be confined exclusively to duly bound apprentices and journeymen printers … and not imparted to all comers'.[140] The executive of the Typographical Association also forbade its members who were instructors in technical schools to teach the trade to anyone who was not a bound apprentice, a restriction that caused disputes for many years. At the Bradford Technical School, teachers and apprentices were withdrawn from classes by the union because the Education Committee insisted on enrolling all those who applied. This dispute lasted many months and was only ended when a compromise was reached, 'that those not following the trade could join the theory classes only, the practical classes being closed against all such'.[141]

In spite of the reservations about trade classes expressed by the Typographical Association, there were good reasons to give it guarded support. It was acknowledged that holding comprehensive craft skills ensured a high degree of employability, thus increasing the chances of full employment. The Typographical Association welcomed any action that raised the status of its members and offered a better basis for improving wages.[142] In 1891, when the Typographical Association made an approach to the master printers for a reduction in hours, it cited the 'physical, mental, domestic, educational, recreational and social grounds why the hours worked should be reduced to 50', claiming the long hours worked prevented attendance at evening classes and lectures.[143]

The gradual acceptance of technical education by the union came about in part because indirectly it provided the union with still another opportunity to exercise control, this time through involvement in the selection of apprentices, a function that had previously been in the hands of the employers. By 1900 it was realized that sound technical training would not be effective unless the right calibre of boy was brought into the trade in the first place. Eventually, in the period following the First World War, the Typographical Association, through the Joint Industrial Council (JIC), followed the example of the American print unions in taking a full part in the selection and training of apprentices. The Typographical Association awarded prizes to its members who gained good results in the City and Guilds examinations and nominated officials to sit on technical-school governing bodies. However, as late as 1930, there was still something of a defensive attitude, the secretary of one branch claiming that 'we have been able to maintain our grip on technical classes and retain them for those following the trade'.[144]

Unlike in Britain, where, in the early years of technical education, the unions took a reactive role regarding technical education, in the USA, from 1899 the International Typographical Union played a central role in the training of apprentices, and founded a technical training school. Additionally, from 1909 every apprentice was compelled by the union to take a correspondence course. This requirement was a condition of admittance to the union and was insisted on regardless of what other training the apprentice may have had.[145] Active co-operation between the American union and the employers appears to have been possible because in the USA there was generally greater recognition and encouragement of, individual merit.[146] For their part, the employers formed the United Typothetae of America (UTA). With 1600 firms grouped into 160 local organizations, the UTA aimed to correct the unfavourable situation of open and non-union shops which, through lack of control of apprentice numbers, threatened to flood the market with partially trained men. This employers' group fully supported vocational education of apprentices through the provision of textbooks, lesson sheets and other literature, providing certificates of proficiency to students completing recognized courses. The UTA took this action in order to 'provide a stonewall insurance against any unreasonable demands of the unions'.

The provision of technical education for printers in Manchester

From 1883 classes in printing were offered in many centres in Britain. The first externally organized classes for the printing trades were begun at the Manchester Technical School and Mechanics' Institute (later the Municipal Technical School) in 1883, to be followed three years later by classes at Leeds, Nottingham and London.[147]

Manchester was the first municipal authority in Britain to provide classes in printing. The Municipal Technical School catered primarily for the needs of the mechanical engineering and textile industries, but courses were offered in a variety of subjects including boardwork (hairdressing), horse-shoeing and dressmaking. By 1902 the Manchester Municipal School of Technology, as it was then named, had a well-established Department of Photography and the Printing Crafts, offering both day and evening classes under the direction of Charles W. Gamble. To meet the needs of the printing trades, courses were offered in lithography, bookbinding, machine printing and compositors' work, but the areas of real importance were the newer fields of photoengraving, photogravure and pure photography. It would appear that the school was well organized and equipped, even at this early date. Facilities were provided for tuition in collotype, electrotyping and stereotyping, the latter two processes being especially relevant to large-scale newspaper production. Photoengraving, too, was of particular importance to the newspaper industry in Manchester, where for the first time newspapers were able to reproduce pictorial news without the use of expensive and laborious hand wood-engraving.

A single comprehensive full-time course in printing was offered, aimed specifically at the needs of young master printers, the prospectus of 1911 declaring that 'the instruction given is especially arranged with a view to the preliminary training of the sons of printers and others who are intending to enter a works'.[148] To gain acceptance on this course, applicants had to be 16 years old and educated to matriculation standard, or have successfully completed an entrance examination which included English, mathematics, drawing, general science and either Latin, French or German. This was the kind of development that caused the Typographical Association some anxiety in that it was seen to bypass the traditional apprenticeship system; the union still held the view that, even for the sons of master printers, the seven-year apprenticeship was the only way to learn the trade.

Clearly there was an element of privilege and class in offering a full-time course of this kind. Apart from the difficulty of paying the fees of 20 guineas per session, most working-class children left school at 13 and would not have been educated to matriculation standard. There was a clear distinction made between 'day students' (i.e. full-time) and evening-class students. Day students were offered the opportunity to join the Officers' Training Corps and take part in a wide range of sporting and social activities, including athletics, debating and literary societies. At a social gathering held at the Manchester Technical School in 1900, students of printing were urged to 'get out of the rut of the common workman'.[149]

Conditions enjoyed by full-time students contrast sharply with those of apprentices attending evening classes. Courses for compositors were held in the evening from 7.00 to 9.30 and ran on two evenings per week for three years and three evenings during the fourth year. Attending classes until 9.30 p.m. would have been hard for apprentices who would already have worked an eight- or nine-hour day. As a concession to compositors working nights, some classes were held on Thursday afternoons.

Tuition in compositors' work paid special attention to 'the cultivation of a simple and good style in display work, and to tabular and technical matter and the arrangement of catalogue text'. The subjects studied included English, practical composing and proofreading. The Linotype machine was demonstrated in order to show its principles, but the school stressed that it did not train operators, possibly an example of the difficult line the school had to tread between satisfying the needs of individual firms without coming into conflict with trade union policy. In the final year, lectures were given in machine printing, photomechanical processes and estimating, the kind of broader knowledge necessary for those who wished to progress in the trade. It was this concern with other trades within the industry that ran counter to the policy of the union regarding rigid lines of demarcation.

By the time technical education was becoming established, the industry was already moving away from sole reliance on hand skills. The title of the department, 'Photography and the Printing Crafts', reflected the changes taking place in the trade itself, where technology was gradually becoming more important than the traditional craft skills. The importance of the application of photography to printing was reflected in both the title of the department and the background of the staff teaching in it. The position of compositors as an elite group of workers at the top of a hierarchy of printing craftsmen was, for the first time, challenged by new trades that demanded knowledge of physics and chemistry as well as artistic skills. Photoengravers, for example, benefited from a scientific training, were better paid and more secure than most craft workers were. Of the three full-time staff teaching in the department in 1911, two were specialists in the science of photography, Charles Gamble and R. B. Fishenden, both who were to become leading figures in the technological development of twentieth-century printing; the third member of staff, W. Buckley, took responsibility for printing craft studies. Even the course structures highlighted the differences in status between craft and technology. Students taking the course in photography and photomechanical processes studied applied chemistry, leading after three years' study to the award of the degree of Bachelor of Technical Science (B.Sc. Tech.) of the University of Manchester.

Catering for the needs of craft apprentices, the City and Guilds of London Institute for the Advancement of Technical Education was formed in 1878 and two years later offered the first examinations in printing. At the start the syllabus content was wide-ranging and very theoretical, ignoring the existing conditions in the trade. The initial examinations were intended to test the competence of journeymen and were beyond the capacity of apprentices, but by 1883 some divisions in the subjects taught were made which still largely ignored the divisions of labour in the trade. In 1886 practical tests for compositors were introduced and by 1893 the tests were divided into general knowledge, composing and machine printing.

Just as the introduction of mechanical composition led to third-party involvement in trade matters, the introduction of technical education also meant that college authorities and elected governing bodies were also having some influence on matters of trade training. Provision of full-time courses introduced a new level in the hierarchy of men entering the trade – men who were equipped to take on managerial roles in the industry without first having completed an apprenticeship. The traditional way into the trade was now under threat, with college-trained managers entering the industry without first having served an apprenticeship. Nevertheless, compositors who attended part-time trade classes increased their opportunities for social and economic mobility, giving those who were successful in their courses the chance to apply for positions of responsibility in the trade. Importantly, attending classes over a long period allowed a degree of socialization between students, increasing the cohesion of men working in the same trade. Unlike full-time college students, who tended to disperse at the end of their course, apprentices usually lived and worked in the same town, producing a network of men who were known to each other, a valuable vehicle for spreading information about conditions in the many printing offices in the city.

Conclusions

What emerges from this brief examination of aspects of industrial relations in the printing trade represents a complex, changing and often contradictory picture, making generalizations difficult to justify.

Employers' associations were often weak and unrepresentative, but this does not mean that individual firms were prepared to concede to the demands of the trade unions. One major problem for the employers was the split between the general trade and the newspaper owners, a situation that allowed the trade union to exploit divisions between the employers to the advantage of tradesmen. Some of the larger firms in the industry were closed to union labour throughout the period, and for most of the nineteenth century there was an excess of skilled labour in the trade, putting master printers in a strong bargaining position. On the other hand, the trade of compositor was a closed one. In the case of a strike it was not possible to bring in 'free labour' in the way employers did in other trades, although there was some risk that unemployed men might be engaged because at certain times there was an excess of labour. For example, when the proprietors of the *Wakefield Journal* took on two extra apprentices, a strike followed. The union sent a circular to every branch in Great Britain and Ireland, but the firm received 20 applications for the jobs of the men who were on strike.[150]

Much of the trade union activity of compositors centred on the chapel, on which the whole union structure was built, although at times the wider concerns of the union were not served by this structure.[151] Inevitably, as Taplin points out in relation to the Liverpool dockers, there were an infinite number of specialisms leading to status based on the work carried out, a situation exacerbated in printing by the large number of small firms.[152] Above all, compositors displayed a strong sense of occupational consciousness and a sense of tradition; nevertheless, the policies and actions of the Typographical Association cannot simply be described as 'old unionism'. While displaying many of the features of traditional craft unions, the Typographical Association did accommodate change and was clearly influenced by some aspects of the 'new model' unions.

During the second quarter of the nineteenth century the main concern of the typographical societies was controlling funds, especially the amount spent on tramp relief. By the third quarter of the century the influence of the Typographical Association was strongly challenged by the introduction of female and boy labour and the introduction of mechanical composition, forcing the union to adopt strategies to retain control. The last quarter saw the unions strengthening their position by increasing membership. Growth was due to an increase in demand for printing and intensification of efforts by the unions to recruit non-society men. Between 1880 and 1890 the Typographical Association increased its numbers from 5350 to 9016, and the Lithographic Printers from 833 to 2235. In the case of both unions, Manchester had the largest branches.[153]

On the whole, good relations existed between printers and their employers.[154] The strength of Typographical Association leadership lay in their recognition of the needs of the master printers. The Typographical Association propounded no revolutionary doctrines, accepting the prevailing social and economic structures, although the union was not always consistent in its application of free trade ideas.[155] Trade practices which restricted the number of apprentices were protective and not in keeping with the principles of *laissez-faire* economics; neither was the union's opposition to the 'taxes on knowledge', while at the same time seeking to maintain duty on foreign books.[156]

Although the Typographical Association avoided overt political action, this did not amount to opposition to the aims of those taking part in labour politics. To describe the change in politicization of printers as cyclic would be an oversimplification, but it would describe the general trend. The radical behaviour of many printers in the Chartist and immediate post-Chartist era gave way to a generally apolitical stance during the next 40 years, only to revert to participation in more radical political activity after 1900.

Until the last decade of the nineteenth century, the stance of the union leadership was the support of Liberal free-trade ideals. As Henry Slatter explained in evidence to the Royal Commission on Labour in 1893, the only area in which the Typographical Association desired state intervention was through improved factory inspection.[157]

The Typographical Association was strong in some ways but the multiplicity of small chapels, branches and local associations left it subject to many minor disagreements that were difficult to resolve through national rules and directives. Poor relations between the Typographical Society and the LSC were particularly damaging.

Ideological and social discord between trade union leaders and their members were not as great in printing as in some trades, although there are unmistakable cases where the union leadership were not acting in accord with the wishes of the members. Smaller branches of the Typographical Association were more democratic and more radical than large branches such as Manchester and Liverpool, where full-time officials were more likely to take decisions on behalf of the rank-and-file membership. Leaders worked with the most influential employers in the city; this hardly suggests that they were confrontational. A common link between the trade union leaders active in the Ship Canal Movement was their involvement in the co-operative movement, the same men working through the Trades Council and the TUC. The London Society of Compositors reaffirmed their moderate stance, declaring that 'Trade unions have specific objectives of their own to carry out, they exceed their functions if they seek to create conditions akin to passive or violent revolution.'[158]

However, slow change did take place as the old leadership was replaced with men who recognized that wider working-class interests could be advanced by the collective actions of a wider community of trade unionists. By the time of the General Strike in 1926, printers were more militant than many workers. Printers on the *Daily Mail* refused to print a particularly severe article attacking the labour side and came out on a lightning strike, an action that led the government to pursue the policy of confrontation. During the strike that followed, printers produced the *British Worker* at the *Daily Herald* office, a response to the government publishing what Cole and Postgate describe as an unscrupulous paper, the *British Gazette*.[159]

Notes

1. Child, J., *Industrial Relations in the British Printing Industry* (London: Allen & Unwin, 1985), p. 174.
2. British Printing Industries Federation, *Centenary Booklet* (London: BPIF, 1974).
3. Manchester Master Printers' Association, first minute book, 1874, ms.
4. Notes of Special General Meeting of the Typographical Association, Manchester, September 1874, ms.
5. Manchester Master Printers' Association. Letter Book, 1874, ms.
6. Fox, A., *History and Heritage: the social origins of British industrial relations* (London: Allen & Unwin, 1985), p. 174.
7. Manchester Master Printers' Association, *Annual Report*, 1876.
8. Child, J., *Industrial Relations*, p. 331.
9. Ibid., p. 91.
10. Saville, J., 'Trade unions and free labour: the background to the Taff Vale decision', in Briggs, A. and Saville, J. (eds), *Essays in Labour History* (London: Macmillan, 1967).
11. Sproat, T., *History and Progress of the Amalgamated Society of Lithographic Printers 1880–1930*, Jubilee Souvenir (Manchester: ASL, 1930).
12. Musson, A. E., *The Typographical Association* (Oxford: Oxford University Press, 1954), p. 135.
13. Price, R., *Labour in British Society: an interpretative history* (London: Croom Helm, 1986), p. 114.
14. Child, *Industrial Relations*, p. 199.
15. Sessions, M., *The Federation of Master Printers: how it began* (York: Sessions, 1950), p. 188.
16. *A brief abstract of the Factory and Workshop Act 1901 so far as applicable to printers* (BPIF archive).
17. BPIF ms.
18. Child, *Industrial Relations*, p. 225.
19. Ibid., p. 202.
20. Ibid., p. 76.
21. Ibid., p. 14.
22. Zeitlin, J. H., 'Craft regulation and the division of labour: engineers and compositors in Britain, 1890–1914', unpublished Ph.D. thesis (Warwick, 1981), p. 86.
23. *Typographical Association 50 year Record* (Manchester: TA, 1899), p. 3.
24. Ibid., p. 14.
25. Ibid., p. 36.
26. Ibid., p. 32.
27. Ibid., p. 52.

28. Roberts, B. C. and Lovell, J., *A Short History of the TUC* (London: Macmillan, 1968), p. 11.
29. Dunning, T. J., *Trades' Unions and Strikes, their philosophy and intention* (London, 1860), p. 73.
30. Child, *Industrial Relations*, p. 120.
31. *Compositors' Chronicle*, No. 12, August 1841, quoted in Musson, A. E., *Trade Union and Social History* (London: Cassell, 1974), p. 87.
32. *Typographical Association Record*, p. 54.
33. 11th and Final Report of Royal Commissioners, *Organisation and Rules of Trade Unions*, Vol. I, PP, 1869, p. 81.
34. *Report on the Royal Commission on Labour*, No. 903, PP, 1892.
35. Industrial Relations, Vol. 36, PP, 1900, p. 325.
36. *British Printer,* Vol. XIII, 1900.
37. Berlanstein, L. R., *Working People of Paris 1871–1914* (Baltimore and London: Johns Hopkins University Press, 1984), p. 171.
38. Sproat, T., *History and Progress*, p. 37.
39. Berlanstein, *Working People of Paris*, p. 177.
40. *Typographical Association Circular*, May 1878.
41. *Typographical Association Record*, p. i.
42. Ibid.
43. *Typographical Association Circular*, January 1900.
44. *Typographical Association Circular*, No. 449, 1896.
45. Thompson, F. L. M., *The Rise of Respectable Society* (London: Fontana, 1988).
46. *British Printer*, Vol. XII, 1900, p. 49.
47. Ibid.
48. Rounsfell, J. W., *On the Road: journey of a tramping printer* (1887; reprinted London, 1982), p. 78.
49. *Typographical Association Record*, p. 32.
50. Ibid.
51. Notes of Special General Meeting of the Typographical Association, Manchester, September 1874, ms.
52. Howe, E. and Waite, H., *The London Society of Compositors* (London: Cassell, 1948), p. 192.
53. Child, *Industrial Relations*, p. 124.
54. Clegg, A. H., Fox, A. and Thompson, A. F., *A History of British trade unions: 1910–1933*, Vol. 2 (Oxford: Clarendon Press, 1985), p. 76.
55. *Typographical Association Record*, p. 28.
56. Willis, F., *The Present Position and Future Prospects of the LSC* (1881), quoted in Child, *Industrial Relations*, p. 119.
57. Clegg, Fox and Thompson, *A History of British Trade Unions since 1889*, Vol. 1 (Oxford: Clarendon Press, 1985), p. 59.
58. Ibid., p. 133.
59. Zeitlin, 'Craft regulation', p. 86.
60. Preece, D. A., 'Social aspects and effects of composing machine adoption in the British printing industry', *Journal of the Printing Historical Society*, No. 18 (1983–4), p. 28.
61. *Typographical Association Circular*, December 1877.
62. Manchester Typographical Society, Minutes of the Quarterly Delegate Meeting, 11 Aug. 1894.
63. *Typographical Association Circular*, April 1887.

64. Bundock, C. J., *The National Union of Printing, Bookbinding and Paper Workers* (Oxford: Oxford University Press, 1959), p. 144.
65. Clegg, Fox and Thompson, *History of British Trade Unions*, Vol. 1, p. 444.
66. Ibid., p. 445.
67. Preece, 'Social aspects', p. 26.
68. *British Printer,* January 1887.
69. Ibid., p. 114.
70. Clegg, Fox and Thompson, *History of British Trade Unions*, Vol. 1, p. 444.
71. *Typographical Association Circular*, May 1879.
72. Ibid.
73. Clegg, Fox and Thompson, *History of British Trade Unions*, Vol. 1, p. 445.
74. Sproat, *History and Progress*, p. 50.
75. *Typographical Association Circular*, April 1899.
76. Ibid.
77. *Typographical Association Circular*, October 1889.
78. Thompson, *Rise of Respectable Society*, p. 14.
79. Musson, *Trade Union and Social History*, p. 125.
80. Musson, *Typographical Association*, p. 76.
81. Thompson, D., *The Chartists: popular politics in the industrial revolution* (Aldershot: Wildwood House, 1986), p. 232.
82. Colthan, S., '*The Bee-Hive*: its origins and early struggles', in Briggs and Saville, *Essays in Labour History*, p. 187.
83. Adams, W. E., *Memoirs of a Social Atom* (1903; reprinted New York: Kelley, 1968), p. 387.
84. Ibid., p. 19.
85. Ibid., p. 599.
86. Musson, *Typographical Association*, p. 77.
87. Burnett, J. (ed.), *Useful Toil: autobiographies of working people from the 1820s to the 1920s* (London: Allen Lane, 1974).
88. Bay, J. O. (ed.), *Biographical Dictionary of Modern British Radicals*, Vol. 2 (Brighton: Harvester, 1988), p. 236.
89. Ibid., p. 238.
90. Ibid., p. 536.
91. Ibid., p. 3.
92. Baker, E. F., *Printers and Technology: a history of the international printing pressmen and assistants' union* (New York: Columbia University Press, 1957), p. xiv.
93. Fraser, W.H., *Trade Unions and Society: the struggle for acceptance 1850–1880* (London: Allen & Unwin, 1974), p. 132.
94. Harford, I., *Manchester Ship Canal Movement* (Keele: Ryburn, 1984), p. 76.
95. Kidd, A. J., *Manchester* (Keele: Keele University Press, 1993), p. 172.
96. Birch, L., *The history of the TUC 1868–1968* (London: TUC, 1968), p. 12.
97. *British Printer*, Vol. iii, No. 15, 1890.
98. Wrigley, C. (ed.), *A History of British Industrial Relations 1875–1914* (Brighton: Harvester, 1982), p. 52.
99. *Manchester Evening News*, 4 July 1902.
100. Musson, *Typographical Association*, p. 306.
101. Ibid., p. 299.
102. Frow, E., *To Make that Future Now: A history of the Manchester and Salford Trades Council* (Manchester: E. T. Morten, 1976).
103. Musson, *Typographical Association*, p. 299.

104. Ibid., p. 304.
105. Manchester Typographical Society, Minutes of branch meeting, 6 April 1896.
106. London Society of Compositors, *A Brief Record of Events* (London: LSC, 1898).
107. Ward, J. T. and Fraser, W. H., *Documents on Trade Unions and Industrial Relations in Britain since the Eighteenth Century* (London: Macmillan , 1980), p. 121.
108. Clegg, Fox and Thompson, *History of British Trade Unions*, Vol. 1, p. 59.
109. Cole, G. D. H. and Postgate, R., *The Common People 1746–1946* (London: Methuen, 1961), p. 60.
110. Musson, *Typographical Association*, p. 307.
111. Kidd, *Manchester*, p. 176.
112. Harford, *Manchester Ship Canal Movement*, p. 74.
113. Stenton, M. and Lees, S. (eds), *Who's Who of British Members of Parliament*, Vol. II, 1886–1918 (Brighton: Harvester, 1978).
114. Burnett, *Useful Toil*, p. 361.
115. Taplin, E. L., *Liverpool Dockers and Seamen 1870–1890* (Hull: University of Hull, 1974), p. 84.
116. *The Bee-Hive*, 25 August 1886.
117. Kidd, *Manchester*, p. 176.
118. Browne, H., *The Rise of British Trade Unions, 1825–1914* (London: Longman, 1979), p. 47.
119. Harford, *Manchester Ship Canal Movement*, p. 11.
120. Ibid., p. 23.
121 Ibid., p. 62.
122. Ibid., p. 24.
123. Ibid., p. 8.
124. *Manchester Evening News*, 10 July 1902.
125. Harford, *Manchester Ship Canal Movement*, p. 65.
126. *Manchester Evening News*, 10 July 1902.
127. Harford, *Manchester Ship Canal Movement*, p. 67.
128. *Courier*, 19 March 1886.
129. Holyoake, G. J., *The Co-operative Movement Today* (London: Methuen, 1903), p. 133.
130. Musson, *Typographical Association*, p. 317.
131. Hall, F., *The History of the Co-operative Printing Society 1869–1919* (Manchester: CPS, 1919), p. 22.
132. Bundock, *The National Union of Printing, Bookbinding and Paper Workers*, p. 135.
133. Fowler, A. and Wyke, T., *Many Arts, Many Skills: the origins of the Manchester Metropolitan University* (Manchester: MMU, 1993), p. 13.
134. *British Printer*, April 1891.
135. *British Printer*, February 1900.
136. *British Printer*, April 1891.
137. Sproat, *History and Progress*, p. 55.
138. Ibid., p. 21.
139. Fox, *History and Heritage*, p. 32.
140. Musson, *Typographical Association*, p. 187.
141. Sproat, *History and Progress*, p. 21.
142. Child, *Industrial relations*, p. 260.
143. Sproat, *History and Progress*, p. 55.

144. Ibid.
145. *British Printer*, May 1928.
146. Fox, *History and Heritage*, p. 227.
147. Calendar, Municipal School of Technology, Manchester, 1911–12.
148. *British Printer*, February 1900.
149. Department of Photography and Printing Crafts, Manchester. First prospectus, 1902.
150. *Compositors' Chronicle*, 1 February 1841.
151. Cole, G. D. H., *Introduction to Trade Unionism* (London: Allen & Unwin, 1953), p. 46.
152. Taplin, *Liverpool Dockers*, p. 10.
153. Musson, *Typographical Association*, p. 78.
154. Child, *Industrial Relations*, p. 120.
155. Musson, *Typographical Association*, p. 77.
156. Ibid., p. 302.
157. *British Printer*, Jan./Feb. 1927.
158. Cole and Postgate, *Common People*, p. 585.
159. Ibid., p. 582.

CHAPTER SIX

Conclusions

It is now appropriate to bring together some of the more significant findings, particularly in respect of the compositor's position in the hierarchy of labour. Study of the experiences of the compositor in the workplace and its institutions reveals complex patterns of continuity and change contiguous to conflict and co-operation. What emerges is a complicated and often contradictory picture, amply illustrating the hazards of making simplistic generalizations about any group of workers.

From the start, two related features of the trade of compositor make it unique: the long continuity of craft practices, which survived more or less unchanged for 500 years, and the ensuing maintenance and respect for tradition at all costs. Although the period between 1850 and 1914 represented a time of rapid change in printing, it is important to note that many compositors in 1914 earned their living in much the same way as their predecessors did, often unaffected by structural changes in the trade, factory legislation or mechanization.

Mechanization in typesetting came very late in the history of the trade and had little impact on the position of the compositor, because with its introduction greater skills were demanded of the hand compositor. Indeed, many aspects of the work did not change at all, for example the preparation of copy, proofreading and the make-up of pages. While the Linotype and Monotype machines facilitated increased output of printed matter and brought issues of quality to the fore, the introduction of these systems opened up new avenues of career progression for the hand compositors. Pride in craftsmanship did not end with the introduction of mechanical composition. In hand composing, there was no narrowing of the gap between the skilled and unskilled as in machine printing, because no unskilled labour came into this part of the trade. There was, however a division between the national newspaper compositors and those working in general printing. The former used only a limited range of skills but received high wages, while the latter needed well-developed skills but received comparatively low wages. The nature of the work carried out meant that compositors needed some autonomy over their work, providing a degree of control that was maintained in the printing workplace longer than in most other trades and to an extent allowing the compositor to function as an independent craftsman.

The very great age of the trade enabled traditions to be established which passed from generation to generation, especially through the long formal apprenticeship and the institution of the chapel. The moral dimension of work was the norm perpetuated by tradition and custom, leading to the frequently used defence 'this is our ancient right'.

Rightly or wrongly, compositors felt that their work deserved respect from the public. Typically, the self-perception of compositors as labour aristocrats was shown by members of the Bradford Typographical Society in a memorial to the employers in June 1904 regarding an advance of wages:

> We submit that it is increasingly difficult upon our present remuneration to maintain that standard of respectability and comfort which is required and expected of us, belonging as we do to what is usually considered to be a superior class amongst working men.[1]

The trade generally was held in high esteem by the public – a situation the unions attempted to reinforce by striving to improve the social and economic status of compositors and to encourage a sense of professional pride, personal dignity and public service. Literacy, relatively high pay and occupational solidarity are the three conditions that have tended to set the compositor apart from workers in many other trades. Compositors differed significantly from other manual workers in that their work, being both manual and intellectual, required them to be literate and to possess a reasonable degree of education. At a basic level it was necessary for a jobbing compositor to be able to read, spell and carry out simple calculations, while compositors working on specialized work, for example scholarly or foreign-language texts, needed at least some appreciation of the content of the work. The *British Printer*, for example, in an article on foreign-language typesetting, went so far as to advocate that 'every youth terminating his apprenticeship should learn a foreign language'.[2]

Trade literature and reports of the Typographical Association contained numerous references to the close association of the printing trades with the 'noble arts' of literature, painting and music and to their connection with science and education. The work of the compositor was often interesting and challenging, particularly so from the 1890s, when demands for creative and technical excellence were growing. The period from 1880 marked a revival in fine printing, inspired partly by William Morris and the Private Press Movement, and partly by commercial competition within the trade. Developing mass markets resulted in demands for advertising and packaging that relied on the imaginative and creative use of printing. Trade journals critically reviewed the work of jobbing printers and organized 'gold medal' competitions for tradesmen, encouraging pride in craftsmanship. At a time when literacy was not universal, the degree of learning needed by compositors earned them a position of respect in the community, at the same time allowing scope for occupational mobility, for example progression into editorial work or management. It is fair to claim that, as a group, compositors were generally able to express themselves both in spoken and printed language, qualities that partially account for the contribution made by individual printers to early radical politics.

Unlike some trades, in which new machinery made craft skills redundant, greater skill levels were demanded of the compositors, allowing them to retain control over relatively scarce skills. Allowing no dilution of labour in the composing room gave compositors added solidarity and exclusiveness in the workplace; these were skilled men following a recognized trade and displaying pride in manual work, a quality which distinguished them from both the labouring and the middle classes.

It is undoubtedly true that there existed a hierarchy among working men, as the *Bee Hive* of 2 March 1872 pointed out:

> There is undeniably a strong aristocratic feeling amongst working men ... the printer looks down on the builder, the builder in his turn looks down on the shoemaker – working men are not prepared to accept that what concerns one, concerns all.

What is much more problematical is to establish precisely what this meant in terms of social mobility and political motivation. Every individual experienced a unique and complex mix of workplace experiences, family life and religious beliefs, features that are so intermingled that it makes little sense to separate out just one sphere. Certainly, in the case of compositors, any notion of belonging to a superior group of men was very much a trade matter not carrying over into politics. Rather than grouping printing workers together, it is essential to recognize that within the trade a hierarchy of compositors developed based on skill and pride in their work rather than high wages. D. B. Updike, the American scholar of typography, used the expression 'commonplace printers' to describe those who put no special thought or craftsmanship into their work, as distinguished from those who looked upon every job as an opportunity for further achievement.[3] Inherited expectations, a sense of their own personal worth and a degree of independence in the workplace were, however, qualities not necessarily connected with the economic values which Hobsbawm described as 'incomparably the most important'.[4]

Difficulties arise in deciding just what the term 'aristocrat of labour' implies, and because there are so many contradictions in the debate it is safer to avoid the all-encompassing term. In his later work Hobsbawm himself expressed caution about the semantics of the term, pointing to the essentially political nature of the labour aristocracy debate: it was not about working-class stratification but the political and ideological consequences of such stratification.[5]

In spite of many signs that compositors belonged to an elite group of workers, other indicators show that their relative position to other workers had declined. By 1900, literacy was widespread and newer 'white-collar' occupations often offered better security and working conditions than did printing. Even within the trade hierarchy the compositor's high position was challenged by the photoengraver and the lithographer, trades that enjoyed high levels of prestige. In the workplace, the gradual introduction of modern management techniques, implemented by foremen and middle managers, resulted in the gradual erosion of control by the compositors over work. The extent of casual work and the retention of tramp relief also suggest a degree of instability of employment through seasonal and cyclical demands on the trade. Large wage differentials were common in the trade; for example, in 1860 newspaper compositors in London and Manchester earned 40s. per week while compositors in market towns earned only half this amount.

The model used by Hobsbawm to identify the aristocracy of labour suggests useful indicators but falls short of providing conclusive answers; this study has demonstrated not the homogeneity of work experience among compositors, but its persistent diversity. Members of the Typographical Association were fragmented in ideological terms and differed in material wealth. It is clearly essential therefore to identify precisely subgroups within the trade in order to explain differences in experience, as skill levels were often not related to wages.

There is perhaps a tendency for some historians to concentrate on the negative aspects of labour in the nineteenth century, dwelling on conflict and hardship while overlooking the positive and pleasurable aspects of work. Without subscribing wholly to the nonconformist ideas of the gospel of work, or indeed the views of William Morris that work was by its nature a self-fulfilling experience, it is reasonable to conclude that many compositors gained satisfaction and enjoyment from carrying out interesting and challenging work. Apart from satisfying the essential needs of living, work allowed social interaction and individual development, the shift patterns employed in newspaper and book production allowing a community of printers to emerge through common leisure and educational activities. In printing, the announcements of retirement that appeared in trade journals provide evidence of the long period worked by many compositors, often with the same company. Many compositors retired between the ages of 75 and 85, having worked for over 60 years. Even in the mid-twentieth century a survey revealed that over 60 per cent of compositors interviewed expressed the view that the general prestige of printing as an occupation was excellent, and over 75 per cent claimed that, given the choice, they would select the job again.[6]

Nor was the working environment as unpleasant and dangerous as in, for example, mining or foundry work. Compositors enjoyed relatively clean working conditions, a fact reflected in their standard of dress which in turn contributed to the notion of a 'clean' job being a 'respectable' one. Work was not simply about earning wages; it was also the focus of social and cultural activities. Within the workplace, the continuous existence of the chapel provided a strong sense of community and allowed the collective views of the members to be articulated, while the 'ship' system of allocating jobs gave compositors a degree of control over their work.

As A. E. Musson noted, the most striking feature of trade union history has always been its profound sectionalism, so often concerned with mundane matters relating to wages, hours and working conditions.[7] This was largely true of the Typographical Association, although a complex and somewhat confused picture emerges which fully backs up the Webbs' contention that the Typographical Association 'passes backwards and forwards from old unionism to new unionism'.[8] The initial aim of the union was to support members out of work and stop strike-breaking, while restricting entry to the trade in order to maintain a relatively privileged position. Typographical societies were determined at all costs to keep the trade free of those who were not fully entitled to membership: the branch minutes record numerous examples of bribes offered to issue membership documents to individuals who had not served the full apprenticeship. In Manchester the society often refused membership, and when they did allow a man to join, they often charged the relatively high entry fee of £5. By mid-century the union concentrated on providing welfare benefits and support for its members and finally, by the end of the century, came to play a full part in labour relations.

The period from 1900 to 1914 was marked by the changing policies of the Typographical Association, which now accommodated machine printers, keyboard operators and readers. The union had increased its membership and, even allowing for a degree of apathy, there remained in the new enlarged union enough politically active men to seek change, although tension still existed between the individualism of the independent craftsman and the prospect of collectivism. The Taff Vale judgment of 1901 and the Osborne case in 1909 served to alert the unions to threats to their status, forcing them to became more effectively organized, with firm leadership and a broader outlook.

Compared to many trades, industrial relations in printing were relatively stable.[9] Until the end of the nineteenth century compositors had the advantage that the Typographical Association represented their interests alone and, despite some criticism of the non-aggressive stance of the union, it is clear that its policies in relation to apprenticeships, female labour and the closed shop were, from the trade union's point of view, successful.

The findings from this work indicate that industrial relations were shaped by trade unions, employers' associations and the P&KTF, rather than by the ideologically driven ideas of individuals. What was important to compositors was how stable the trade was, what demands it made and what prospects it held for the future. In the context of the rank-and-file debate, which assumes a fundamental division between workers and trade union leadership, no clear, consistent differences can be determined. Leadership of the Typographical Association was drawn from right across the political spectrum. On some occasions union officials took a more militant line than the membership, and at other times the members were less willing to accept the moderate recommendations of the leadership. As Geary argues, there was little reason for workers in Britain to turn to political action as they negotiated collective wage agreements.[10] What is clear is the major part played by the union leadership in civic affairs, which considerably reinforced the idea of printing as a respectable and responsible trade, different to the general mass of trade unionists.

Work does not just happen, but has to be planned and organized by employers. As Musson noted, too little account has been taken of the role of employers as entrepreneurs, providing capital, taking risks, supporting technical innovation and organizing work – often acting as the driving force to increase production, trade and wealth.[11] Too often employers were portrayed as the enemy and yet there is ample evidence to show that there were many genuinely benevolent employers in the trade.

Because of the relatively small scale of the printing industry, there tended to be little in the way of a culture of the factory-owner 'feudalism' common in some trades. Instead, in many small or even medium-sized printing offices, the employer himself would have served his time as an apprentice, the interests of the employer being close to those of his skilled employees, each having an understanding of the other's problems. Of course in these circumstances, unlike in some trades, there were no common conditions of work, and men had limited opportunities to function as a united workforce. It is not surprising, then, that the Typographical Association did little to promote a homogeneous class-based movement.

Printing employers themselves were rarely united in the way that coal-owners and the dock employers were. Perhaps the most significant feature of industrial relations in the trade was divisions among employers – divisions which the Typographical Association was able to exploit in negotiating conditions among the three main sectors of the trade: the provincial press, national newspapers and general commercial printing.

It would be a mistake to leave the impression that all employers were favourably disposed towards the union. Even when printing offices were deemed to be fair, employers did not always welcome the third-party intervention of the trade unions. In a letter to the Manchester Society, dated 13 June 1867, the proprietor of the *Manchester Times* stated:

> I have no desire to be recognised by a society whose rules are so arbitrary and unreasonable. I am determined that no society shall ever again be in a position to dictate to me what wages I must pay.

The retention of tramp relief until 1914 provides an outstanding example of conservatism by the Typographical Association.[12] Generally the printing unions adopted a voluntarist ethos of non-intervention. In 1887, when the National Union of Printing, Bookbinding and Paper Workers put the question of the eight-hour day Bill to their membership, they voted against it, claiming: 'the interference of Parliament in matters of this kind is open to grave objection ... the union is our parliament in such matters as affect our business'.[13] The conservative stance of the union is again in evidence on the question of female employment. Objections to the employment of women as compositors were vociferous, usually underpinned by notions that women were not suited to the robust labour in the printing office, concern being expressed that 'hard toiling housewives had enough to do in washing, baking, cooking, dairy work and mending the duds of the bairns [clothes of the children]'.[14]

One of the main inferences to be drawn from the evidence gathered is the folly of suggesting that because some workers were better paid they were 'more respectable and politically more moderate than the rest of the proletariat'.[15] Attention throughout this work has emphasized the long history of the trade and the importance of tradition. Divisions between skilled and unskilled workers which gave rise to the notion of a labour aristocracy were not new in the nineteenth century, and concentration on the idea of a labour aristocracy as a product of industrialization distracts attention from social continuity and tradition, leading to oversimplification.[16] Grouping together factory hands, tradesmen and small-scale employers is unhelpful. All had relatively low incomes and depended on the owners of capital for their wages, or for the purchase of the goods they produced, but each differed in patterns of residence, religious belief, culture and leisure.[17] Differences between workers in the past were manifest in diverse ways. For example, on occasions puritan strains of self-righteous virtue and notions of temperance and respectability were sufficient to guarantee vertical class bonding.[18]

Further research into the living conditions of compositors would be necessary to reach firm conclusions. Nevertheless, the indications are that these skilled tradesmen experienced similar conditions to other workers, with no apparent benefit in terms of housing and general environment. As R. Dennis points out, many skilled artisans' families were brought up with a meagre housekeeping allowance and exposed to poor physical and moral standards. Some geographical separation within the working class took place, but not according to any measurable criteria such as income.[19] The number of dependent children and relatives was important, a large family making heavy demands even on a high wage, and it has been shown that the wives of skilled workers often did not work outside the home.

The brief comparison made between the experiences of compositors in different countries reveals a similarity of conduct that defies so-called national characteristics, particularly in respect of their political behaviour. Just as in Britain, printers in France and Germany deliberately avoided political matters, although this is not to suggest that union organization and political radicalism were mutually exclusive.[20] In France the unions were less successful in maintaining the closed shop, and in Germany there was often a high rate of unemployment among compositors, which tended to depress wages; nevertheless there existed the same pride in craftsmanship and sense of tradition.

In comparing British and American printers, more marked differences are seen. Unlike in Britain, where nonconformism played an important role in the development of labour consciousness, in the USA the trade was more diverse ethnically. Patriotism overtook any narrow trade sectionalism, self-interest coming second to the demands created by the new nation. American compositors insisted they be treated as their employers' equals and foremen were recruited into the union with the specific aim to ensure that chapel rules were adhered to.[21] Just as in Britain, the International Typographical Union (formed in 1851) comprised a loose federation of local unions which maintained their independence, although the ITU was clearly more politically motivated than its British counterpart. Throughout its existence a two-party system operated in the ITU with a split between conservative and liberal/socialist groups.

In Britain the general use of moveable type ended during the 1980s with the introduction of computer typesetting and the implementation of legislation that restricted the powers of the trade unions. After more than 500 years the skilled trade of compositor ceased, together with many of the ancient customs and practices.

Notes

1. Preece, D., 'Social aspects and effects of composing machine adoption in the British printing industry', *Journal of the Printing Historical Society*, No. 18 (1983–4), p. 50.
2. *British Printer*, Vol. 39, January 1927.
3. Ibid.
4. Hobsbawm, E. J., *Labouring Men: studies in the history of labour* (London: Weidenfeld & Nicolson, 1964), p. 273.
5. Hobsbawm, E. J., *Worlds of Labour* (London: Weidenfeld & Nicolson, 1984), p. 215.
6. Lipset, M., Trow M. and Coleman, J., *Union Democracy: the internal politics of the International Typographical Union* (New York: Free Press, 1968), p. 31.
7. Musson, A. E., *Trade Union and Social History* (London: Cassell, 1974), p. 5.
8. Clegg, A. H., Fox, A. and Thompson, A. F., *A History of British Trade Unions*, Vol. 1, p. 415.
9. Zeitlin, J. H., 'Craft regulation and the division of labour: engineers and compositors in Britain, 1890–1914', unpublished Ph.D. thesis (Warwick, 1981), p. 96.
10. Geary, D., *European Labour Protest 1848–1939* (New York: St Martin's Press, 1981), p. 57.
11. Musson, *Trade Union and Social History* (London: Cassell, 1974).
12. Child, J., *Industrial Relations in the British Printing Industry* (London: Allen & Unwin, 1967), p. 121.

13. Bundock, C. J., *The National Union of Printing, Bookbinding and Paper Workers* (Oxford: Oxford University Press, 1959), p. 43.

14. *Blackwood's Edinburgh Magazine*, Vol. 92, August 1862.

15. Hobsbawm, *Labouring Men*, p. 272.

16. Berg, M. (ed.), *Technology and Toil in Nineteenth Century Britain* (London: CSE, 1979), p. 11.

17. Dennis, R., *English Industrial Cities of the Nineteenth Century: a social geography* (Cambridge: Cambridge University Press, 1984), p. 193.

18. Fox, A., *History and Heritage: the social origins of the British industrial relations system* (London: Allen & Unwin, 1986), p. 143.

19. Dennis, *English Industrial Cities*, p. 193.

20. Geary, D., *European Labour Protest*, p. 46.

21. Lause, M. A., *Some Degree of Power* (Arkansas: University of Arkansas Press, 1991), p. 119.

Glossary of slang and trade terms

Balancing time
The practice of stopping men's overtime pay until they had worked the maximum number of hours ordinary time. A cause of many disputes in the trade.

Blacks
Name given by union members to non-society men working in a 'fair office'. Refers to the black-tailed rat.

Borrowing matter
For reprint work, transferring type formes between offices, thus saving costs in resetting the copy. Compositors took strong objection to this, especially when unfair offices were involved. In 1866, when men claimed for 'standing matter' (type already used previously), arbitration found against the men but on an appeal to court the men won their case.

Chapel
Used to describe the organization of workmen in a printing office. The term, dating from at least the early seventeenth century, is still in use today. Although some functions of the chapel have changed over time, its main purpose was to enforce rules of conduct and negotiate with the master printer.

Ens and ems
Printer's unit of measurement corresponding to the width of the letters 'n' and 'm'. Standard used to record output of both hand and machine compositors.

Fair list
List of printing offices employing trade union labour and judged by the Typographical Association as 'fair'. Offices employing non-society men were deemed 'unfair'. In the late nineteenth century a number of firms objected to the term, taking court action against the union.

Farming
Breaking the union rule against contracting labour to carry out a certain amount of work for a lump sum.

Fat copy
Straightforward, simple text, short pages and blank pages were classed as 'fat'. This kind of work allowed men on piecework to work with little interuption, earning good rates of pay. Lean copy, on the other hand, involved complex text, foriegn languages and small sizes of type, making it difficult for men on piecework to work fast.

Gifts
Sub-group of men forming secret clique in order to share information about jobs and to provide mutual support in times of hardship. Strongly opposed by the Typographical Association.

Grass
To have two jobs, for example working overtime in another office. On occasions compositors took time off, 'selling their galley' to another man.

Horse flesh
The action by compositors of setting down on their bill more work than had been done.

Jeffing
Game played by compositors in the nineteenth century, involving throwing pieces of type like dice. Called by typefounders 'bogleing' and by twentieth-century compositors 'nicks-up'.

Jerrying
Ancient custom of loud singing, shouting or banging galleys. Used on occasions of celebration or as a form of protest.

Ship
Abrieviation of companionship and referring to a form of organization in the composing room where between three and six men worked together. Men elected a leader called a 'clicker' who was responsible for the distribution of copy and the billing of the master printer for the ens set. Term in use from the early eighteenth century to the present.

Slating
Time spent waiting for copy. Names of men waiting for work were marked on a slate in strict order. Long waiting times meant that compositors on piece work were losing wages.

Smooting or smouting
Transgression of the rule against working in more than one office.

Stab
Short for establishment wage. Time rates, as opposed to piecework.

Supping
In mixed news and jobbing offices the practice was to lay off jobbing compositors when work was short and for their work to be undertaken by the news compositors.

Turnovers
Apprentices who commenced work with one firm and then moved to another to complete their apprenticeship.

Twicing

Working both as a compositor and a machine printer. Against society rules but a common practice in small offices.

Wayzgoose

Ancient chapel custom of celebrating St Bartholomew-tide, marking the time in the year when men could use candles to work by. In the nineteenth century it took the form of a dinner or a day of recreation.

Bibliography

Archive material

Manchester Typographical Society

Minutes of branch meetings
Balance sheets, 1832–87
Quarterly reports, statements of account and half-yearly reports
Minutes of annual general meetings
Reports of quinquennial delegate meetings

Stockport Typographical Society

Record of foundations, 1871
List of members, 1888

British Federation of Master Printers

Minutes and annual reports, 1874–1914
Letter books, 1874–1914
Printed notices and members' circulars
Wages book, 1877–82, Megson & Son, Manchester

Official and other reports

Report from the Select Committee of the House of Lords on Poor Relief (PP 1888, Vol. XV)
Reports of the Inspectors of Factories (PP 1878–81, Vols XVI, XX, XXIII)
Royal Commission on Labour: Foreign reports (PP 1892–4, Vols I–XI)
Reports of the Commissioners appointed to inquire into the organisation and rules of Trades Unions and other Associations (PP 1867–8, 24 vols)
Reports from Commissioners, Inspectors and Others: Royal Commission on Labour (PP 1892, Vol. XVIII)
Trade societies and strikes: report of the commission on trade societies, National Association for the promotion of social science (London, 1860)

MacDonald, J. R. (ed.), *Women in the Printing Trades: a sociological study* (London: WIC, 1904)

Trade publications

Compositors' Chronicle
British Printer
British and Colonial Printer
Linotype Record
Monotype Recorder
Monotype Newsletter
Printers' Register
Printers' Specimen Exchange
Printing World
Provincial Typographical Circular
Typographical Circular
Typographical Gazette

Newspapers and periodicals

The Bee Hive
Blackwood's Edinburgh Magazine
Gentleman's Magazine
Manchester Guardian
Manchester Evening News
Manchester Examiner and Times
Manchester City News
Notes and Queries
The Penny Magazine

Contemporary books and reports

Adams, W. E., *Memoirs of a Social Atom* (1903; reprinted New York: Kelley, 1968)
Bigmore, E. C. and Wyman, C. W. H., *A Bibliography of Printing* (1880; reprinted London: Holland Press, 1978)
Carey, A., *The History of a Book* (London: Cassell, 1873)
Hall, F., *History of the Co-operative Printing Society 1869–1919* (Manchester: CPS, 1919)
Keefe, H. J., *A Century in Print 1839–1939* (London: Hazell, Watson & Viney, 1939)
Knight, C., *Passage of a Working Life*, 3 vols (London, 1845; reprinted 1971)
Lefevre, T., *Guide pratique du compositeur d'imprimerie* (Paris, 1873)

Moxon, J., *Mechanick Exercises on the Whole Art of Printing* (1683–4; reprinted London: Oxford University Press, 1962)

Odhams, W. J. B., *The Business and I* (London: Odhams, 1935)

Rounsfell, J. W., *On the Road: journey of a tramping printer* (1887; reprinted London, 1982)

Savage, W., *Dictionary of the Art of Printing* (London, 1841; reprinted New York: Franklin, 1964)

Smith, C. M., *The Working Man's Way in the World: autobiography of a journeyman printer* (1857; reprinted London: PHS, 1967)

Southward, J., *Practical Printing* (London: Raithby Lawrence, 1882)

Suthers, R. B., *The Story of Natsopa* (London, 1929)

Thomas, A., *The Beginnings of Printing in London* (London, 1928)

Timperley, C. H., *Encyclopaedia of Literary and Typographical Anecdote*, Vol. II (1842; reprinted New York and London: Garland, 1977)

Secondary sources

Ashworth, W., *An Economic History of England 1870–1939* (London: Methuen, 1982)

Astle, W. (ed.), *History of Stockport* (York: Scolar, 1971), p. 52.

Baker, E. F., *Printers and Technology* (Columbia: Columbia University Press, 1957)

Baron, A. (ed.), *Work Engendered: towards a new history of American labor* (London: Cornell University Press, 1993)

Bay, J. O. (ed.), *Biographical Dictionary of Modern British Radicals*, Vol. 2 (Brighton: Harvester, 1988)

Bell, M., *A Dictionary of Women in the London Book Trades 1540–1730* (unpublished MA thesis, Loughborough University of Technology 1983)

Benson, J., (ed.), *The Working Class in England 1875–1914* (London: Croom Helm, 1985)

Berg, M. (ed.), *Technology and Toil in Nineteenth Century Britain* (London: CSE, 1979)

Berlanstein, L., *The Industrial Revolution and Work in Nineteenth Century Europe* (London: Routledge, 1992)

Berlanstein, L., *Working People of Paris 1871–1914* (Baltimore and London: Johns Hopkins University Press, 1984)

Berry, W. T. and Poole, H. E., *Annals of Printing* (London: Blandford, 1966)

Best, G., *Mid-Victorian Britain 1851–75* (London: Weidenfeld & Nicolson, 1971)

Bienefield, M. A., *Working Hours in British Industry* (London: Weidenfeld & Nicolson, 1972)

Binns, N., *An Introduction to Historical Bibliography* (London: AAL, 1969)

Birch, L., *The History of the TUC 1868–1968* (London: TUC, 1968)

Boyce, G., Curran, J. and Wingate, P. (eds), *Newspaper History from the Seventeenth Century to the Present Day* (London: Constable, 1978)

Briggs, A. and Saville, J. (eds), *Essays in Labour History* (London: Macmillan, 1967)

Brown, E. H. P., *The Growth of British Industrial Relations* (London: Macmillan, 1959)

Brown, E. H. P., *The Origins of Trade Union Power* (Oxford: Clarendon Press, 1983)

Browne, H., *The Rise of British Trade Unions, 1825–1914* (London: Longman, 1979)

Burnett, J. (ed.), *Useful Toil: autobiographies of working people from the 1820s to the 1920s* (London: Allen Lane, 1974)

Burnett, J., *Idle Hands: the experience of unemployment 1790–1990* (London: Routledge, 1994)

Calhoun, C., *The Question of Class Struggle* (Chicago: Chicago University Press, 1983)

Challinor, W. H. and Musson, A. E., *Industry and Technology* (London: Vista, 1965)

Child, J., *Industrial Relations in the British Printing Industry* (London: Allen & Unwin, 1967)

Clair, C., *A History of Printing in Britain* (London: Cassell, 1965)

Clair, C., *A History of European Printing* (London: Academic Press, 1976)

Clapham, J. H., *An Economic History of Modern Britain* (Cambridge: Cambridge University Press, 1965)

Clegg, H. A., Fox, A. and Thompson, A. F., *A History of British Trade Unions since 1889*, Vol. 1, and *A History of British Trade Unions: 1910–1933*, Vol. 2 (Oxford: Clarendon Press, 1985)

Cockburn, C., *Brothers: male dominance and technological change* (London: Pluto, 1983)

Cole, G. D. H., *Introduction to Trade Unionism* (London: Allen & Unwin, 1953)

Cole, G. D. H. and Postgate, R., *The Common People 1746–1946* (London: Methuen, 1961)

Cook, C. and Keith, B., *British Historical Facts 1830–1900* (London, Macmillan, 1975)

Cranfield, G. A. *The Press and Society* (Harlow: Longman, 1978)

Crossick, G. J., *An Artisan Elite in Victorian Society* (London, 1978)

Cunningham, H., *Leisure in the Industrial Revolution 1780–1880* (London: Croom Helm, 1980)

Curran, J. and Seaton, J., *Power without Responsibility* (London: Routledge, 1992)

Davies, A., *Leisure, Gender and Poverty: working class culture in Salford and Manchester 1900–1939* (Buckingham: Open University, 1992)

Dennis, R., *English Industrial Cities of the Nineteenth Century: a social geography* (Cambridge: Cambridge University Press, 1984)

Drake, B., *Women in Trade Unions* (London: Virago, 1984)

Feltes, N. N., *Modes of Production of Victorian Novels* (Chicago: Chicago University Press, 1986)

Foster, J., *Class Struggle and the Industrial Revolution* (London: Methuen, 1977)

Fowler, A. and Wyke, T., *Many Arts, Many Skills: the origins of the Manchester Metropolitan University* (Manchester: MMU, 1993)

Fox, A., *History and Heritage: the social origins of the British industrial relations system* (London: Allen & Unwin, 1986)

Fraser, W. H., *Trade Unions and Society: the struggle for acceptance 1850–1880* (London: Allen & Unwin, 1974)

Frow, E., *To Make That Future Now: A history of the Manchester and Salford Trades Council* (Manchester, 1976)

Geary, D., *European Labour Protest 1848–1939* (New York: St Martin's Press, 1981)

Gillespie, S. C., *A Hundred Years of Progress: a record of the Scottish Typographical Association 1853–1953* (Glasgow: Maclehose, 1953)

Gray, R., *The Aristocracy of Labour in Nineteenth Century Britain c 1850–1900* (London: Macmillan, 1981)

Hansard, L., *Biographical Memoir of Luke Hansard, Esq.* (London, 1829)

Harford, I., *Manchester Ship Canal Movement* (Keele: Ryburn, 1994)

Harris, J., *Private Lives, Public spirit: a social history of Britain 1870–1914* (Oxford: Oxford University Press, 1993)

Harrison, R. and Zeitlin, J., *Divisions of Labour* (Brighton: Harvester, 1985)

Harrison, S., *Poor Men's Guardians: a record of the struggles for a democratic newspaper* (London: Lawrence & Wishart, 1974)

Heinemann, J. W., *Heinemann: a century of publishing* (London: Heinemann, 1990)

Hobsbawm, E. J., *Labouring Men: studies in the history of labour* (London: Weidenfeld & Nicolson, 1964)

Hobsbawm, E. J., *Worlds of Labour* (London: Weidenfeld & Nicolson, 1984)

Hopkins, E., *Working Class Self Help in Nineteenth Century England* (London: UCL, 1995)

Howe, E. (ed.), *The London Compositor, 1785–1900* (London: Bibliographical Society, 1947)

Howe, E., *The London Society of Compositors* (London: Cassell, 1948)

Hudak, L., *Early American Women Printers and Publishers* (New York and London: N. J. Scarecrow Press, 1978)

Hunt, E. A., *Regional Wage Variations in Britain 1850–1914* (Oxford, Clarendon Press, 1973)

Johnson, J., *The Printer, his Customer and his Men* (London: Dent, 1993)

Jones, G. S., *Outcast London: a study in the relationships between classes in Victorian society* (Oxford: Clarendon Press, 1971)

Joyce, P., *Work, Society and Politics* (New Brunswick: Rutgers University Press, 1980)

Joyce, P., *The Historical Meanings of Work* (Cambridge: Cambridge University Press, 1987)

Kennedy, R., *A Boy at the Hogarth Press* (London: Heinemann, 1972)

Kidd, A. J., *Manchester* (Keele: Keele University Press, 1993)

Kirk, N., *The Growth of Working Class Reformism in Mid-Victorian England* (London: Croom Helm, 1985)

Kirk, N., *Labour and Society in Britain and the USA*, 2 vols (Aldershot: Scolar, 1994)

Lause, M. A., *Some Degree of Power* (Arkansas: University of Arkansas Press, 1991)

Leeson, R. A., *Travelling Brothers: the six centuries road from craft fellowship to trade* (London: Allen & Unwin, 1979)

Lipset, M., Trow, M. and Coleman, J., *Union Democracy: the internal politics of the International Typographic Union* (New York: Free Press, 1968)

Lummis, T., *The Labour Aristocracy 1851–1914* (Aldershot: Scolar, 1994)

Mann, K., *The Making of an English Underclass: the social divisions of welfare* (Milton Keynes: Open University Press, 1992)

McDougal, H. (ed.), *Reputation for Excellence: a history of printing in Edinburgh* (Edinburgh: Napier, 1990)

Meacham, S., *A Life Apart: the English working class 1890–1914* (London: Thames & Hudson, 1977)

Montgomery, D., *The Fall of the House of Labour: the workplace, the state and American labour* (Cambridge: Cambridge University Press, 1987)

Moran, J., *Printing Presses: History and development from the fifteenth century to modern times* (Berkeley: University of California Press, 1973)

More, C., *Skill and the English Working Class* (London: Croom Helm, 1980)

Morris, R. J., *Class and Class Consciousness in the Industrial Revolution 1780–1850* (London: Macmillan, 1979)

Musson, A. E., *The Typographical Association* (Oxford: Oxford University Press, 1954)

Musson, A. E., *Trade Union and Social History* (London: Cassell, 1974)

Pelling, H., *A History of British Trade Unionism* (Harmondsworth: Penguin, 1987)

Penn, R., *Skilled Workers in the Class Structure* (Cambridge: Cambridge University Press, 1985)

Plant, M., *The English Book Trade* (London: Allen & Unwin, 1965)

Price, R., *Labour in British Society: an interpretative history* (London: Croom Helm, 1986)

Ratcliffe, E., *The Caxton of her Age* (Upton-upon-Severn: Images, 1993)

Reynolds, S., *Britannica's Typesetters: women compositors in Edwardian Edinburgh* (Edinburgh: Edinburgh University Press, 1989)

Roberts, B. C. and Lovell, J., *A Short History of the TUC* (London: Macmillan, 1968)

Ryder, J., *Printing for Pleasure* (London: EUP, 1957)

Savage, M. and Miles, A., *The Re-making of the British Working Class 1840–1940* (London: Routledge, 1994)

Saville, J., *Democracy and the Labour Movement* (London: Lawrence & Wishart, 1954)

Sessions, M., *The Federation of Master Printers: how it began* (York: Sessions, 1950)

Singleton, F., *Tillotsons 1850–1950* (Bolton: Tillotsons, 1950)

Skelley, J. (ed.), *The General Strike 1926* (London: Lawrence & Wishart, 1976)

Sproat, T., *History and Progress of the Amalgamated Society of Lithographic Printers 1880–1930*, Jubilee Souvenir (Manchester: ASL, 1930)

Stearns, P. and Walkowitz, D., *Workers in the Industrial Revolution* (New Brunswick: Transactions, 1974)

Stearns, P. N., *Lives of Labour: work in a maturing industrial society* (London: Croom Helm, 1975)

Steinberg, S. H., *Five Hundred Years of Printing* (Harmondsworth: Penguin, 1974)

St John, J., *Heinemann: a century of publishing* (London: Heinemann, 1990)

Stenton, M. and Lees, S. (eds), *Who's Who of British Members of Parliament*, Vol. II, 1886–1918 (Brighton: Harvester, 1978)

Thompson, D., *The Chartists: popular politics in the industrial revolution* (Aldershot: Wildwood House, 1986)

Thompson, E. P., *The Making of the English Working Class* (Harmondsworth: Penguin, 1968)

Thompson, F. M. L., *The Rise of Respectable Society* (London: Fontana, 1988)

Thompson, P., *The Nature of Work: an introduction to debates on the labour process* (Basingstoke: Macmillan, 1989)

Turner, H. A., *Trade Union Growth, Structure and Policy: a comparative study of the cotton unions* (London: Allen and Unwin, 1962)

Twyman, M., *Printing 1770–1970: an illustrated history of its development and uses* (London: Eyre & Spottiswoode, 1970)

Ward, J. T. and Fraser, W. H. (eds), *Workers and Employers: documents on trade unions and industrial relations in Britain since the eighteenth century* (London: Macmillan, 1980)

Webb, S. and Webb, B., *The History of Trade Unionism 1666–1920* (London: Longmans, Green, 1919)

Webb, S. and Webb, B., *Industrial Democracy* (London: Allen & Unwin, 1920 edition)

Wiener, J. H., *The War of the Unstamped* (New York: Cornell University Press, 1969)

Woodword, E. L., *The Age of Reform 1815–1870* (Oxford: Clarendon Press, 1938)

Wright, B. D., *Women, Work and Technology: transformations* (Michigan, Ann Arbour: University of Michigan Press, 1987)

Wrigley, C. (ed.), *A History of British Industrial Relations 1875–1914* (Brighton: Harvester, 1982)

Journals

Journal of the Printing Historical Society
Printing Historical Society Bulletin
Printing History, Journal of the American History Association
Society for the Study of Labour History Bulletin
Journal of Interdisciplinary History
American Historical Review
Past and Present
Historical Journal

Theses and unpublished papers

Barker, H., 'Female involvement in the English printing trades c 1700–1840' (unpublished paper, Keele University, 1996)

Cannon, I. C., 'Social situation of skilled workers: London compositors' (Ph.D., London, 1961)

Kassel, B., 'Training and qualifications in the German metal industries before 1930' (unpublished paper, Technical University of Berlin, 1995)

Masten, V., 'Women's work in provincial newspapers 1750–1800' (unpublished paper, University of Cambridge, 1995)

Richards, J. H., 'Social and economic aspects of combinations in the printing trades before 1875' (MA, University of Liverpool, 1956)

Zeitlin, J. H., 'Craft regulation and the division of labour: engineers and compositors in Britain 1890–1914' (Ph.D. thesis, Warwick, 1981)

Internet sources

Internet library of early journals: www.bodley.ox.ac.uk/ilej/
The Penny Magazine: www.history.rochester.edu/pennymag/
Victoria research web: www.indiana.edu/victoria/libraries
The Victorian web: http://landow.stg.brown.edu/victorian
Lause, M., *New York Typographical Union*: H-CIVWAR@MSU.EDU
Jepson, T. C., My sisters Telegraphic: the letters of nineteenth century women
    telegraphers: www.mindspring.com
Sparticus Internet Encyclopaedia: British history 1700–1950: www.sparticus.
    schoolnet.co.uk
Concise history of the British Newspaper: The British Library: http://
    portico.bluk/collections/newspapers
Wiesner-Hanks, M., The world of the renaissance print shop, Dept. of His-
    tory, University of Wisconsin-Milwaukee: www.uwm.edu/Dept/Library/
    special

Miscellaneous

Manchester Municipal Technical College Calendar
*An historical account of the origin and development of the Municipal College
    of Technology* (booklet, 1923)
Printing and the mind of man (exhibition catalogue, 1963)
The craft lectures of the Stationers' Company and the printing Industry
    Technical Board (London School of Printing, 1928–39)
The jubilee souvenir of the London Society of Compositors (1898)

Index